Ballads, Songs and Snatches

Ballads, Songs and Snatches

The Appropriation of Folk Song and Popular Culture in British Nineteenth-century Realist Prose

C. M. JACKSON-HOULSTON

Ashgate

Aldershot • Brookfield USA • Singapore • Sydney

Published by
Ashgate Publishing Limited
Gower House, Croft Road
Aldershot
Hants GU11 3HR
United Kingdom

Ashgate Publishing Company
Old Post Road
Brookfield
Vermont 05036-9704
USA

ISBN 1-84014-296-0

The author has asserted her right under the Copyright, Designs and Patents Act, 1988, to be identified as the Author of this work.

British Library Cataloguing-in-Publication Data
Jackson-Houlston, Caroline Mary
Ballads, Songs and Snatches: the Appropriation of Folk Song and Popular Culture in British Nineteenth-century Realist Prose
(Nineteenth Century series)
1. English fiction—19th century—History and criticism.
2. Folk songs in literature. 3. Popular culture in literature. 4. Allusions.
5. Authors and readers—Great Britain—History—19th century. I. Title.
823.8'09357

US Library of Congress Cataloguing-in-Publication Data
Jackson-Houlston, C. M., 1950-
Ballads, songs and snatches: the appropriation of folk song and popular culture in British nineteenth-century realist prose/C. M. Jackson-Houlston
Includes bibliographical material and index.
1. English fiction—19th century—History and criticism.
2. Folklore and literature—Great Britain—History—19th century.
3. Folk songs, British—Great Britain—History and criticism.
4. Ballads, British—Great Britain—History and criticism.
5. Popular culture in literature. 6. Folk songs in literature.
7. Folklore in literature. 8. Realism in literature.
9. Intertextuality. 10. Allusions. I. Title.
PR 868.F64J33 1999
823.8'09357—dc21

98-42922
CIP

Typeset in Times New Roman by the Author and A. D. Townsend.

Printed and bound in Great Britain by MPG Books Ltd, Bodmin, Cornwall

Contents

The Nineteenth Century
General Editors' Preface

The aim of this series is to reflect, develop and extend the great burgeoning of interest in the nineteenth century that has been an inevitable feature of recent decades, as that former epoch has come more sharply into focus as a locus for our understanding not only of the past but of the contours of our modernity. Though it is dedicated principally to the publication of original monographs and symposia in literature, history, cultural analysis, and associated fields, there will be a salient role for reprints of significant texts from, or about, the period. Our overarching policy is to address the spectrum of nineteenth-century studies without exception, achieving the widest scope in chronology, approach and range of concern. This, we believe, distinguishes our project from comparable ones, and means, for example, that in the relevant areas of scholarship we both recognize and cut innovatively across such parameters as those suggested by the designations 'Romance' and 'Victorian'. We welcome new ideas, while valuing tradition. It is hoped that the world which predates yet so forcibly predicts and engages our own will emerge in parts, as a whole, and in the lively currents of debate and change that are so manifest an aspect of its intellectual, artistic and social landscape.

Vincent Newey
Joanne Shattock

University of Leicester

Acknowledgements

No such book as this could be written without the help of librarians and archivists. I would like to record my thanks to the librarians, curators and staff (past and present) of the following libraries and archive collections: the Bodleian Library, Oxford, for the daily grind; the Brotherton Library of the University of Leeds, for material associated with gipsies and Gaskell; the Dorset County Library, for the Lock Collection, and local records; the Dorset County Museum, for the Thomas Hardy Memorial Collection; Edinburgh University Library; the Gaskell Collection in Manchester Central Reference Library, for allowing me to consult music books and other material associated with the Gaskells; the National Library of Scotland in Edinburgh, for access to manuscripts of Lady John Scott, Thomas Wilkie, Charles Kirkpatrick Sharpe and others, and the Materials for Scott's *Minstrelsy*; Norwich City Library, for Borrow material; the Pierpoint Morgan Library in New York, for answering a query about a Gaskell letter; earlier, the Swindon Public Reference Library, and latterly the Wiltshire and Swindon County Record Office in Trowbridge, for material collected by Alfred Williams, and parish records; the Vaughan Williams Memorial Library of the English Folk Dance and Song Society in London (with special thanks to Malcolm Taylor) for folk songs collected by Hammond, Gardiner and others, for unique collections of broadsides, and for helping me to search the Roud database. Mrs P. Maxwell Scott most kindly allowed me to consult the private Library of Sir Walter Scott at Abbotsford House by arrangement with the Keeper of the Advocates Library, Edinburgh, with Catherine Smith, and Douglas Gifford.

For permission to refer to or reproduce material I am grateful to: the National Library of Scotland, for the manuscripts mentioned above; H. E. F. Lock, for the Lock Collection in Dorset County Library; the Keeper of the Advocates Library in Edinburgh, for material from Scott's Library at Abbotsford; the Trustees of the Thomas Hardy Estate, for the Hardy family manuscript books and Hardy's Collection of Country Songs; Mrs Ursula Vaughan Williams and the Vaughan Williams Memorial Library, for the manuscripts of Hammond, Gardiner and others, and for various broadside collections.

I am also grateful to Angus Fraser for answering enquiries about Borrow, Vic Gammon for allowing me to refer to his unpublished essay on seventeenth-century political balladry, and to Hamish Henderson and others too numerous to mention for enlightening discussion.

For permission to reprint the substance of articles on Hardy, Gaskell and Scott I am indebted to the University of California Press, the Gaskell Society, and the Association for Scottish Literary Studies. Chapter 8 is substantially 'Thomas

Hardy's Use of Traditional Song', © 1989 by *The Regents of the University of California*, reprinted from *Nineteenth Century Literature*, vol. **44** no. **3**, December 1989, pp. 301-34. Chapter 5 is an expanded version of a paper given to the Gaskell Society Conference in 1995 and part-published as 'Mrs Gaskell, "Manchester Song" and its Contexts' in the *Gaskell Society Journal*, **10** (March 1996), 27-41. Some of Chapter 2 was published as '"Scoundrel Minstrels":. Some Allusions to Song in Two Scott Novels' in *Scott in Carnival: Selected Papers from the Fourth International Scott Conference, 1991*, edited by J. H. Alexander and D. Hewitt (Aberdeen: Association for Scottish Literary Studies, 1993). The Jefferies Society kindly invited me to give their Birthday Lecture in 1989 and may recognise its substance here, as may the organisers and audiences of various conferences around the world where most of the chapters got tried out.

This book would probably never have been started but for Dave Townsend and the enthusiasm for Hardy and for folk music we found we shared. Music is not my first language; it is his, and he gave advice on musical technicalities and very kindly typed out the music in Appendix 1. The book would certainly never have been finished but for my long-suffering husband Andy Gosler, who patiently got the writer out of the incessant difficulties generated by asking a computer Luddite to produce camera-ready copy.

For my mother and father

To revive gross ribaldry and witty obscenity, would be the last wish of any well-conditioned mind, though much which comes under that sweeping denomination in a sanctimonious, formal, and puritanical age, has no claim to such a distinction. But to engraft on some ancient loose ditty, a modern composition which, in so far as words go, offers no outrage to the delicately sensitive ear; but in its spirit and covert allusion, smacks of the elder devil which it has supplanted ... is positively doing more harm to sound morality, than ever its rude prototype in the unvarnished grossness of its strains, could ... have effected. ... When a song is inimical to virtue, and unfit to be heard by modest ears, let it utterly perish without a sigh, and above all ... without a comment. To give part and withhold part, while that which is withheld furnishes the scrupulous editor for some smart and sly note, only provokes curiosity, and becomes the sure means of perpetuating what otherwise would have soon ... silently slid into oblivion.

William Motherwell, *Minstrelsy Ancient & Modern* (1827), xcvii

1

Introduction

Classical quotation is the *parole* of literary men all over the world, but as
to those scraps and orts of songs that seem to have been written merely for
the people, I am in doubt whether, in the present state of improved
literature, they could be deemed worthy the attention of the public.

Allusion is seldom regarded as anything more than literary small potatoes.
Anyone who pursues echoes obsessively can be branded as a mere parasite—'a
louse upon the locks of literature', as Tennyson said of Churton Collins.[1] Yet
there are both traditional and more modern justifications for the pursuit of
textual cross-referencing in literary studies. First, it helps to establish the links
of influence which constitute literary history, giving texts a locatable
relationship through influences from the past and into the future.   This is
essentially a literary or cultural-historical exercise.   Secondly, and more
recently, interest has focused on the interdependent nature of all texts created in
verbal language. Thus, as Jonathan Culler points out, using Julia Kristeva as a
starting point:

> 'every text takes shape as a mosaic of citations, every text is the
> absorption and transformation of other texts' ... A work can only be read
> in connection with or against other texts, which provide the grid through
> which it is read and structured by establishing expectations which enable
> one to pick out salient features and give them a structure.[2]

This claim is part of a much wider structuralist and post-structuralist analysis
of language, not only as part of culture but as what actually constructs cultures
and the individuals who inhabit them. The first kind of search tends to assume a
reader who is fully cognisant of the widest possible range of reference, or who
can be made to feel guilty if he (usually) is not. The second allows for a variety
of readers who may, quite permissibly, respond in different ways. I hope this
book will provide material that will interest both kinds of critic.

However, this is not a book on allusion in general. It focuses on what might
seem an impossibly narrowly limited area of allusion, to traditional folk song,
though subsidiary reference will be made to a variety of other forms of song and
of popular culture. The actual proportion of each text that this involves is
extremely small, though the scarcity of material available for comment may in
itself be significant. I am claiming that such reference forms a major part of the
cultural coding of the work for only two of the writers discussed: Scott and

Hardy. However, the tightness of focus allows for very precise comparisons to be made between authors. At the same time, the implications of authorial decisions about how to handle the cultural life of working-class characters within the framework of a broadly realist fiction (or descriptive essays) designed to appeal to a middle-class readership are extremely wide-ranging, and throw light on other, more commonly considered, aspects of the texts.

Useful and informative work on allusion already exists in the shape of multitudinous articles on a wide range of authors, such as Dieter Berger's '"Damn the Mottoe": Scott and the Epigraph' (1982) and even books, such as Michael Wheeler's *The Art of Allusion in Victorian Fiction* (1979) and Joan Grundy's *Hardy and the Sister Arts* (1979).[3] However, almost all of these concentrate on 'high' culture allusions implying a middle-class audience (like the W. S. Gilbert words from *The Mikado* which form the title of this book). To date, literary scholarship has tended to avoid the discussion of intertexts from traditional and popular sources, while folk song scholars have tended to avoid the literary matrix in which these allusions occur. As an active performer and researcher in both fields I aim to bring them together and to redress the balance.

Folk song allusion is a Cinderella area of scholarship because the texts cited are protean ones. As part of traditional oral culture they do not have fixed, unitary sources. They use formulaic phrasing and plot motifs, thus making references difficult to trace. For example, even with on-line searches, someone looking for the complete text of something from which Scott is quoting two verses, and which refers to a 'Captain Glen', is going to have something of a hunt to locate it as a ballad known as 'William Guiseman'.[4] A 'floater' verse such as

> A man may drink and not be drunk;
> A man may fight and not be slain;
> A man may kiss a bonny lass,
> And yet be welcome back again.

(quoted in *Woodstock*, Chapter 27) is probably most familiar nowadays as part of the Scottish ploughman's song 'The Barnyards of Delgaty', but Scott's audience might have known it best as part of a song of successful love, 'Duncan Davison'.[5] Many songs were reworked one or more times by fashionable popularisers like Allan Ramsay or Robert Burns, who might themselves have at least one foot in the tradition. Either old or new words might be fitted to a traditional or new instrumental tune. This might be difficult to sing—pipes and fiddle have a greater range than the average human voice. These words (or tune) might then be set to an easier tune (or different words) but keep the original title. One of the purposes of this book is to try to outline the most likely sources for intertexts drawn from traditional song and to recreate their probable implications for the original readers of the novels.

Even today, folk song material is seldom admitted to literary study, whereas all the named authors in this book are given a place in the canon, even if a very minor one. It is sometimes still tacitly assumed that those sections of British society whose verbal culture was oral rather than primarily written *had* no verbal culture, or none worth serious consideration. In the nineteenth century this was the dominant assumption, yet many authors chose to mediate the culture(s) of the working classes for the enjoyment of predominantly middle-class audiences. In so doing they employed a variety of strategies, which often romanticised, falsified or denigrated what the novels and stories claimed to represent. Almost all the texts I discuss exhibit some feature of this tendency.

'High' culture allusions construct two possible subject positions for the reader to occupy. They may act to reaffirm a sense of cultural solidarity with the reader through his or her active recognition of the references. Such readers would be able to produce such references themselves as equal participants with the narrator in that high culture. Alternatively, readers may accept such references as belonging to the culture to which they aspire; they are within the readers' receptive comprehension, and, in accepting them, readers occupy the position of active and successful candidates for admission to high culture; they take pleasure in learning. However, familiarity with the 'low' culture allusions offers the audience a more equivocal position because of the implications of this knowledge. The advantages of congratulating oneself on the possession of a cosmopolitan knowledge and sensibility are off-set by awkward questions about how such knowledge was acquired. The author can be lifted above such doubts by the conventional assumptions of his or her narratorial omniscience. S/he can presume to instruct the audience as to the nature of this world, which their class or gender position implicitly forbids them to recognise. However, one of the assumptions generated by the use of realist conventions is that the author is telling the truth.

To test these assumptions, please consider the epigraph to this Introduction. This was constructed using the principles—or lack of them—of Sir Walter Scott:

> The scraps of poetry which have been in most cases tacked to the beginning of chapters in these Novels are sometimes quoted either from reading or from memory, but, in the general case, are pure invention. I found it too troublesome to turn to the collection of the British poets to discover apposite mottoes ... I drew on my memory as long as I could, and when that failed, eked it out with invention. I believe that, in some cases, where actual names are affixed to the supposed quotations, it would be to little purpose to seek them in the works of the authors referred to.[6]

The first part of my 'quotation', up to 'world', is a real quotation from James Boswell's *Life of Johnson* for 8 May 1781. The second part is adapted by me from a remark made by Thomas Percy on page ix of the Preface to his *Reliques of Ancient English Poetry* (1765), and applied to the first part with a little Shakespearean cement. Of course, you may have spotted this, but probably you did not. I have exploited the presumption that you as reader probably have about the moral obligations of the author of a scholarly text not to mislead. These are greater than those of a writer of realist fiction, but similar in kind. How do you react now you know? How far would this reaction be similar if you were reading a work purporting to represent real life, or does all fiction, or even all language, give out the signal famously articulated by Sir Philip Sidney in his *Apologie for Poetry* (1595), 'for the poet, he nothing affirmeth, and therefore never lieth'? This tension between the expectations of realist descriptive writing, whether overtly fictional or supposed reporting, and the expectations of romance is one I shall discuss in more detail in relation to Scott, who quite consciously manipulates these genre expectations. This manipulation is particularly prominent where the author is also articulating expectations about the original musical milieu of the allusions.

Readings of the texts discussed are therefore likely to depend on the audience's horizons of expectation and their degrees of knowledge, which vary according to their historical circumstances.[7] This book aims to recreate the circumstances of the audience originally anticipated by the writers. Many authors assume a readership whose knowledge is divided along class or gender lines, and offer the reader a variety of subject positions on this basis. The Johnson quote establishes a dominant expectation that the reader is male, and of a high enough social class to have had a classical education. This has the advantage of establishing a community of culture across national divisions, though Johnson's idea of the world implicitly excludes non-western cultures. Various kinds of allusion, including both classical and, as I hope to show, folk song, introduce to the texts in which they occur subtexts only accessible to some of the audience. They are, therefore, commonly used to refer to sexuality, especially in nineteenth-century texts constrained by the expectation that nothing will be said that could bring a blush to the cheek of a young female reader. Only those already familiar with the intertextual material, and therefore already 'corrupted', can recognise the reference.

Percy's remarks imply a complete separation of 'the people' from 'the public', the latter being (implicitly) defined as those who can read, and can afford to buy books or subscribe to libraries. Such an absolute division would have been neither tenable nor tactful a century later, yet the fact remains that the majority of the characters Hardy writes about in his tales of rural life would not have been in a position to read his work. Authors working in a high culture context were reluctant to admit the existence of a creative impulse among the unlettered and ill-educated, and typically operated a number of devices to avoid such a recognition. One of these was straight denial: there was no such culture. Another was the denigration of the value of this culture, especially of street songs derived from the music-hall. A third is the recuperation of the popular art of the past by ascribing it to a mythologised minstrel figure and by absorbing it into the *literary* culture of the present through such collections as Percy's *Reliques*, which by the Victorian period was a literary classic. Ballads are distanced from a modern labouring poor by time. One of the commonest strategies for English writers was a displacement of tradition-based creativity out of their own community onto another, especially that of Scotland, and especially the songs of the safely dead democrat Burns. Lyrical works from Scots tradition were sung round pianos in English parlours; the songs still sung by their servants were not.[8] These last two distancing strategies are what I have called cross-class cultural colonialism.

Alternatively, the verbal signs of this culture have actually been erased, and inventions of the author substituted. Even as generalised imitations of a kind of discourse these are usually feeble and misleading. These apparent representations of a different discourse I have called false intertexts. Scott was largely responsible for this. Though the discourses used by Johnson and Percy are compatible (and genuine), the epigraph to this introduction is a false intertext since it is presented in a way that implies a single source. Since the critical enterprise of this book rests (*pace* Culler and Kristeva) on maintaining a distinction between language that has the function of referring to actual events in the non-verbal world and language that is more playfully and self-referentially constructed, I shall not play this trick again. The other quotations in this book are authentic!

Some Definitions and Assumptions

Folk Song: a folk song can be defined as a composition of moderate (i.e. easily memorable) length in a metrical form designed to fit the musical phrasing of (usually) a fairly limited number of patterns. Its author is likely to be an otherwise ordinary member of the community that forms his or her audience. Traditional folk songs, ballads, carols and instrumental tunes are *performed*, being handed down, shaped, and partially re-created through transmission by ear. This mode of preservation may be modified by cross-fertilisation with printed texts on broadsides and elsewhere. Also, songs from other sources can be subjected to traditional modes of transmission and re-creation. Though definition through a qualitative preference for certain forms or subjects is suspect, we can distinguish between the narrative ballad, with its typically dramatic presentation, its progression through incremental repetition, its direct and uncompromising concentration on action, and the lyric, which concentrates on a mood resulting from circumstances described only briefly, if at all, and which often reflects on the position of the speaker with the aid of a subtle natural symbolism. Both types contain a wide range of mood, by no means as tragic as is sometimes assumed. There are also celebrations of seasons and festivals (including carols) as well as more jocular pieces, such as drinking songs. Sometimes we need to call in distinctions of this kind but the original singers did not necessarily do so. They sang what they liked when it came their way, whatever its source.[9]

Because oral transmission is facilitated by repetition within familiar social contexts, folk song tends to be associated with stable communities. Within such communities, especially when they are largely pre-literate, 'folk' songs are not the exclusive property of any particular class. However, with the newly emerging class divisions of the eighteenth century, the creation and transmission of folk song tended to be concentrated in the less literate classes, giving them a distinct verbal and musical art of their own. These communities are often assumed to be rural, because the deracination caused by urbanisation in the late eighteenth and nineteenth centuries coincided with the decline of folk song. However, there is nothing intrinsically inimical to oral transmission in an urban environment, and nineteenth century towns did have lively oral urban cultures, though we tend to categorise them rather differently (see below). (Today, oral transmission of songs in adult life is most obvious in ritualised social gatherings such as those of sports clubs and the armed forces.)

Popular Song: I have used this as an umbrella term to cover several rather different types. What they have in common is that they were short pieces capable of standing on their own, composed for comparatively simple settings, and mostly suitable for unaccompanied performance, though they were often accompanied. They could be subdivided into *factional, parlour* and *street songs*.

Factional songs are the earliest type discussed here. They were designed to reinforce political solidarities, especially Royalist and Jacobite ones. Politics often went hand in hand with the celebration of conviviality through drinking, usually in all-male gatherings.[10] My treatment of Scott makes some reference to this kind of song.

'Popular song' in the nineteenth century was heterogeneous. What I have called *parlour song* would include those literary songs from Shakespeare, Ben Jonson, etc. that had a continuing history of canonical popularity and newer genteel pieces by Romantic versifiers like Thomas Moore. Others might have risen up the social scale from the early music-hall, or have been excerpted from stage pieces or, occasionally, opera. Later they often included 'nigger minstrel' pieces. They had settings and tunes appropriate to the skills and vocal ranges of domestic performers and audiences of both sexes with a social status high enough to afford a piano. If not comic, the recently composed pieces tended to be sentimental in that they relied on contrived situations to generate extreme feelings.

Following on from Restoration and eighteenth-century models, they sometimes attempted to imitate folk songs (especially Scottish ones) through the use of artless and simple language, and were often called 'ballads' even when they had no narrative. They were often artless. They were often simple. What they were not was folk songs; their own formulas often parasitised and undermined the strengths of their originals. A good example would be 'Monk' Lewis's 'Banks of Allan Water', discussed below in relation to Hardy. Most of these appeared too late to be 'taken over by the folk and transformed into the folk idiom through oral transmission', as Maud Karpeles notes:

> The creation of folk songs in an industrialized country is hardly possible.
> ... Any popular composed song is immediately stereotyped by means of
> mechanical recording [print, in the nineteenth century] and it is in this
> standardized form that it is purveyed to the members of the public and in
> this form that it remains. The processes of oral transmission have no
> opportunity of operating because the song is constantly being referred
> back to the original.[11]

These songs are popular in that, given increasingly fluid class divisions, growing literacy, and a diversifying reading public, they became widely available not in expensive sheet music form, but in cheap collections, sometimes issued in parts. An early example would be *Davidson's Universal Melodist* (1847) which was issued in weekly parts at threepence each or monthly parts at a shilling; the two volumes contain about 1,600 songs (not all different!) and one got about 125 songs for one's shilling. Collections of the lyrics alone are also common, for example *The Vauxhall Comic Song Book*, edited by J. W. Sharp (n.d.) or *The Red, White and Blue Monster Song Book* 'containing all the standard favourites and an immense number of new and popular copyright songs' (n.d. but c. late 1860s). It is noticeable that the purveyors of such songs thought that they were filling a gap in the musical life of the nation. The preface of the *Universal Melodist* suggests this and so does *A Short History of Cheap Music* forty years later, claiming that 'the people' were longing for music but did not have any: 'There were no cheap publications, and there were no cheap concerts. The taxes on knowledge and the vexatious rules observed by the printing trades laid an embargo upon all attempts at reform in this direction.'[12]

There were also raunchier songs, often derived from the music-halls which sprang out of the exclusively male song-and-supper rooms of the 1830s and 1840s.[13] The gender implications of reference to these are discussed in relation to Thackeray. These overlapped with the *street songs*, the ballads and lyrics composed for the consumption of the very poorest (and often by them) and marketed on broadsheets, without music, containing only one or a very few songs, printed on one side only and often pasted up on walls. Small collections, known as chapbooks or garlands, could be bought for a penny. A little later, small song books retailed at twopence or threepence. The Victorians thought of these songs as vulgar and degraded, and some of them certainly were indecent, but prolixity, a tendency to moralising, and poor grammar are usually their worst faults.[14] (Many folk songs were printed in this way, which was partly why Victorian commentators tarred them with the same brush, but popular songs from composers higher up the social scale eventually filtered into this market too.)

All these types of song might on occasion be sung by those usually thought of as constituting the community of tradition, if they came their way.

Working Class: the terminology of class is also a contested area. Here, 'working class' refers to the majority of the British population, who belonged to families where the main income was derived from wages for agricultural or manufacturing manual labour, or from domestic service in small households or 'below stairs' in large ones, those who engaged primarily in trade or services for such people (e.g. tailors, pedlars, tinkers) and the destitute from these categories. Some of the artisans and skilled craftsmen (like Thomas Hardy's father) might have been quite prosperous, and more comfortably off than some of those clinging on desperately to the lower fringes of the middle classes by virtue of parentage or upbringing. Traditional folk song is usually associated with relatively stable rural labouring communities but in some chapters I shall refer to the urban proletariat, and to those who moved from a rural way of life into the towns and hence had experience of both old and new cultures.

Middle Class is another big baggy monster term used to delineate the sizeable and increasing proportion of the population from small capitalists and upper servants (e.g. stewards) 'upwards' (but not major landowners or members of the aristocracy). These people formed the bulk of the book-owning, library-subscribing, comfortably literate public, though throughout the late eighteenth and nineteenth century there had always been some determined and serious working-class readers. Although book prices increased to a peak around 1830, most technological and social development led to an expansion of readership. For example, steam-driven printing machines were in general use by the 1840s. Increased education and decreasing printing costs and newspaper duties inevitably led to an expansion of the reading public and to a blurring of distinctions between various kinds of audience for printed material.[15]

Allusion: this term has been used to cover several kinds of intertextuality, primarily, here, the *marked* quotation of song titles or all or part of their texts. This is fairly standard modern usage; the development of the term is discussed by Michael Wheeler in the first chapter of his *Art of Allusion in Victorian*

Fiction. Sometimes the phrasing of a song may be incorporated without any indication into the main text. Sometimes the author refers to an alternative discourse, but substitutes his own imitation of it for a genuine example. This 'intertext' can only be a generalised allusion to a *kind* of discourse.

Throughout, I make the assumption that when a reader comes across a noticeable allusion of any kind this triggers one or more responses. The first is the sense of the intrusion of one discourse into another, especially the intrusion of verse into prose, leading to recognition of the plurality of discourses within the text. This may lead to a sense of the text as a constructed thing, and hence to a greater sense of its fictionality, a recognition that literature is a licensed form of play. Alternatively, allusion to an unfamiliar culture may also be taken as evidence of authentic reference, presented as part of historical or social evidence. Dieter Berger argues that only the first of these responses matters:

> It is irrelevant whether or not Scott had himself invented these scraps of poetry because the irony of the fakes was never recognised by his admirers. What counts is the reference itself, which takes the reader's imagination back to the past, to a poetical, enchanting, mysterious past. (Berger, 381)

In terms of the actual experience of some readers this must carry conviction. However, I would contend that not all readers of nineteenth-century fiction were so passive and that their reading experiences varied. I also assume that authors as individuals are of some importance as the generators of the meanings of their work. They hold a uniquely privileged position in that as authors they are the only individuals who can occupy the positions at both ends of of a paradigm of communication such as Jakobson's, in which there is an implicit lopsidedness not apparent from the diagrammatical symmetry between addresser and addressee.[16] Writers are not only the addressers of texts but also their first and most significant addressees.

A further assumption is that there is an implicit contract issued by the realist writer to his readers about the nature of his subject. Readers still make this assumption, and they certainly made it when this fiction was published. Hazlitt, for example, praises Scott in these terms in 1825:

> Our author has conjured up the actual people he has to deal with ... and by borrowing of others, has enriched his own genius with everlasting variety, truth, and freedom. He has take his materials from the original, authentic sources, in large concrete masses, and not tampered with or too much frittered them away. He is only the amanuensis of truth and history.[17]

Realism (like folksong) is identified not by the absolute congruence between a text and an abstract definition as by the predominance of several features from a suite of characteristics.   For realism, these are: *verisimilitude* in the description of settings in time and place, a plausibly *linear chronology scheme*, reference to the *external* and supposedly objective features of an *extensive range* of the experience of *ordinary people,* who are *rounded characters* rather than types, in *language used as a transparent medium* of representation, by an *omniscient third-person narrator*, in a form with a firm narrative *closure*. Realism of content is not the same as realism of presentation; a full-blooded realist text would have both. Nineteenth-century fiction is pervasively under the influence of realist conventions but texts can be classified along a continuum according to the proportion of their realist features.   The effect of a realist text is to confirm to the reader the order and stability of his or her known world, which is why it has in the latter part of this century been regarded as an untrustworthy instrument of social and political hegemony.[18]

David Lodge suggests in *The Modes of Modern Writing* that realist texts convince us not so much because they resemble reality as because they remind us of texts which we take to be non-fictional.   Thus, the historical novel resembles history, the social novel resembles reporting (while the descriptive essay actually is reporting).   This is how allusion fits into this hypothesis: 'where one kind of aesthetic presentation is embedded in another, the 'reality' of the embedded form is weaker than that of the framing form' (37).

Certainly if Scott quotes from an 'old song' we usually take the content of that song to be fiction.   However, Scott himself frequently uses such references as historical evidence, notoriously in the lengthy notes to *Rob Roy*, where he cites several ballads.   Moreover, where the embedded form is supposed to be the index of an alternative cultural world from that of the novel, it has a status as evidence that reveals the literary matrix to be the more fictional of the two discourses.

Different kinds of writing make different kinds of guarantees about their own referentiality.   Of course, this generates problems of epistemology; there are always awkward questions to be asked about how we know things.   But this should not be a pretext for arguing that epistemological problems are the same as ontological ones.   My argument is that there can be such a thing as *mis*representation, and that if nineteenth-century realist writers misrepresent their subjects, this matters.   It matters in the world of social realities where a vote or a wage may be part of a whole web of complex signifying systems but they are not *only* important as signs.   It matters to people, and although it would be possible to put the material of this book to a variety of critical uses, my own perspective is basically a materialist-historicist one.   I have also a residual belief that knowing a subject to have been misrepresented affects our aesthetic enjoyment as well as our historical conscience.

Endnotes

1. C. Tennyson, *Alfred Tennyson* (1968), 490.
2. J. Culler, *Structuralist Poetics* (1975), 139.
3. D. Berger, *Anglia* **100:3-4** (1982), 373-96; M. Wheeler, *The Art of Allusion in Victorian Fiction* (1979); J. Grundy, *Hardy and the Sister Arts* (1979).
4. An extract from this appears in Chapter 36 of Scott's *The Pirate*. Note that because of the multiplicity of editions of Scott's work I shall give chapter references for verse quotations, which are fairly easily found. Where the new Edinburgh edition volume is currently in print I shall also give page references for that, and sources for traceable folk song allusions in Scott's novels should eventually appear in that edition. Those already available are: *The Antiquary, The Black Dwarf, The Bride of Lammermoor, Kenilworth, A Legend of the Wars of Montrose, Redgauntlet, St. Ronan's Well, The Tale of Old Mortality*. These use the volume numbering, but the continuous chapter numbering is given at the top of the page. If the appropriate volume has not yet appeared any necessary page references will be to the Dryburgh edition. There are similar words and a tune in W. Christie (ed.), *Traditional Ballad Airs* (1876), **1**, 240-41, and Scott's own note to C. K. Sharpe's *A Ballad Book* is printed on p. 156 of the 1880 edition by David Laing. However, the printed version likely to be best known in Scott's lifetime—though it post-dates the novel—was called 'William Guiseman' and is to be found in G. R. Kinloch (ed.), *Ancient Scottish Ballads* (1827), 156. In the novel, Bunce very reasonably dislikes this 'long and disastrous ballad' in which the Captain turns out to be a murderer.
5. J. Johnson (ed.), *The Scots Musical Museum*, 6 vols (1787-1803), **2**, no. 149. Hereafter this will be referred to as *SMM*. A popular modern version of 'The Barnyards of Delgaty' can be found in *The Clancy Brothers and Tommy Makem Song Book* (1964), 38.
6. Chronicles of the Canongate, First Series, 1827 introduction (Dryburgh edn, **19**, 324). For Scott's admission that he did not know himself how much was genuine, see E. Johnson, *Sir Walter Scott: The Great Unknown* (1970), 784.
7. For the dynamic effects of Scott's novels on readers, see W. Iser, *The Implied Reader* (1974), and R. L. Stein, 'Historical Fiction and the Implied Reader: Scott and Iser', in *Novel*, **14:3** (Spring 1981), 213-31. For the idea of an 'horizon of expectations' (*sic*), see H. R. Jauss (1974), 'Literary History as a Challenge to Literary Theory', in R. Cohen (ed.), *New Directions in Literary History* (1974), 11-41.
8. Maud Karpeles claims that even at the end of the nineteenth century 'outside the village communities, English folk song was almost unknown. French and German folk songs and even Scottish and Irish, but English—no. It was commonly supposed that we had none; or if we ever had, they were all bad.' 'The Distinction between Folk and Popular Music', *Journal of the International Folk Music Council*, **20** (1968), 11. These strategies of denial are commonly applied to the achievements of all kinds of disadvantaged groups, and feminists will like to compare Joanna Russ, *How to Suppress Women's Writing* (1984).
9. See P. Barry, 'The Part of the Folk Singer in the Making of Folk Balladry', in M. Leach and T.P. Coffin (eds), *The Critics and the Ballad* (1961), 61, 68-71; A. E. Green's foreword to Frank Kidson, *Traditional Tunes* (Wakefield: E. P. Publishing reprint, 1970), viii-xii; Michael Pickering, *Village Song and Culture* (1982), 51, 54; D. Harker, *Fakesong: The Manufacture of British 'Folksong' 1700 to the Present* (1985),

passim, but especially 247-50. Karpeles quotes the standard IFMC definition of folk music, op. cit., 9.

10.   For more detailed information, see H. Rollins, *Cavalier and Puritan* (1923), and V. Gammon, *The Broadside Ballad as a Form of Political Propaganda During the English Revolution 1640-60*, typescript in the Vaughan Williams Memorial Library of the English Folk Dance and Song Society in London (1976), especially Section 4.

11.   Karpeles, 10-11. For contemporary and later accounts of popular song, from a variety of viewpoints, see J. S. Bratton, *The Victorian Popular Ballad* (1975); J. Hullah, 'Popular Songs of the Last Half Century', in *Macmillan's Magazine*, **21** (1869-70), 127-34; E. D. Mackerness, *A Social History of English Music* (1964); R. Nettel, *A Social History of Traditional Song* (1969), especially Chapter 9; R. Pearsall, *Victorian Popular Music* (1973). For an attempt to separate out those songs more likely to be sung in prosperous parlours, see D. Scott, *The Singing Bourgeois: Songs of the Victorian Drawing Room and Parlour* (1989).

12.   *Davidson's Universal Melodist, Consisting of the Music and Words of Popular, Standard, and Original Songs* (1847), preface; anon., *A Short History of Cheap Music, as exemplified in the Records of the House of Novello, Ewer & Co.*, 22.

13.   G. Speaight (ed.), *Bawdy Songs of the Early Music Hall* (1975).

14.   For discussion and examples, see J. Ashton, *Modern Street Ballads* (1888); Bratton, op. cit., 24-25; R. Collison, *The Story of Street Literature* (1973); V. E. Neuburg, 'The Literature of the Streets', in H. J. Dyos & M. Wolff (eds), *The Victorian City* (1973) **1**, 191-209; R. Palmer, *The Sound of History* (1988); W. Tomlinson, *Papers of the Manchester Literary Club*, **5** (1886), 305-16; M. Vicinus, *The Industrial Muse* (1974). Even recent commentators feel a need to apologize for their interest, e.g. Collison, who says 'there are no masterpieces and no works of true literary merit, but there are flashes of a natural instinct for the apt phrase that rescue the whole from mere drivel' (9).

15.   Collison, 9. R. Altick, *The English Common Reader: A Social History of the Mass Reading Public, 1800-1900* (1963), especially 49-66, 274-77, 306-09, 379-80.

16.   'Closing Statement: Linguistics and Poetics', in T. A. Sebeok (ed.), *Style in Language* (1960), 353.

17.   W. Hazlitt, *Lectures on the English Poets* and *The Spirit of the Age*, intro. C. M. Maclean (1967 repr.), 228-29.

18.   For discussions, see D. Lodge, *The Modes of Modern Writing* (1979); R. Selden (1981), 'Realism and Country People', in K. Parkinson and M. Priestman (eds), *Peasants and Countrymen in Literature: A Symposium Organised by the English Department of the Roehampton Institute in February 1981* (1982), 39-58; R. Williams, *The Long Revolution* (1992), chapter 7, 'Realism and the Contemporary Novel'.

2

Scott

> I have tagged with rhyme and blank verse the subdivisions of this important narrative, in order to seduce your continued attention by powers of composition of stronger attraction than my own.[1]

So says Frank Osbaldistone, the narrator of *Rob Roy* (1817), and surely his faintly ironic tone here represents Scott himself. Among the wildly heterogeneous examples of this 'superior composition' are five labelled 'old ballad', 'old song', or by the names of specific pieces of this type: five out of thirty-nine—about 13%, a significant proportion. Such chapter tags are also prominent in Scott's work as a whole. Similar kinds of quotation play intimate parts in the main texts of the novels. Why did Scott use them? How far do Frank's words offer a credible explanation, and what is the reader's reaction? Is his or her attention successfully seduced?

The answers to these obvious questions are further complicated by the unreliability of 'the Author of the Waverley Novels'. Lines like

> Yon lamp its line of quivering light
>   Shoots from my lady's bower;
> But why should Beauty's lamp be bright
>   At midnight's lonely hour?[2]

sound less like the Old Ballad they purport to be than a piece of contemporary fustian added to manufacture a suspenseful curiosity about Diana Vernon's unknown visitor. Tom Haber claims, with partial justification, that 'nearly all of the "Old Ballad" tags in the novels ... are of Scott's own manufacture'.[3] Moreover, as pointed out in the introduction, we have Scott's own authority for our suspicions. And if he really wanted the support of other authors, why did he himself compose the Ballad of the Red Harlaw sung by Elspeth Mucklebackit in Chapter 40 of *The Antiquary* when he could have got a genuinely old—if unimpressive—version from Allan Ramsay's *Evergreen* (1724), James Johnson's *Scots Musical Museum* (1787-1803), or David Herd's *Antient and Modern Scottish Songs* (1791)?[4] How much of a fool is Oldbuck supposed to be in taking it as genuine?

At this rate it would look as if Scott's claim to be introducing examples of a stronger power of composition than the narrator's own is just one more of the layers of obfuscation which constitute his introductory narrative technique. But how much of his apparent allusion did Scott invent, and how much remember?

Of the fourteen chapter tags Haber implies may be examples of fake 'Old Ballads', at least ten can be traced to some original Scott could have been remembering, however loosely. And the narrative parts of the texts show a similar blend of manufacture and memory in allusion.

Of course, what I have been saying about Scott's habits in quotation is applicable to his use of all kinds of texts. However, the use of quotation from folk song poses particularly interesting questions about the nature of Scott's writing and the implications this has for our ideas of the relation between his texts and their audience.

Scott's Audiences, Knowledge and Inclinations

One needs to point out that if one were talking about an English novelist and an exclusively English audience of Scott's period one would have to draw the lines in different places. This is because in Scotland there was far less of a cultural division between classes. David Craig, in *Scottish Literature and the Scottish People 1680-1830,* ably outlines the eighteenth-century situation. Housing in Edinburgh and Glasgow mixed the classes till the end of the century.[5] A comparatively high literacy rate allowed more of the lower classes to assimilate printed material.[6] It was a common amusement with all classes in the early nineteenth century to repeat proverbs, lines of Scotch poetry, songs, etc. (Craig, 24) Certainly by the time Scott wrote his novels this position was changing. But a taste for old ballads and vernacular songs was not so much a revival, as in England, as a continuation of a preference for verbal art of a different kind from the 'elegant' and 'refined'.

I would just like to stress these points about these songs. Folk song in Scott's day included the 'muckle sangs' beloved of scholarly and literary tradition, but also much more. It was not rigidly confined to a certain class in a rural area. It existed in a dynamic state with input from various sources. In time oral tradition might well have operated to prune the redundant and affected false refinement which appealed to late eighteenth- and early nineteenth-century cultured taste, but the intervention of printing radically and irreversibly altered the processes of transmission, more especially for the likely audience of Scott's novels. It is worth remembering that one of Scott's informants, Mrs Hogg, condemned him for putting the words of her songs into print at all:

> There war never ane o' my songs prentit till ye prentit them yoursel', an' ye hae spoilt them awthegither. They were made for singin' an' no for readin'; but ye hae broke the charm noo, an' they'll never be sung mair.[7]

One of the consequences of this kind of culture then was an intense cross-fertilisation of kinds of writing. Texts which had been passed on largely orally for scores or hundreds of years were set down in print. Their words might be partially or wholly rewritten, either for a more 'refined' taste, or for a more depraved one. Burns engaged in both these kinds of rewriting, for Johnson's *Scots Musical Museum,* and in the *Merry Muses of Caledonia* (c. 1800) for the Crochallan Fencibles.[8] But this was not a one-way process. Writers whose compositions might formerly have spread no further than their own communities approached the literary establishment with pieces based on and using the same conventions as the pieces they had heard from a more purely oral tradition did. And these pieces returned, both in print and orally, to undergo further variation and re-creation through performance. But a fixed form available in a popular book, rather than on ephemeral sheets or in chapbooks, did tend to restrict variation. It sometimes acquired a superior status on the grounds of its printed authority, and many of the songs rewritten by Allan Ramsay for the *Tea-table Miscellany* (1724) or by Burns for Johnson and others actually replaced the originals. Ramsay's love-song version of 'Bessy Bell and Mary Gray', which Scott uses as the epigraph to Chapter 3 of *The Pirate*, was better known than the tragic original, in which the two die of the plague. David Craig testifies to the popularity among all classes of Burns and Ramsay. He quotes John Fraser's *Humorous Chapbooks* as saying that in 1800 Ramsay's work was '*universally* read' by the peasantry (Craig, 112-13, 121).

But if it was universally *read*, what happened to the singing? Scott was writing at a time when the texts from which he quotes might have had two kinds of life—one, stabilised by print, was a life as a read text, and one, still subject to variation by those who used memory rather than print authority, was a life as a sung text. We cannot always be sure which kind Scott had in mind or whether his audience's memory would have referred to the same version as the author. They were certainly meeting these allusions shorn of their immediate musical context in a form designed for consumption in private, by a silent individual reader, or a family group listening to a text read aloud. It is worth asking what this new form of consumption did to the original texts, but this is not my main concern here.

The texts of the novels (and of quotes from canonical poets) are effectively static. The texts of much of the material I shall be discussing are only partially stabilised by print. In ballads and folk songs, the formulaic nature of the writing leads to overlap between texts. Readers' reactions, then, would differ according to the context recognised by them. Whichever version they knew they might have significant non-verbal associations with it. The possession of a recognised musical element alters the way a reader responds. The reader, who is immersed in a verbal element, receives a kind of shock at recognising a disjuncture in the discourse, and the aural memory is stimulated by reference to a known piece just as the visual memory is stimulated by reference when Scott refers to a painter like David Wilkie, for example, in Chapter 31 of *The Antiquary* (346). The imaginative response is different if the reader has had a sensuous response to some recognised original.

Some readers would have this, some would not. But they might not be responding to what Scott had in mind. It is obvious that Scott himself quoted from different versions of some ballads and songs such as his favourite 'The Battle of Otterbourne'.[9] He knew at least three very different versions of 'My Heart's in the Highlands' and used at least two, the Burns version in chapters 9/10 of *Redgauntlet* and the version in chapter 28 of *Waverley*. The second verse of this is not by Scott himself. His friend Wilkie collected a similar but slightly longer version at about same time as *Waverley* came out.[10] It would be unsafe to say that Scott did *not* know a particular song or variant. I shall be drawing my illustrations from works which Scott himself knew or possessed, as far as possible in the editions known to him, such as Herd's *Antient Songs* (Edinburgh, 1791), Ramsay's *Evergreen* (Edinburgh, 1724) and *Tea-table Miscellany* (Edinburgh, 1762), Johnson's *Scots Musical Museum* (Edinburgh, 1788-1803), Percy's *Reliques* (London, 1794), James Hogg's *Jacobite Relics* (Edinburgh, 1819-21), William Thomson's *Orpheus Caledonius* (London, 1733), etc., and from manuscripts compiled by Scott himself or by those he knew or could be associated with such as Charles Kirkpatrick Sharpe, Thomas Wilkie, Herd or Lady John Scott. One might have nagging doubts that Scott had contributed his own pennyworth to later records of the tradition—'Jock of Hazeldean' is a notorious example—but reference to earlier texts usually allows us to avoid this pitfall.[11]

I should like first to say a little about the compilers of some of the books I shall refer to most. David Herd (c.1732-1810) came from a farming family and became a clerk in Edinburgh, where he 'took an active part ... in Edinburgh's all-male convivial clubs'.[12] He had first-hand knowledge of the culture he was striving to record and even by today's standards was an accurate and honest recorder, even when dealing with material which mentioned sex. *The Scots Musical Museum* was the brainchild of James Johnson, an Edinburgh engraver and music seller (d. 1811). Its first volume was largely culled from Allan Ramsay's extraordinarily popular collection *The Tea-table Miscellany* (1724). This was made up of new lyrics written for old Scots tunes by Ramsay and his acquaintances, and retouched folk songs. After Johnson met Robert Burns, however, in 1787, the emphasis shifted as Burns became in effect the editor, collecting, writing, and rewriting songs as well as rooting out those of other people from printed sources. The collection was more varied than Herd's. Burns, who played the fiddle, and could read and probably write music to some extent, was actually more interested in preserving the tunes.[13] Although the music was printed in an unfashionable way and the collection never became really popular,[14] the pieces were accompanied by their music.

Having tried to suggest that some of his own songs were 'Scotland's voice', Burns was perhaps reluctant to spell out how much was his own,[15] and Burns's idolaters have been readier to credit him as composer than as collector, so the traditional status of the *Museum* texts has been much debated. Burns really did spring from the milieu in which such songs had been and were still being composed, and many of his compositions have passed back into tradition. He made extensive use of Herd's collection. However, it must be admitted that, unlike Herd, but like Ramsay, Burns was very alive to contemporary demands for delicacy in a collection at six shillings a volume or two guineas a set, and aimed at the female owners of harpsichords and pianos (*SMM*, preface to vol. 5). This was not so much a matter of internalising social repressions as of policing his own tastes, for what he cleaned up for *SMM* he dirtied down for the male Crochallan Fencibles Club. Burns knew 'certain subjects were taboo in polite society.'[16] For this collection he removed sexual references from texts which we know he knew from current tradition. Presumably others did too. The collection also avoids political controversy.

So, in quoting from texts available in print in these two collections, Scott was evoking a particular social milieu for his audience, but one with the potential to raise associations beyond or even antagonistic to the world of a genteel readership. Neither the antiquarian Herd nor the light-entertainment *SMM* was specially popular, but they were both readily available. Both were part of a second generation interest in native Scots material which had developed throughout the eighteenth century and which is charted by David Johnson in *Music and Society in Scotland in the Eighteenth Century*. Allan Ramsay had been largely responsible in Scotland for the development of the so-called 'Scottish national song', 'a kind of pseudo-folk-song, designed for a genteel class of people who regard real folk-songs as crude and beneath their attention ... a national song is usually made by taking a folk-song and rewriting first the words and then the tune' (D. Johnson, 130). This tendency formed part of a reaction to the loss of Scottish independence, constitutionally after the Act of Union in 1707, and politically and militarily after the failure of the Jacobite risings in 1715 and 1745. It is worth remembering that nearly all the songs now commonly thought of as representing authentic Jacobite feeling were written as part of a later political nostalgia in the later eighteenth and early nineteeth century, 'as an act of self-conscious nationalism', by (for example) James Hogg and Lady Nairne, as well as Burns himself.[17] As David Johnson shows (145), by the 1780s there was a critical tension between national songs and folk songs proper which the many collections of the Romantic period all failed to resolve.

This is not to say that such tensions led to any polarisation of choice in the songs sung. One of the notable features of the *audience* for such work was its catholicity of taste, especially in Scotland, as is pointed by David Johnson and by David Craig. In the England of the late eighteenth century, and still more when Scott was writing, folk song was not unselfconsciously enjoyed by members of the middle and upper classes (those Percy called 'the public', as opposed to 'the people'). However, Scotland was different; folk and classical music 'co-existed within the same cultural framework', and 'the leisured and professional classes ... were also very much in touch with folk music (D. Johnson, 3, 15-18). The manuscript collections made by fiddlers—whose instrument was coming to dominate folk music in the eighteenth century—show an eclectic mixture of pieces (D. Johnson, 18-19, 111). Scott's own family habitually performed traditional Scottish material, which was much more to his taste than German or Italian classical music.[18]

Thomas Crawford has described Scott's ideal reader as 'a gentleman steeped in the folk and popular literature of both England and Scotland, who would greet such allusions with delight'.[19] Certainly Scott's implied reader is genteel. In *Guy Mannering* Chapter 5, Scott seems to imply that every reader will be able to observe country justices (from the right side of the dock, of course), and in *The Heart of Midlothian* Chapter 5, the narrator obviously expects the reader to pick up a Latin joke. But, as M. R. Dobie points out, Scott as a child was 'one of the audience for whom [ballads] were composed,'[20] and this cultural amphibiousness must have been characteristic of at least some of his readers as well.

So, the Scottish audience of Scott's novels would probably have had quite a wide acquaintance with traditional material, but the nationality of the readership would affect the degree of their familiarity with it. Even in Scotland, though, there would have been a difference in cultural knowledge between that of the characters Scott represents and members of his audience in similar class positions, since 'during the eighteenth century the social gap between the upper and lower classes had widened' (D. Johnson, 197). The former had become both more anglified and, in their reactive nationalism, more interested in 'national songs' and in instrumental music than in folk lyrics. Knowledge of songs dealing openly with sexuality would also have had both a class and gender bias; as far as Scott's readership is concerned, it is the gender bias that is important. Squeamishness about sexuality was found as early as Ramsay, who boasted in the preface to the fifth edition of *The Tea-table Miscellany* (1730) that he had 'kept out all Smut and Ribaldry, that the modest Voice and Ear of the fair Singer might meet with no affront.' Such fastidiousness—or, at least, the appearance of it—was a developing feature of the Romantic period.

Scott himself was subject to an increasing strictness of moral taste, as detailed in his anecdote about his great aunt, who persisted in asking him to send her Mrs Behn's novels in spite of his warning that she would not like the manners or language. Commenting on her later reaction, 'Take back your bonny Mrs Behn; and ... put her in the fire', Scott says this revulsion was 'owing to the gradual improvement of the national taste and delicacy.'[21] Scott felt himself to be part of this; he was not struggling against it. But it must have influenced the material he was prepared to quote explicitly. For example, the lines

>   O, in Skipton-in-Craven,
> Is never a haven,
>   But many a day foul weather;
> And he that would say
> A pretty girl nay,
>   I wish for his cravat a tether

from Chapter 8 of *Rob Roy* nicely fit their context: Diana Vernon is just about to try to soft soap Justice Inglewood. But Scott would seem to have adapted them from lines he could have found in Joseph Ritson's *Ancient Songs* (London, 1792, 190):

>   At Skipton in Craven there's never a haven,
>   Yet many a time foul weather;
>   He that will not lie a fair woman by,
>   I wish he were hang'd in a tether.

Surely even for the purposes of realistic reflection of Inglewood's coarseness he would hardly have thrust such indelicate lines on a gentle reader.

However, he had no objection to activating any latent knowledge in a reader already familiar with the texts quoted. I shall discuss later a couple of Effie's references in *The Heart of Midlothian*. One of Scott's favourite songs for quotation seems to have been 'The Bob of Dumblane', mentioned in *The Heart of Midlothian*, Chapter 40, *The Monastery* (Introduction) and privately.[22] Versions of this, probably by Ramsay, can be found in *TTM* (p. 34), Herd (**2**, 161) and William Thomson's *Orpheus Caledonius* (1733, no. 45). But none of these contains the lines Scott quotes, which seem to have attained a separate quasi-proverbial status. They are found in a version Burns is said to have heard in Dumblane, which is splendidly frank in its economical announcement of seduction and pregnancy:

>   Lassie, lend me your braw hemp heckle,
>   And I'll lend you my thripling kame;

My heckle is broken, it canna be gotten,
  And we'll gae dance the Bob-o-Dunblane.

Twa gaed to the wood, to the wood, to the wood,
Twa gaed to the wood, three came hame;
An' it be nae weel bobbit, weel bobbit, weel bobbit,
An' it be na we'll bobbit, we'll bob it again.[23]

Did this spring to the minds of Argyle's daughters in *The Heart of Midlothian* when their father quoted it? And how many of the audience remembered the old songs? Contemporary commentators certainly anticipated the complicit recognition Scott's methods imply, as we can see from the quotation from the indignant Motherwell on the title page of this book, with its suspicion of any rewritten song which in 'its spirit and covert allusion smacks of the elder devil which it has supplanted'.

All these factors introduce curious uncertainties into our ideas of the reception of the texts of his novels as a whole. Scott's novels are more, and more obviously than most, a patchwork of citations. One of the expectations readers tend to have about the genre 'novel' is that it emphasises its continuity with the 'text' we call 'reality'. Scott's novels don't conform consistently to this expectation. Neither do hundreds of others written before and since, but it is worth noting the ways in which Scott challenges it. The two most important are his use of layers of nominal narrators and his use of quotation. Scott didn't invent the latter technique. As Maryhelen Mayorkas points out in her thesis *Minstrels and Minstrelsy: Their Function in the Works of Sir Walter Scott* 'incorporating songs and ballads into the narrative' was a 'typically Gothic device.'[24] She cites 'Monk' Lewis, and it is a habit of Mrs Radcliffe as well, and Scott comments fairly favourably on it in his life of her.[25] However, Gothic writers were not given to quoting traditional and popular material. There was also a slight precedent in Maria Edgeworth's Irish regional novel *Castle Rackrent* (1800). Here one quotation from the folk song 'Landlord Fill the Flowing Bowl' in the text, and one of a formulaic ballad verse in the notes, add local colour to a comically exaggerated but realistically detailed tale.[26]

Conventionally literary sources may not, though, have been the only literary influences on Scott. When he was young, Scott himself was an avid collector of popular printed ephemera, and this collection, bound into six volumes in 1810, is preserved in the Library at Abbotsford. On the flyleaf of the first volume Scott explains its provenance and likely audience:

This little collection of stall tracts and ballads was formd by me when a boy from the baskets of the travelling pedlars. Untill [*sic*] put into its present decent binding it had such charms for the servants that it was

repeatedly and with difficulty rescued from their clutches. It contains
most of the pieces that were popular about 30 years since and I dare say
many that could not now be purchased for any price[27]

In spite of its title, 'Popular Ballads and Stories', which implies Scott
considered the ballads to be more important than the rest, the majority of the
collection is in prose. Many of the prose pieces display a vigorous straight-
forward narrative style, and they include lively vernacular speech from ordinary
people. One could argue that some of the forthrightness of Scott's lower-class
characters was derived from such models. More surprisingly, they too
interpolate quotations from songs, for example, 'The History of the Young
Coalman's Courtship to the Creelwife's Daughter', in which the hero sings a
quatrain from 'For the Sake of Somebody'; another version of the whole song
is found in a garland elsewhere in the collection.[28] Some pieces also have
vaguely relevant songs included at the end as a kind of makeweight, which is
not so far from Scott's practice in some of his notes to the novels.

We could, of course, escape from some of the dilemmas of classification
by claiming that the author of the Waverley Novels was in fact the author of the
Waverley Romances. This view could be supported by quoting some of Scott's
numerous self-deprecating comments about the value of the fiction writer's art
in general and his own in particular, for example, 'I was far from thinking that
the novelist or romance-writer stands high in the ranks of literature' (*The
Abbot*, introduction, ix). In spite of the distinction offered at the beginning of
the *Essay on Romance*[29] Scott admits that many works can be a mixture of
novel and romance. He frequently calls both the work of other writers like
Defoe and his own work 'romance'.[30] We could then claim that a gallimaufry
of allusion introduces a deliberate heterogeneity of form and content which
constantly insists on the fictionality of the text. For an audience familiar with
reading matter as mixed as that in publications like the *Gentleman's Magazine*
this might even be a preferred form of fiction.

This seems to me an element which requires recognition in Scott, and it
may even prove a satisfactory way of treating some of the novels with
Elizabethan, medieval or earlier settings. But it ignores several awkward
points, namely, that Scott's use of notes and his interweaving of historical
characters, his insistence on the constraints of contingent time and place on
human behaviour, all suggest that he wished the reader to relate the text(s) of
the novel to his/her experience of reality. Moreover, Scott constantly uses the
contrast between 'romance' in various forms and sober everyday experience as
part of a structure of moral contrasts which allows us to judge the progress of
the heroes' maturity (for example, Waverley's) and the relative value of the
causes competing for his commitment. Scott is well aware of the irony of this,

but if we relegate the whole of the novel to the status of 'romance' its Aristotelian didactic function collapses.

What is more, though it is not inevitable, calling the novels 'romances' can be just a way of being kind to sloppy writing. The tensions and self-contradictions of Scott's practice in the mode of the novel need recognition if we want to explain why we would advise a newcomer to Scott to read *Old Mortality* or *The Heart of Midlothian* rather than *Count Robert of Paris* or *The Betrothed*. To claim that all texts are intertexts says nothing interesting about specific works unless one establishes which expectations are aroused and what salient structural features are apparent; this provides at least some grounds for judging a text, and I would certainly argue that Scott is most successful when he roots his fiction in a world where all his characters have a credible cultural and social life, and where he uses his allusions to create a structure of moral paradigms which assumes the readers' approval or persuades them into it. A discussion of every example of Scott's folk song allusion would fill a large book (and comments on it are currently appearing in the notes to the new Edinburgh edition of his work) but the same broadly similar range of points would arise from each discussion.[31]

Some of the most obvious general points are these. Scott uses ballads as markers of heroic gallantry, irrespective of whether the intertext matches its frame in terms of period or subject. In its original context the heroism, violent though it may be, is usually seen as admirable, if only because circumstances allow of nothing more civilised. On the other hand, he is suspicious of cultured heroes who mistakenly find or deliberately manipulate a factitious charm in such simplicity of action, to the detriment of political realism and moral rectitude. This sometimes, but not usually, reflects back on the originals. Thus, in *The Black Dwarf* (1816, set shortly after the Union of 1707) Hobbie Elliott keeps up his spirits by whistling 'Jock o' the Side' (Chapter 2; 17). Chapter 8, about the pursuit of those who have raided his homestead, has an epigraph including lines from 'Jamie Telfer o' the Fair Dodhead'.[32] Marischal displays his defiant insouciance in the face of his possible fate by singing part of 'MacPherson's Lament':

> Sae dauntonly, sae wantonly,
> Sae rantingly gaed he,
> He play'd a spring and danced a round
> Beneath the gallows tree.[33]

Similarly, Dalgetty in Chapter 6 of *A Legend of [the Wars of] Montrose* (1819) cheers his spirits by singing the butt-end of a seventeenth-ventury military song.[34] The epigraph to Chapter 7 of *The Bride of Lammermoor* (1819) is from 'Bewick and Graeme'. In the original ballad, Christy Graham, egged on by his father, challenges his better-learned friend Bewick to combat, kills him, and commits suicide.[35] The characters of the two combatants in the novel, outlined by Craigengelt in the previous chapter, fit Bucklaw and Ravenswood. Although it is not pursued to the death here, the theme of the pointless duel is appropriate to the novel. So is the theme of the relentless parent sacrificing the child to his/her own pride, though this is displaced onto Lucy Ashton.

Scott takes ballads seriously, though not uncritically, as historical authorities, as for example in the note to *Waverley* on 'Field-piece in the Highland Army' (1829 onwards, 480). He uses them to give colouring to his pictures of the past. Thus, in Chapter 9 of *The Abbot* (82) Magdalen Graeme refers to her grandson Roland as her gay goss-hawk. This allows Scott to cite three verses of 'Fause Foodrage' (C89, and in the *Minstrelsy*) later, in Note 3 (430). As it happens, the ballad has considerable thematic relevance, since it deals with a deposed queen. Roland has been trained in falconry, and originally brought up in obscurity cherishing the possibility of revenge. The ballad also contains the theme of the deprived heir, though his case is more unjust than Roland's. This example also illustrates how often Scott uses ballad-type situations in his plots, but this is only one of a mixture of influences, and conventionally formulaic plots such as that of *The Bride of Lammermoor* do not owe their being only to traditional ballads.

To avoid repetition, and to give a more extended sense of the effects of individual novels, I therefore propose to continue by using four case studies. The first two examine Scott's use of false intertexts in novels set in two historical periods. One of these is set in the comparatively recent Scottish past; such a time and place usually encourages the more realist side of Scott. The other is set in the mid-seventeenth century, in England, and thus displays more of Scott the romance writer. In each of these novels there is a dense background consideration of different kinds of tradition, sometimes social, sometimes literary. The second two case studies deal with two Scottish novels which are clear candidates for recommendation as Scott's best work, and both of them involve copious allusion to song. They also involve manipulation of the intertexts, for although a distinction between 'false' and 'real' intertexts is a tidy one, all the writers discussed in this book adapt what they allude to to suit their own artistic purposes and for their audiences and thus mediate or misrepresent those texts in ways much more drastic than what is implied in the simple transposition of the text to a context alien to the original.

Scott, Tradition, and False Intertexts

This is a comparison of Scott's procedures in two very different novels. *The Antiquary* (1816) was written in the days of Scott's fresh success as a novelist, whilst *Woodstock* (1826) was composed very fast during the crisis of his life caused by the failure of Ballantyne and Constable.   Both novels are structured on cultural antitheses which are represented by different kinds of intertextual allusion and quotation, or apparent quotation. Each includes a major character from an older generation whose conversation consistently refers us to Shakespeare. Such reference is emblematic of the characters and cultural allegiances of these figures. It forms part of a pattern of allusion in the novel to which popular songs of some sort also make an important contribution. This pattern demonstrates the ambivalent attitudes towards tradition and the past in both the texts and their author.

First, what status did Shakespeare hold in the minds of Scott's likely readers?   And how far did their ideas correspond to Scott's? Scott himself undoubtedly found that his early and thorough knowledge of Shakespeare had helped to form his own idiolect; in his *Journal* for 1826 he admits: 'when I want to express a sentiment which I feel strongly, I find the phrase in Shakespeare'—or, as we shall see, in one or two other types of text.[36] Wilmon Brewer claims with reason that 'Scott assumes without difficulty that interest in Shakespeare is characteristic of every well-educated person'.[37] This applies to both his characters and his readers. Indeed, a reviewer of Scott's work in 1826—including *Woodstock*—devotes a long section of his article to listing echoes of Shakespeare, noting not only direct quotation, but also the 'unconscious adoption of Shakspearian forms of speech by almost every character'.[38] Such interest presumably suggests that allusion of this sort would be interesting to the reader, though perhaps also that some readers might like to be alerted to the extent of it. Brewer gives evidence for the continuing popularity of Shakespeare in Scott's day (16-17, 33-34).   Perhaps Jeffrey's review of Bowdler's censored edition of Shakespeare in 1818 may be seen as typical of Romantic attitudes. He credits Shakespeare with 'the most luxurious fancy which ever fell to the lot of a mortal' and claims that any indecency is incidental, and due to 'the misdirected wantonness of too lively a fancy'.[39]

With these things in mind I wish to move to a discussion of the first of the two novels, *The Antiquary*.   Like Scott himself in a wider context, the novel adopts an ambivalent attitude towards tradition.   On the one hand there is tradition as gossip and rumour.   This is the sort we see operating in Mrs Mailsetter's post office (Chapter 15), in the rapid perversion of the facts about Lovel's rescue of the Wardours and Edie, and about Sir Arthur's good fortune (Chapter 26). Rumour increases the death toll for the incident in which Steenie Mucklebackit (or Meiklebackit, as Scott originally wrote) is drowned by 400% (Chapter 29). There are varied popular expectations as to why Caxon has been given the job of watching the invasion beacon (Chapter 43).

On the other hand, popular memory is also presented as an accurate if somewhat selective record. Legend preserves the reputation of the inhabitants of a castle, if not of the monks: 'the shepherd will tell you with accuracy the names and feats of its inhabitants' (Chapter 17; 133). Even what is supposed to be the most closely guarded secret, and source of the plot mystery, the recent history of the Glenallans, is apparently known to local folk memory: 'there was queer things said about a leddy and a bairn or she left the Craigburnfoot' (Chapter 40; 316). Francie is able to fill in more of the story for Edie's benefit (Chapter 29). Most importantly, two characters now in very humble social positions are seen as accurate vessels of history. These two are Edie Ochiltree and Elspeth Mucklebackit. Indeed, in Elspeth's case almost the only coherent knowledge remaining to her is that of the Glenallan family. Saunders disparages the value of his mother's 'auld warld stories' (Chapter 32; 257), but the reader is twice assured that her information has the authority more readily recognised by a modern audience in that 'she can speak like a prent buke'. Significantly, this involves the diminution of her attachment to merely local community with the dwindling of her accent: 'she gets to her English' (Chapters 26, 39; 214, 309).

The existence of this kind of authority in Elspeth brings us to a question posed by the title of the novel. The deictic 'The' leads us to suppose that only one antiquary is intended, but the definite article may rather be used here in a generic sense. Certainly, if we ask the obvious question 'which character represents the figure of the title?' the answer is much less obvious. Oldbuck is a strong candidate, but even such minor figures as Sir Arthur and Blattergowl act as antiquaries at some point (Chapters 5, 19). Moreover, there is some tension between those who might claim to be antiquaries at the genteel level of society to whose members the term is most likely to be applied (primarily Oldbuck and Sir Arthur) and those who preserve and celebrate the past at a lower social level (primarily Edie Ochiltree and Elspeth Mucklebackit).[40]

The typography of Chapter 1 insists that Oldbuck is the ANTIQUARY. He is certainly a collector of objects from the past. He lays claim to an intention of intellectual rigour which is certainly manifested more often by him than by Sir Arthur, and which appears in his dismissal of the exaggerated claims made about Macpherson's *Ossian* in his discussion with Hector (Chapter 30). However, he is himself most optimistically credulous on other points, easily deceived by Edie, and comically rebuked by him about his supposed Praetorian *vallum*: 'Praetorian here, Praetorian there, I mind the bigging o't' (Chapter 4; 30). He is introduced as ridiculously irascible, and this quality in what is nominally the central figure of the novel is one of the prime reasons why, as David Daiches points out, 'in *The Antiquary* the prevailing atmosphere is comic [which] is unusual in Scott.'[41]

This feature is made more interesting by the fact that Oldbuck is in part a satirical portrait of Scott himself. In spite of the later versions of the Advertisement, and in spite of some commentators' claims that Oldbuck is a portrait of John Constable[42] one needs only a cursory acquaintance with Scott's tastes to notice some of him in Oldbuck. Both were trained as lawyers. Oldbuck is well-versed in the ancient dramatists, especially Shakespeare. He is a veteran collector, especially of ballads, including one 'thrice and four times rare broadside' of which the narrator claims to possess an exemplar (Chapter 3, 1829 onwards). The last sentence of the novel reveals that Oldbuck has completed his notes. These notes, of course, are for the *Caledoniad*, but the reader of later editions is irresistibly led on to the final section of Scott's text, which is—the Notes. Scott is introducing sly parallels between Oldbuck and himself both as personality and as narrator of the text.

However, this does not mean that he wishes to endow Oldbuck with authoritative judgement either about the past or the present. Many of his judgements are comically undermined. Moreover, in so far as the novel depends on character contrast rather than on the rather feeble love and deception plots for its structure, Oldbuck is paralleled throughout with Edie. As we have already seen, Edie is liable to have the upper hand when it comes to local history. If Edie is in no way a collector of historical objects, he is nevertheless both a repository of, and one who takes an interest in, that local history, in a way quite consistent with the earlier meaning of the word 'antiquary'. Scott is obviously striving for a nicely balanced response to Edie, an approval of his antiquarian function combined with a leavening of suspicion about his personality and his social role. Thus, in his (later) introductory material he cites a seventeenth-century opinion that 'many of the old Scottish mendicants' were 'descended from the ancient bards' and capable of reciting the slogans 'of most of the true ancient surnames of Scotland'. Edie, it is suggested, then, has the status of both inspired creative genius ('bard') and historian. Scott adds a note of literary approval in comparing Edie (through his model Andrew Gemmells) to one of Shakespeare's jesters. On the other hand, though beggars like Gemmells are licensed satirists, Scott places them ideologically by stressing their separation from the world of productive society: 'these indolent peripatetics suffered much less real hardship and want of food than the poor peasants from whom they received alms.' Oldbuck takes a similarly balanced view: a 'privileged nuisance' but also 'the minstrel, and sometimes the historian of the district' (Chapter 4; 33). However, although Edie is allowed to deceive Oldbuck there is no indication that he is anything other than a reliable channel of information on local pastimes, language, and, most importantly, the Glenallan history (Chapters 29, 30, 27). This latter point is also true of Elspeth, whose absolute accuracy on this matter is not to be doubted. Thus, both characters' memories act as substitutes for the narrator's authority. Edie also contributes to the foreshadowing of the resolution of the Wardour part of the plot in his relation of a traditional oral prophecy about Sir Arthur's estate (Chapter 23).

As one would expect, the major vehicle of Shakespearean allusion is Oldbuck; with the use of allusions to traditional phrasing or song the situation is more complicated. One or two of the text's references to Shakespeare serve to introduce an appropriately sombre note. One example would be the quotation from *King Lear* which forms the epigraph to Chapter 8, and its reinforcement by Oldbuck later, but these have no more than local appropriateness to a cliff and a storm. A parallel between Hector and Hotspur is developed; both are rash-tempered, but Hector comes no nearer to an early death than is required to cause the temporary disappearance of Lovel.[43]

On the whole, however, references to Shakespeare, though frequent, have a very limited propriety, and are often the result of intentional frivolity by Scott as narrator or through the person of Oldbuck, who is given to drastic parody of serious lines, as in his jokes to Hector about the seal, where he alludes to *King John*, and to Shylock's lament for his ring.[44] If *Lear* is used seriously earlier, it is used entirely frivolously in Oldbuck's attempts to prolong Lovel's stay (Chapter 11). Indeed, out of what I take to be thirty references to Shakespeare's plays in the novel, at least twenty-one are in contexts which reduce the seriousness of the original. For all Scott's fondness for Shakespeare, this is entirely characteristic of him in both his public and private writing. In his journal for 13 December, 1826, just after expressing his overwhelming admiration for Shakespeare, Scott makes a rather vulgar adaptation of *Romeo and Juliet* about his *bottom's* lord.[45]

If this was how Scott operated with a source which he venerated and believed that others venerated, what did he do with material which he believed to be valuable, but felt ambivalent about, and certainly felt defensive about before his public, to wit, the songs of tradition? As he did with Shakespeare, Scott assimilated odds and ends of traditional phrasing into his own habitual mode of expression, and such phrases operated with the status of a proverb—collocations complete in themselves rather than reminiscent of particular contexts. An example relevant to *The Antiquary* is in the *Journal* for 13 August, 1826:

> No wonder if I must sing at last—
>> Thus says the auld man to the Aik tree,
>> Sair faild, hinny, since I kend thee. (*Journal*, 184)

These lines, which come from a North Country song, have been absorbed in the texture of Edie's speech in Chapter 12, 'I am no that sair failed yet' (92).[46]

Scott is using what is a marked allusion in his journal, but a tacit one in his creation of Edie's speech, an idiolect supposedly dignified by traditional phrasing. In the previous chapter, Oldbuck has used both a typographically marked quotation from Shakespeare, and, unmarked, what is taken to be a familiar quotation from an historical ballad known to literati through Percy's *Reliques* (87).[47] Of course, Scott cannot make publicly recognisable jokes without publicly recognisable material, and it may be that this is the constraint that tends to restrict his reference to ballad phrasing and contexts to more sober occasions, but it is also feasible that this sobriety is out of a respect for a marginalised body of texts and subculture.

In some cases the original is comic. Oldbuck comes home in Chapter 9 to find the minister has eaten his supper and, with entire appropriateness, half-whistles and half-hums

the end of the old Scottish ditty,

> O, first they eated the white puddings,
> And then they eated the black, O,
> And thought the gudeman unto himsell,
> The de'il clink down wi' that, O![48]

On other occasions the implications are more sombre. Chapter 4, which introduces Edie, is prefixed with the first four lines of 'The Gaberlunzie Man', his theme tune, as it were. This well-known ballad[49] is cheerful in tone with a happy ending, but when Edie is relating the history of the Wardour family in Chapter 24, he quotes a line from it recalling the violent conventional endings for sexual wrongdoers in the ballad world: 'she's be burnt, and he's be slain' (199).

Indeed, Edie and Elspeth live in a world partly constructed of ballad vocabulary and expectations. Edie stresses Oldbuck's relationship with Hector in terms of the closest relationship in ballad families: 'the blood o' your sister's son' (Chapter 44; 345). What is left of Elspeth's mind formulates matters in ballad terms. The death she expects from Lord Glenallan in Chapter 33 is to be burnt in a fire prepared by his 'merry men', as befalls the treacherous women in ballads like 'Earl Richard' or 'Lamkin'.[50] This brings her mental world a lot closer to that of the ballad than to Shakespeare's, in spite of Brewer's insistence that her actual death resembles that of Cardinal Winchester in *Henry VI* (253-54). Even the rejection of Eveline Neville by her mother-in-law through a false story and her death by or after immersion in the sea has some similarities with the story of 'The Lass of Lochroyan'.[51] In Chapter 40 Elspeth revamps a verse from 'The Douglas Tragedy' to suit her version of the situation:

He turned him right and round again,
  Said, Scorn na at my mither;

Light loves I may get mony a ane,
  But minnie ne'er anither.

She has changed the sexes round; in the original the girl begs her lover not to kill the father who is attacking him.[52] Elspeth projects onto Lord Glenallan the passionate feeling of loyalty she herself had for her mistress, and changes '*true* loves' to '*light* loves' to denigrate the romantic feeling between Glenallan and Eveline.

This chapter in fact opens with four lines of apparent nonsense about the preferences of fish and shellfish, developed from a traditional kernel in a song Scott could have found in Herd's collection.[53] They suggest, in their illogicality, an eerie atmosphere, and set the scene for a climactic chapter that combines comedy and tragedy in its focus on the most extensive 'song' in the book, 'The Ballad of the Red Harlaw'. The tragedy lies in the matter of the ballad: the great loss on both sides in the battle. The comedy lies in the inadequate reactions of all the bystanders to Elspeth, apparently deranged, singing to children who are not there, but also fey, a Fate still spinning in her dotage. Edie has a simple practical but obtuse response: 'it is a sad thing to see human nature sae far owerta'en as to be skirling at auld sangs on the back of a loss like her's' (310-11). Hector is too angered at the denigration of the Highlanders to hear any more than 'a silly old woman sing a silly old song'; 'I have not seen or heard a worse half-penny ballad' (312).

Oldbuck, however, is entranced by the prospect of so many 'legendary scraps of ancient poetry', and eagerly latches on to what he takes to be 'a genuine and undoubted fragment of minstrelsy! Percy would admire its simplicity—Ritson could not impugn its authenticity' (310). Now, though I fear that Percy might well have admired its 'simplicity', Ritson would certainly not have had much difficulty in impugning its authenticity. For the most important feature of this 'traditional ballad' is its *absence* from the text. As traditional ballad, it isn't *there*, since it is Scott's own composition. Ritson would no doubt have been rightly suspicious of its vocabulary—words like 'chafron' (which so much excites Oldbuck), and 'jeopardie', let alone a phrasing that might look forward to Tennyson, but looks backward to nothing: 'Then ne'er let the gentle Norman blood/Grow cauld for Hieland kerne'. Though Scott has put together a number of ballad formulae, such as the saddling of the steeds, and an interchange between two leaders as to whether to fight or flee, much of the language is in fact a dead give-away.

One of the reasons this is so interesting in the context of intertextuality is that there were extant in Scott's day at least two 'ballads' on the Battle of

Harlaw. One of these was well-known to Scott and probably to many of his readers since it was printed in Ramsay's *The Evergreen* (1724, **1**, 78-90) and elsewhere (for example, in part in the *Scots Musical Museum* **5**, no. 512). As Child says in his headnote to the ballad (C163) this poem 'is not in the least of a popular character' and has more elaborate stanzas of eight lines each.

However, there was another more authentically traditional one from Aberdeenshire.[54] The problem is that so far I have found no evidence that Scott knew of its existence. Had he done so, it seems inconceivable that he would not have included it in his notes, or even somewhere—in spite of the provenance—in the making or remaking of the *Minstrelsy*. However, the tune is recorded twice in the manuscript music of Lady John Scott, and the copy of it printed in 1858[55] by Aytoun was derived by her from a friend of Mr. Dalrymple, the source of Child 163A. C. K. Sharpe, who had sent Scott ballads from 1802,[56] was the source of much of Lady John's knowledge of folk music. The most likely explanation is that Scott thought of the traditional version as lost—a mention of one is made in *The Complaynte of Scotland* of 1549—and decided to reconstruct it in a way appropriate to the motivation of Elspeth's vengeful pride.

In turning to *Woodstock* we see a comparable set of oppositions structuring the novel, though with wider historico-political resonances. Again we have an elderly afficianado of Shakespeare in Sir Henry Lee, and again, his allusions are often of a superficial character and he is undermined by comic touches. As Scott himself points out, Lee's applications of Shakespeare do not display either real taste for him, or skill in application, but are partly manifestations of loyalty, since Charles I was supposedly an enthusiast for the Bard. Indeed, some of Charles II's unsoundness appears in his own distaste for Shakespeare, though *Richard II* was hardly a tactful choice of reading matter on Lee's part.[57] In this novel, unlike *The Antiquary*, Shakespeare and song are manifestly on the same side. The Royalists are associated with a plurality of kinds of diversion which includes not only Shakespeare and Cavalier songs, but also the world of Romance—which forms part of a set of binary oppositions in many of Scott's novels from *Waverley* onwards—and of what might loosely be called the pursuits of 'merrie England', such as folk song, maypole celebrations and morris dancing. This cluster is set against an almost entirely hypocritical language of inflated Biblical phrasing from the Roundhead side.[58] There is considerable historical warrant for the Puritan opposition to every feature of this association.[59] In the novel this is represented largely by the turncoat Tomkins in a significant discussion in Chapter 3. Here he lays all 'lawless idleness and immodest folly' to Shakespeare's charge, and compares the healthy amorous behaviour of the pertinently-named Joliffe and Phoebe to a dancing school 'where the scoundrel minstrels make their ungodly weapons to squeak, "Kiss and be kind, the fiddler's blind"' (41).

At first glance one might assume that the frequency of Shakespearean allusion and phrasing is an attempt to short-circuit imagination by a desperate man—Scott writing against time and circumstance. Brewer finds sixty-nine allusions from twenty five plays in *Woodstock*, more than in any other novel (367). At the time of writing, Scott was (abortively) editing Shakespeare and had finished three volumes by 1826 (Brewer, 42). Yet Scott's journal gives the impression of some elation at his elasticity under pressure, rather than desperation, and much of the novel was rapidly written. The baldness with which love of Shakespeare is used as a touchstone suggests deliberate if crude planning, and Scott seems to have thought the use of Shakespeare an entirely appropriate mode of engaging the reader's sense of historical context.

Even though he was not above mischievously planting 'an anachronism for some sly rogue to detect'[60] one can also see Scott's sense of history in his song references. In *Woodstock* these are not, of course, predominantly either folk songs or traditional classic ballads, although Chapter 34 opens with an appropriate memory of 'Fair Rosamond', who was imprisoned in Woodstock.[61] The songs here are from a popular tradition of a different sort. In the battle of ephemeral publications during the Commonwealth, the small arms fire of song was very largely Royalist, and established men of letters did not scruple to add their own verses to those from humbler writers (Rollins, 14). Few of these texts outlived their times and they are no longer represented in sung tradition,[62] not even Martin Parker's 'When the King Enjoys his Own Again'. Rollins says this 'is universally admitted to have played no small part in keeping up the spirits of the Royalists and in bringing about the Restoration' (20). Scott would seem, therefore, to be entirely justified in using it as a key-note reference for Wildrake; substantial references to it occur four times, though the words are not always those of Parker's original. The song was fairly well-known and widely printed, so Scott could have expected at least some of his readers to recognise it.[63]

However, it is not the most lengthily 'quoted' Cavalier lyric in *Woodstock*. This honour goes to the glee supposedly composed by Dr. Rochecliffe and given in Chapter 20. Once again a major 'allusion' in the novel is to a piece by Scott. Readers of Scott's note on Rochecliffe would realise he was fictitious, but unless they also had access to Scott's journal (for 6 February 1826) they could not be sure that the glee also is invented, and Scott presents it, once again, as if it were a genuine Cavalier song. In fact it's a much better imitation than the 'Ballad of the Red Harlaw'. The more varied lyric measures of Cavalier songs suited Scott's gift of easy versification and he catches accurately the combination of alcoholic enthusiasm and Royalist loyalty. Here, though,

Scott is not really improving on history for the sake of his plot, for Cavalier popular lyrics, like this glee, are often unspecific enough to fit anything. We must, I think, conclude that Scott inserts this glee largely because he wants to try his hand at such a composition.

Here, therefore, we have two novels with quite different settings: the Scotland of recent time—the 1790s—within the memory of a few generations, and of Scott's native culture, and the England of 1652, reconstructed from Scott's historical reading. These two broad types have been seen as characteristic of Scott's successful and unsuccessful novels respectively.[64] However, these two novels exhibit strong similarities of structure and role with regard to their uses of intertextuality. Notably, both offer the appearance of reference to pre-existing texts when in fact these do not exist, thus producing in the reader a false 'recognition' of the materials of historical discourse.

In order to place this in a critical context we might do better to turn from Culler and Kristeva to their model Bakhtin. For if Scott is not referring to supposedly identifiable texts he is certainly imitating the discourse out of which such texts sprang. In Bakhtin's terms, such allusion is the discourse of an incorporated genre, and would stand as part of the third category of discourse: doubly-oriented speech.[65] Moreover, both novels contain obvious elements of what for Bakhtin is a distinguishing feature of the genre: the carnivalesque.[66] *The Antiquary* has Edie as its licensed representative, and in *Woodstock* the Puritan hegemony is undermined by the ex-Morris man Joliffe. It is easy to align these characters with the positive sides of the oppositions I have outlined. Since these oppositions are both ambivalent, and composed of heterogeneous materials, there is no necessary contradiction between their broadly binary nature and Bakhtin's concept of polyphony, in spite of the time of writing. Scott's narrative voice certainly operates to exert some degree of control, but until the final resolution the text is highly conscious of the dialogue of differing voices.[67]

Such a theoretical framework does not, however, necessarily provide a method of evaluating Scott's novels. Neither does it do away with the realist-oriented reader's sneaking suspicion that Scott is cheating. However, it does help to clarify similarities of structure in differing types of Scott's fiction, and to illuminate a procedure which was as typical of Scott the personality as it was of Scott the novelist.[68]

Scott's Use of Allusion to Traditional Song

Scott's use of allusion to folk song faces us with some of the problems of intertextuality in their most extreme form, in switching not only from prose to verse, but to verse of such varying kinds, some of which has overtones of a quite different, and non-verbal, art form. His allusions could be classified as follows:

  a) simple display,
  b) allusion which seems to imply audience recognition of common material,
  c) the ingenious selection of unlikely quotation for its local verbal propriety,
  d) selection for significant intertextual propriety.

This is not meant to be a hierarchy; the types can be combined; (d) could go along with either (a), where Scott's sense of the significance of a quote would be largely hidden, or with (b).

A good example of (a) would be 'no end of popular ballads' as the source for King Richard's disguise in *Ivanhoe*, and especially 'The Kyng and the Hermite'. This was 'first communicated to the public in that curious record by ... Sir Egerton Brydges and Mr. Hazlewood, in the periodical work entitled *The British Bibliographer*' and then by Charles Hartshorne's *Ancient Metrical Tales* (xiii). By citing the second book even Scott seems to imply that few would have met the first, and as he points out in this 1830 introduction, the second was not published until 1829, nine years after the first edition of the novel. It would be expecting rather a lot to demand recognition of a possible source here.

Looking at just Scott's references to his source, some readers of Chapter 15 of *The Abbot* might think that 'The Paip, that pagan full of pride', a 'ballad popular among the lower classes' was pretty abstruse. But they could also have found it in Ramsay's *Evergreen* (2, 236-39), and if they had met this compilation (2nd ed. 1761) would be able to read this as a type (b) allusion. They might even know how much of the ribald criticism of the clergy Scott had cut out and replaced with something more decorous.[69]

These two divisions—(a) and (b)—focus on the way the text constructs relations between its sender and its addressees. The second pair shifts the focus to the relation between the text itself and other texts (including, for the sake of argument, 'reality') and on the text's internal relations. Thomas Crawford picks out the effect of this division. He says Scott's 'novelty consists in the contradictoriness of the strands combining to form his texture rather than in the originality of each strand considered in isolation' (1965, 84). This would cover (c)—a purely verbal propriety which ignores anachronisms such as an Elizabethan ballad as an epigraph to Chapter 26 of a story about ancient Byzantium, or a song about a minister who took part in the battle of Killiecrankie (1689) being 'remembered' at the time of Cromwell in *Woodstock* (Chapter 28; 339). It would also cover examples where a knowledge of the context is positively unhelpful, e.g. the epigraph to Chapter 18 of *Peveril of the Peak*:

> Now rede me, rede me, brother dear,
>   Throughout Merry England,
> Where will I find a messenger,
>   Betwixt us two to send.

The words quoted fit the idea of the selection of a messenger, in this case Julian Peveril's being sent to London on behalf of the Countess of Derby. But in the original 'Ballad of King Estmere', easily available in Percy's *Reliques* (**1**, 62-78), the enquirer goes himself.

Crawford also says, rightly, that 'each novel has its own kind of song, its own special pattern of *pastiche*' and that in many novels 'allusion to ballad *motifs* has almost the function of imagery' (1965, 83-4). I would extend the latter comment to cover texts as well as motifs. As we have seen, even a comparatively undistinguished novel like *Woodstock* has an ingenious structure of contrasts of intertextual loyalties and there is a similar contrast in *The Heart of Midlothian* and *Redgauntlet*. But if this claim is true, Scott is here using allusion to unify his work and bind it together, something he is not always given credit for. I wish to contend that this is the case and that there are plenty of examples of various shades of (d) to prove it.

This leads me to my second set of case studies. One example that Scott himself seems to call our attention to is the tune conversation between Darsie and Willie in Chapters 9/10 of *Redgauntlet*. This is possible, Scott says, (through Darsie) because 'in Scotland, where there is so much national music, the words and airs of which are generally known, there is a kind of free-masonry amongst performers, by which they can, by a mere choice of a tune, express a great deal to the hearers' (200-01). This section is obviously a *tour de force*, a display like Wandering Willie's Tale itself. It forms part of a structural contrast in which gaiety and a certain degree of lawlessness are set against the ultimately victorious stolid compromise of Alan's world of Edinburgh law. However, the musical element is marginalised to the more attractive and sympathetic of the rogues, such as Willie himself and Nanty Ewart. Neither of them offers either the virtues or the tedium of ideological commitment, though it is worth noting that Willie ends his days as a sort of retainer in 'Sir Arthur Redgauntlet's ha' neuk' (379), the kind of position he had indignantly repudiated earlier, in Letter 10. Redgauntlet's cause is so hopelessly anachronistic that it isn't offered even the spurious attractions of a musical trapping, except briefly in Chapters 11/12, when Summertrees embarrasses Crosbie by singing a Jacobite song.

One of the functions of this conversation is to enhance Scott's limited but sincere claim that men are brothers. This is set against Darsie's sometimes snobbish condescension. In Letter 10 Darsie recounts how he came upon a man and (apparently) two boys singing a catch from Cowley: the voices 'were

rough, but kept good time, and were managed with too much skill to belong to
the ordinary country people' (78). But Willie, Maggie and Benjie *are* ordinary
country people except for their musicianship. What is more, it is Willie who
relates what is often regarded as one of Scott's tightest and best-told tales.
Willie gives Darsie a lesson in both fiddling and politesse, and ends with a
claim of his own superiority: 'if he was ten gentles, he canna draw a bow like
me' (Letter 10, 82). Willie's familiarity with both a sonata of Corelli's and
traditional-type tunes like 'Galashiels' is not an invention of Scott, but a fair
observation of the likely repertoire of professional musicians of the period of
even a humble sort.[70]

Scott's assumption of a community of culture between his characters is a fair
one. It is one that can also be applied to his audience; the setting of the novel is
near enough in time and culture to the time of writing for some of them to have
remembered it. Nevertheless, Scott is cautious to spell out by copious quotation
the exact wording of the messages, for the benefit of those who might not be so
familiar with them. This, and the fact that this promising intrigue never actually
comes to anything, might make us suspicious that Scott is having a bit of fun in
showing off his ingenuity as well as applying a little sticking plaster to class
relations. But perhaps this little episode of Darsie as imprisoned King Richard
and Willie as faithful minstrel is precisely part of the romance that our two
heroes need educating out of and can play no part in the real world. In any case,
it is well worth looking at the works Scott quoted in a little more detail. Let us
look at the sequence, omitting just one untraced reply from Darsie. I am using
verses selected from wherever in the song seems appropriate. Then I shall run
over the items separately in discussion.

> Here awa', there awa here awa', Willie,
> Here awa', there awa', here awa', hame.
> Lang have I sought thee, dear have I bought thee,
> Now I ha'e gotten my Willie again.

> When as we sat in Babylon
>   the rivers round about,
> And in remembrance of Sion
>   the tears for grief burst out.
> We hang'd out [*sic*] harps and instruments
>   the willow trees upon:
> For in that place men for their use
>   had planted many a one.

> Then they to whom we prisoners were
>   said to us tauntingly,
> Now let us hear your Hebrew songs,

and pleasant melodie.
Alas said we, who can once frame
 his sorrowful heart to sing,
The praises of our living God
  thus under a strange king?

O whistle an' I'll come to you, my lad;
O whistle an' I'll come to you, my lad:
Though father and mither should baith gae mad,
O whistle, an' I'll come to you, my lad.
Come down the back stairs when ye come to court me;
Come down the back stairs when ye come to court me;
Come down the back stairs, and let naebody see;
And come as ye were na' coming to me,
And come as ye were na' coming to me.

Dearest Maid nay do not fly me
Let your Pride no more deny me
Never doubt your faithfull Willie,
There's my Thumb, I'll ne'er beguile ye.

The night is my departing night,
 The morn's the day I maun awa,
 There's no a friend or fae o' mine,
  But wishes that I were awa.
What I hae done for lack o' wit
 I never never can reca'
I trust ye're a' my friends as yet,
 Gude night and joy be wi' you a'.

When first my brave Johnnie lad came to this town,
He had a blue bonnet that wanted the crown;
But now he has gotten a hat and a feather.
Hey, brave Johnnie lad, cock up your beaver!
Cock up your beaver, and cock it fu' sprush;
We'll over the Border and gie them a brush:
There's somebody there we'll teach better behaviour.
Hey, brave Johnnie lad, cock up your beaver!

My heart's in the Highlands, my heart is not here;
My heart's in the Highlands a chasing the deer;
A chasing the wild deer, and following the roe,
My heart's in the Highlands, wherever I go.
Farewell to the Highlands, farewell to the north,
The birthplace of Valour, the country of Worth,

Wherever I wander, wherever I rove,
The hills of the Highlands for ever I love.

Though Geordie reigns in Jamie's stead,
I'm griev'd, yet scorn to shaw that;
I'll ne'er look down, nor hang my head
On rebel Whig, for a' that.
For a' that, and a' that,
And thrice as muckle's a' that,
He's far beyond Dumblane the night,
That shall be king, for a' that.

Whare will I get a bonny boy
That will win hose and shoon;
That will gae down to Durisdeer,
And bid my merry-men come?

Robin is my ain dear jo,
Robin kens the way to woo,
And to his suit I mean to bow,
For Robin says he loes me.

Heigh hey, Robin, quo she,
Heigh hey, Robin now;
Heigh hey, Robin, quo she,
Kind Robin loes me!

Bid iceshogles hammer red gads on the studdy,
And fair simmer mornings nae mair appear ruddy;
Bid Britons think ae gait, and when they obey ye,
But never till that time believe I'll betray ye.
Leave thee, leave thee, I'll never leave thee;
The starns shall gang withershins e'er I deceive thee.[71]

Obviously, the whole point of this sequence is that the sections used should
have verbal propriety of type (c) and there is a slight degree of type (d)
propriety. Out of the twelve songs used in the text six (half) seem to be love
songs, four songs of political activity or exile. If one includes the psalm this
makes five. Though it is from a very different context it certainly fits the theme
of captive exile, and perhaps hints at a Protestant allegiance rather than a
Catholic one. One of the extracts is from a ballad. There is a loose general
appropriateness about the songs of political activity and exile to the Jacobite
theme, though they all align the sympathy with the defeated Jacobites. I would
like to be able to argue that the use of the love songs can be connected to the

humiliating period Darsie spends disguised as a woman, an outward image of his impotence in the world of masculine action, but in fact he is allotted the man's part in at least half, and in the last quote Scott even changes the words to give this effect. The snatch of ballad, as Scott points out, is a floater found in many ballads and this version seems to have been put together by Scott: the name Durisdeer and this plot motif suggest 'Johnnie o'Breadislee', but these lines are not in Scott's version.

'Wandering Willie' (Herd **2**, 253), (*SMM* **1**, no. 57) presents the image of searching for a favoured person, and, of course, the title coincides with the fiddler's soubriquet. There are many translations of Psalm 137; I selected this one because of the widespread use of Sternhold and Hopkins, because Scott owned a copy of an edition of this year (1649), and because the last line quoted, 'thus under a strange king' does not appear in other versions from the eighteenth century which I have checked, yet it seems to have a sly relevance to the Jacobite theme. 'Whistle and I'll Come T'ye, my Lad' (*SMM* **2**, no. 106) has words by Burns enjoining secrecy in making a visit. 'There's My Thumb' appears in very different versions in different sources. There is one version in Herd **2**, 200, one in *TTM*, 70, and one in Thomson's *Orpheus Caledonius*, no. 42. It produces the most comically odd effect as soon as we move beyond the one line Scott quotes. Keen memories of the love song context in Herd would certainly add unexpected implications to this relationship:

> Thy bosom white, and legs sae fine are,
> That, when in pools I see thee clean 'em
> They carry away my heart between 'em.

The one quoted in the song sequence is from Thomson. If Scott was thinking of this version he selected it for its apt introduction of the fidelity of a character called Willie. 'Goodnight and Joy be wi' ye all' is the well-known fragment 'Armstrong's Goodnight' which Scott printed in the *Minstrelsy*, and he also mentions it in *Waverley*, Chapter 43 (277). It is also in Herd **2**, 182, and *SMM* **6**, no. 600. According to Scott, Armstrong is supposed to be fleeing his native land for murder, but Henderson in his edition of the *Minstrelsy* suggests a Jacobite application.[72] It continues the flight theme and introduces the idea of conflict. This is picked up more specifically in the Jacobite 'Hey, Johnnie Lad, Cock Up Your Beaver' (*SMM* **4**, no. 309 and *Jacobite Relics* **2**, 127). This relates the conflict specifically to the Border, Darsie's troubles arising because for him the Scotland/England border divides laws as well as geographical areas. 'My Heart's in the Highlands', though, is a more generalised expression of longing for one's native land, and Darsie is hardly a Highlander. This is part of the Romantic political geography that aligns Jacobitism with picturesque scenery and costume. Scott knew at least three versions of this song[73] and here chooses the Burns one, perhaps the most likely to be familiar to his audience. He makes it clear, however, that the version of 'For a' That' he has in mind is 'the fine old Jacobite air', (*Relics* **2**, 55) i.e. neither the Burns universal brotherhood version, nor the love-song in *SMM* **2**, no. 290.[74]

The four lines about getting a messenger to effect a rescue are common form in many ballads, as already mentioned. Willie presumably thinks Darsie is taking risks in being so explicit, but the tune he uses to cover Darsie's words puzzles him, as well it might. There are varying versions of 'Kind Robin Loes Me'[75] but all are love songs assuring fidelity, as is the final piece to which Willie retreats. Some variants of 'Kind Robin' deal with the girl's preference of a kiss from her lover over fine clothes. Darsie is about to be forcibly disguised in woman's clothes, but he doesn't know this, and there is no reason to suppose Willie does either. It doesn't help much to see these love songs as a hint of the relationship between Darsie and Greenmantle, who is the subject of the next paragraph and represents 'another quarter from which [he] looks for succour'. Whatever Darsie may think, her goodwill is based on sisterly rather than sexual affection. The quotations are carefully chosen for their local significance but have only a rough general fit with the book's themes. This carefully controlled sequence seems to have as its main function the establishment of community of culture between author and readers and characters of different classes. This is achieved by the articulation of a range of intertexts which assume common participation in the process of mediating folk culture into popular middle-class culture through a process of nationalist sentimentalising.

If we look at *The Heart of Midlothian* we can see working examples of all four of my categories. Scott's scintillating allusiveness here, as elsewhere, ranges over an enormous breadth of reference. He can hardly have expected his average reader to have called to mind without his prompting an appropriate piece of Fletcher (Chapter 42) or the 'The Elegy on Mrs. Anne Killigrew' (Chapter 43). In this novel too, though, he is using false intertexts, and is often bluffing in his attribution of 'old songs' to the fragments sung by Madge Wildfire.

Of course, Madge is more a creature of literary tradition than of observation, even given her alleged prototype in Feckless Fannie.[76] Scott himself directs us to this conclusion in comparing her to Ophelia at the end of Chapter 16 (170). We might then expect her to create pathos by quoting, as Ophelia does, from simple popular ditties. Scott says that 'it was remarkable, that there could always be traced in her songs something appropriate, though perhaps only obliquely or collaterally so, to her present situation' (Chapter 40; 418). But when the 'something appropriate' seems to have been invented by Scott rather than discovered elsewhere, one feels he is not playing the game. When Madge is dying (Chapter 40) he introduces some of her fragments with typical equivocations: 'a part of the chorus and words of what had been *perhaps*, [my italics] the song of a jolly harvest-home' (417) or 'her next *seemed* [my italics] to be the fragment of some old ballad' (418). I have not found any likely origin for 'Our work is over—over now' (417) or 'Cauld is my bed, Lord Archibald' (418) in popular song. Nor would I expect to find them. Vocabulary, sentence structure and linguistic devices mark Scott's own intervention, for example, the feminine ending in repeated rhymes, with a rather stiff hyperbaton: 'And sad my sleep of sorrow ... Though death your mistress borrow.' This is not to decry the achievement of 'Proud Maisrie' (419) but this is in itself a much better piece. Its dramatic structure of question and answer and the common-core vocabulary of the first two and a half verses at least produce both a closer and a more dynamic approximation to the feeling of an 'old ballad' like 'Proud Lady Margaret' in the *Minstrelsy*.

Much of the material that is genuine quotation shows genuine care in selection and adaptation on Scott's part, so that it fits well into category (c) at least and usually makes the leap into (d). His source was probably an entirely literary one for the words Madge uses to describe Bedlam to Jeanie at the end of Chapter 29:

> In the bonny cells of Bedlam,
>   Ere I was ane-and-twenty,
> I had hempen bracelets strong,
> And merry whips, ding-dong,
>   And prayer and fasting plenty.

This is from one of the mad songs in vogue in the sixteenth and seventeenth centuries and Scott could have found it in Ritson's *Ancient Songs* (1829, **2**, 248) where it is attributed to a miscellany of 1660, *Le Prince d'Amour*. Although Madge sings it, it is doubtful that Scott would have heard it. Ritson says the tune is in D'Urfey's *Pills to Purge Melancholy* (**4**, 189) which contains a whole group of mad songs, but in fact the one cited has a different set of words and would not easily fit these. Ritson's version runs:

> 'Of' thirty bare years, have I
>   Twice twenty been inraged,
>   And of forty, been
>   Three times fifteen
>   In durance soundly caged,
> On the lordly lofts of Bedlam,
>   With stubble soft and dainty,
>   Brave bracelets strong,
>   And whips ding dong,
> And wholesome hunger plenty.

Another example, though, was heading at least half way to tradition, in that what is recognisably the original piece can be found in *TTM* **1**, 73, and was recorded by Charles Kirkpatrick Sharpe.[77] Scott's snippet is 'Up in the air,/On my bonny grey mare,/And I see, and I see, and I see her yet.' Ramsay's runs

> Now the sun's gane out o' sight,
> Beet the ingle, and snuff the light;
>   In glens the fairies skip and dance,
> And witches wallop o'er to *France*.
>   Up in the air
>   On my bonny gray mare,
> And I see her yet, and I see her yet.

At this point in Chapter 18 Madge is being questioned about the disappearance of 'Robertson', who seems, like the rider in the song, to have vanished into thin air. The song ends with the injunction 'To my wife's first husband me commend' and it's worth remembering that at this point Madge, a former lover of 'Robertson', is supposed to be in court to testify to her knowledge of him, when he has just written a letter to the magistrate in support of the innocence of Effie, his new mistress. So the idea of an individual with two sexual partners is backed up by the full original context of the song.

Unequivocally popular song material is also carefully selected for its oblique appropriateness, as in another snippet from Madge's interrogation a little earlier in Chapter 16:

> What did ye wi' the bridal ring—bridal ring—bridal ring
> What did ye wi' your bridal ring, ye little cutty quean, O?
>   I gied it till a sodger, a sodger, a sodger,
>   I gied it till a sodger, an auld true love o' mine, O.

This is from a piece that probably had a political original (or adaptation) but survived as a nonsense song dialogue between a robin and a wren, 'The Wren', or 'Lennox's Love to Blantyre'. Scott could have met this in Herd (**2**, 281) or in *SMM* **5**, no 483.[78] The Herd version runs:

> And qhere's the ring that I gied ye,
> That I gied ye, that I gied ye;
> And qhere's the ring that I gied ye,
> Ye little cutty quean-O
>   I gied it till a soger,
>   A soger, a soger
>   I gied it till a soger,
>   A kynd sweet-heart o' myne-O.

The tone of irritated interrogation is entirely appropriate to the situation. Madge is being asked about something she has given to 'Robertson' (Staunton)—her clothes, but the 'wedding ring' idea reflects her sexual relationship with him.

Nor is this care simply a feature of Scott's creation of Madge, with her Shakespearean precedent; it is—intermittently at least—a feature of the novel as a whole. Certainly there are examples of a less rigorous propriety. The epigraph from Chapter 8 is an example of my category (b), and one of the rare examples when the quotation has no immediate relevance—a category so rare I felt free to omit it from my scheme. It consists of four lines from an 'Old Song', 'Waly Waly Gin Love Be Bonny' to be found in Herd (**1**, 140-41), *TTM* 170-71, Percy (**3**, 144-46) and *SMM* **2**, no. 158:

> Arthur's Seat shall be my bed,
>   The sheets shall ne'er be pressed by me;
> St. Anton's well shall be my drink,
>   Sin' my true-love's forsaken me.[79]

One might think that this would be appropriate for part of Effie's story, but in fact this chapter deals only with the history of Butler and his neighbours, so this easily recognisable quotation has no relevance to what follows, at least in this chapter.

However, there are numerous examples of (c) and (d). An example for (c) is the epigraph for Chapter 12,

> Then she stretch'd out her lily hand,
>   And for to do her best;
> 'Hae back thy faith and troth, Willie,
>   God gie thy soul good rest.'

Jeanie offers in this chapter to revoke her understanding with Reuben because of her sister's loss of character. But the original context, in which the lover is returning from the dead, is not relevant here, though since the ballad, 'Sweet William's Ghost', with much the same words, was available in Herd (**1**, 134-37), Ramsay (*TTM*, 324-25) and *SMM* **4**, no. 363, this context would have been easily recognised. So here, then, we have a neat verbal propriety, but limited to the amount of text quoted.

Category (d) quotes are, if anything, even more plentiful, even where the reference is but fleeting. There's a splendid economy in Scott's choice of the last song sung by Old Dumbiedykes, 'Deil Stick the Minister' (Chapter 8; 77). Its title alone picks up the old Laird's reputed contempt for the Church. Its content neatly embodies the entirely justified jealousy felt by his son for Jeanie's preference for Reuben Butler:

> Our wife she keeps baith beef and yell,
>   And tea to treat the Minister;
> There's nowt for me but sup the kale,
>   The beef's for the Minister.
> Besides, a bottle keeps in by
> To warm his breast, when he's no dry;
> While I the water-stand maun try.
> May the Deil stick the Minister.[80]

This song is not as common in print as the last few examples I have been discussing, which might also support the idea that Scott was planning what he was doing.

This is one of the novels in which Scott erects a structure of cultural contrasts indicated by allusion. In characterising Reuben Butler he naturally draws on the classical for Reuben's slightly pedantic insinuation of superiority. But a larger scale contrast is that between the upright but rigid traditions of Presbyterianism and the enticing but dangerous world of romantic excitement represented by a range of characters from Madge to Staunton and represented by song. Scott makes it clear that a denial of the life of secular music and song is cramping and even oppressive. His audience would have agreed, for by the 1770s dancing was 'a major national pastime' (D. Johnson, 121). David Deans's attitudes are a rigid and narrow development of an act of the General Assembly of Scotland of 1649 (reaffirmed in 1701) against mixed-sex dancing (D. Johnson, 120). David Deans denounces Effie for going to a dance in Chapter 10 in these terms, among others: 'I hae often wondered that ony ane that ever bent a knee for the right purpose should ever daur to crook a hough to fyke and fling at piper's wind and fiddler's squealing.' He then threatens to disown his daughters if either even name a dance to him again. The effect of this is to create 'a division of feelings in Effie's bosom' and deter her 'from her intended confidence in her sister' (**7**, 99). This, it could be argued, sows the seed of her later disaster. Scott later ensures that we take this cultural opposition seriously by later giving a lengthy note citing an original for this diatribe against dancing. If we needed confirmation, we could note that Hogg points out in the *Relics* (**1**, 209) that strict Covenanters used at Mass formally to debar from the table all those who had ever danced facing one of the opposite sex. Effie, of course, has just danced with Staunton five times.

To submit entirely to the world of music is to confound all rational distinctions and moral behaviour. Madge Wildfire represents the extreme of this position and her voluminous quotations evoke a sense of pathos rather than sympathy. The major characters, unsurprisingly, are somewhere in the middle. Jeanie herself is no singer, though she is not as unsympathetic to harmless entertainment as her father. Effie, however, affects liveliness when returning home late in Chapter 10 by carolling as she comes—first, a portmanteau ballad with a refrain suggesting sexual experience in its mention of the broom and probably constructed by Scott out of several originals.[81] Then she sings 'a scrap of an old Scotch song':

> Through the kirkyard
> I met wi' the Laird;
> The silly puir body he said me nae harm.
> But just ere 'twas dark,
> I met wi' the clerk—.

Scott almost certainly got this from Herd; it is in both his manuscript and 2, 189.[82] The manuscript version has the title 'or cushen dance'; in other words, these are words to fit what is obviously a dance tune. The cushion dance involved a certain amount of horseplay and even kissing in its genteel Renaissance form.[83] The words probably fit something like this:

> I'll trip upon trenchers, I'll dance upon dishes;
> My mither sent me for barm, for barm:
> And through the kirk-yard I met wi' the laird,
> The silly poor body could do me no harm.

> But down i' the park, I met with the clerk,
> And he gaed me my barm, my barm.

What Effie is doing is trying to cover her own misdemeanours by taking a fling at Jeanie's lovers—the impotent, stick-in-the-mud Dumbiedykes and the apprentice minister. Reuben is hardly the traditional lecherous clerk, so Jeanie's rebuke is justified: 'if ye will learn fule sangs, ye might make a kinder use of them' (98). What Scott has omitted is also interesting, both in the context of the Deans family within the novel and in the context of his audience beyond it. Barm, i.e. the froth from yeast, is a fairly obvious sexual metaphor whose meaning is quite apparent in the Herd version. Presumably the propriety of his novel would have prevented Scott from quoting the fragment entire in any case, but had he done so he would certainly have risked alienating the sympathies of some of his audience from Effie. He has a tricky job on hand gaining sympathy for a girl who bears an illegitimate child; he chooses not to give too much away. One can only speculate as to how many of his audience would have heard the piece, understood it, or been affected one way or the other by their knowledge, but it seems reasonable to suppose an interesting diversity of response. The tune alone is found as an instrumental in Lady John Scott's collection (NLS MS 836, p. 17). A knowledge of the context certainly makes Effie's singing it within David Deans's hearing an act of recklessness.

What conclusions, then, could we draw about Scott's use of folk song allusion? First, that it may not always have represented 'superior composition' for him, hence his own pastiches. After all, he denied charges of forgery in the *Minstrelsy* on the grounds that he would have written better than the original composers.[84] Secondly, its use can either pull the novels apart, or pull them together. It is not the mere inclusion of allusion that is significant. This was just Scott's characteristic way of writing, as amply evidenced by his Journal. What matters is the kind and degree of integration of the quoted material with the rest of the text. Sometimes the most prominent features are Scott's love of display and a kind of open game playing. If we are still old-fashioned enough to value a unity underlying the diversity of Scott's world then we cannot avoid seeing writing of this kind as belonging to a lesser genre and admitting that there is a lot of it in Scott.

There are occasions, though, when even references that seem superficially incongruous can represent a crucial point about Scott's view of the world. When Scott characterises David Deans's emotions in Chapter 12 in terms of 'Chevy Chase', 'Earl Percy sees my fall',[85] he is seeking to dignify the old man by relating him to the heroic noble in what was one of his favourite ballads. *Waverley* is about the passions common to all men (Chapter 1; **1**, 3), and the Dedicatory Epistle to *Ivanhoe* claims that 'the passions ... are generally the same in all ranks and conditions, all countries and ages (**9**, xxv). The use of apparently incongruous quotation links apparently very widely differing areas of humanity by asserting a community of experience between them. Ballads and popular songs provide particularly marked contrasts. Here the ballad provides the heroic and David Deans the ordinary; on other occasions—with the Duke of Argyle, for example—popular song provides evidence of the common touch. Argyle is even said to have composed the song used as epigraph to Chapter 35, and which he sings in Chapter 38.[86] Even without this usage, however, it seems to me that Scott shows enough care in his selection of quotation from folk song and in his weaving it into the thematic fabric of his novels for us to have extra evidence for claiming that in the curate's egg of his *oeuvre* at least parts of it are excellent.

Endnotes

1.   *Rob Roy*, Chapter 3, 22. Chapter numbers refer to the continuous numbering common to most editions and available in the running heads of the Edinburgh edition. Page numbers refer to the Edinburgh edition where that is available, i.e. for *The Antiquary, The Black Dwarf, The Bride of Lammermoor, A Legend of the Wars of Montrose,*

Redgauntlet, St Ronan's Well, The Tale of Old Mortality, and the Dryburgh edition where it is not, or for later editorial editions by Scott. Page numbers will be given for prose quotations only.

2.   Ibid., Chapter 14.

3.   T. B. Haber, 'The Chapter-Tags in the Waverley Novels,' *PMLA*, **45** (1930), 1145.

4.   A. Ramsay, *The Evergreen* (1724), **1**, 78; *SMM*, **6**, no. 512; D. Herd, *Antient and Modern Scotish Songs* (1791), **1**, 73-82. Different words to this title, apparently from oral tradition, are recorded in the manuscript music books compiled by Lady John Scott in the possession of the National Library of Scotland, to whom I am indebted for permission to consult and use both Lady John Scott's MSS and those of Charles Kirkpatrick Sharpe and Thomas Wilkie. Lady John Scott was the wife of a younger son of the fourth Duke of Buccleuch and her extensive collection of traditional songs may give some indication of what songs Scott would have encountered in his contacts with the Buccleuch circle, since his friend Sharpe instructed her in folk music. However, the dates of the MSS are uncertain and even the earliest was probably not compiled until late in Scott's career as a novelist. It is difficult to believe that Scott would not have wanted to use the song recorded in NLS MSS 835 (p. 18) and 840 (unpaginated) somehow, though since Harlaw is near Aberdeen it would have been stretching the point to put it in a later edition of the *Minstrelsy*. See also below, p. 30, and note 55. For versions and discussion, see B. H. Bronson, *The Traditional Tunes of the Child Ballads* (1962), **3**, no. 163.

5.   David Craig, *Scottish Literature and the Scottish People 1680-1830* (1961), 28-29.

6.   R. D. Altick, *The English Common Reader* (1963), 9-10.

7.   E. Johnson, *Sir Walter Scott: The Great Unknown* (1970), 2 vols, **1**, 192.

8.   R. Burns, *The Merry Muses of Caledonia,* ed. J. Barke & S. Goodsir Smith (1982), introduction.

9.   Much of the substance of this ballad overlaps with that of 'Chevy Chase', another favourite of Scott's. Ritson (*Ancient Songs*, 1829, **1**, 94-105) and Percy, *Reliques of Ancient English Poetry* (1794), **1**, 18-38, both provide literary versions. Future references to Percy will be to this 1794 edition, unless there is some indication to the contrary, since this is the one Scott owned. Hogg contributed versions in the *Materials* (NLS MS 877, nos. 5 and 132).

10.   NLS MS 123 (1815) p. 5. Wilkie claims to have collected most of his material from tradition, though very close parallels with Herd suggest that some scepticism is prudent.

11.   For the debate about 'Jock of Hazeldean', see Charles D. Zug, 'Scott's "Jock of Hazeldean": The Re-creation of a Traditional Ballad', *Journal of American Folklore*, **86** (1973), 152-60. A traditional original can be found in NLS MS 210 (Sharpe), ff.64-65, Christie **1**, 124-5, G. R. Kinloch, *Ancient Scottish Ballads* (1827), 206-09.

12.   Dave Harker, *Fakesong* (1985), 15-17.

13.   For Burns's knowledge of folk tunes, see M. E. B. Lewis, '"The Joy of my Heart": Robert Burns as Folklorist', *Scottish Studies*, **20** (1976), 65. For Burns, the music was more important, and he was prepared to provide what he called 'many silly compositions' to preserve the tunes as singable, because 'many beautiful airs wanted words' (48).

14.   David Johnson, *Music and Society in Lowland Scotland in the Eighteenth Century* (1972), 148-49. Hereafter cited in text as 'D. Johnson'.

15.   Harker, 36; Lewis, 59-60.

16.   Quoted by Lewis, 52.

17.   D. Johnson, 4. For a fuller study, see William Donaldson, *The Jacobite Song: Political Myth and National Identity* (1988). There is an excellent discussion of Scott's practice

in C. Lamont, 'Jacobite Songs as Intertexts in *Waverley* and *The Highland Widow*' in *Scott in Carnival*, ed. I. Alexander and D. Hewitt (1993), 110-121.

18. For a discussion of Scott's family musical milieu, see Ailie Munro, '"Abbotsford Collection of Border Ballads": Sophia Scott's Manuscript Book with Airs', *Scottish Studies*, **20** (1976), 91-108.

19. T. Crawford, *Scott* (1965), 83.

20. M. R. Dobie, 'The Development of Scott's "Minstrelsy"', *Transactions of the Edinburgh Bibliographical Society*, n.s. **2** (1940), 67.

21. J. G. Lockhart, *The Life of Sir Walter Scott* (1906), 412 (Chapter 12). However, by 1830 he had rather changed his mind; noting after a dinner at the Bannatyne Club that modern songs were free from the 'naughty innuendos' of his youth, but that this was not necessarily an improvement (E. Johnson, *Sir Walter Scott: The Great Unknown* [1970], 1138).

22. E. Johnson, 701.

23. Allan Cunningham, *The Songs of Scotland, Ancient and Modern* (1825), **3**, 167-68. Tune in William Thomson, *Orpheus Caledonius* (1833) no. 45.

24. M. Mayorkas, 'Minstrels and Minstrelsy: Their Function in the Works of Sir Walter Scott' (Ph. D. 1975), 42.

25. Scott, *Miscellaneous Works*, **3**, 384.

26. M. Edgeworth, *Castle Rackrent* (1972 reprint of 1910 Dent edn), 5, 78.

27. I am indebted to Mrs P. Maxwell-Scott and to the Keeper of the Advocates Library in Edinburgh for granting me access to Scott's Library and for permission to quote and to make use of information derived from Scott's collection. Other information about the Library can be found in J. G. Cochrane, *Catalogue of the Library at Abbotsford* (1838), and J. C. Corson's 'Sir Walter Scott's Boyhood Collection of Chapbooks in Abbotsford Library', *The Bibliotheck*, **3:6** (1962), 202-17. Both cite Scott's flyleaf note, but Corson is more accurate (203).

28. 'The History of the Young Coalman's Courtship to the Creelwife's Daughter' (n. d.) is no. 11 in volume **2** of Scott's collection 'Popular Ballads and Stories'.

29. Scott, *Miscellaneous Works*, **6**, 129.

30. Ibid., **6**, 216; **4**, 252. The ensuing novel is called a romance in the introductions to *The Antiquary*, *The Monastery* and *The Pirate*.

31. For other discussions, see C. Lamont, op. cit. and 'The Poetry of the Early Waverley Novels', *Proceedings of the British Academy*, **61**, 315-36.

32. See the Edinburgh edition of *The Black Dwarf* by P. D. Garside (1993) for notes on the ballads in the novel, 131, 200-05, 212, 220, 224-25. Both these ballads are in the *Minstrelsy*, **1**, 97-113, **1**, 172-81. Hobbie Noble is a character in 'Jock o' the Side' (C187) who rescues Jock and he also has his own ballad (**1**,182-93). Scott has altered the first two lines of the quatrain of 'Jamie Telfer o' the Fair Dodhead' (C190) which he uses here.

33. *BD* Chapter 12; 85. See *SMM*, **2**, no. 114, for words and tune. For the history of the song, see J. C. Dick, *Notes on Scottish Song by Robert Burns, Written in an Interleaved Copy of* <u>*The Scots Musical Museum*</u> *with Additions by Robert Riddell and Others* (1908), xlvii, 63, 114-15, and his edition of *The Songs of Robert Burns* (1903) 475-77. Hereafter 'Dick, *Notes*' and 'Dick, *Songs*'.

34. Edinburgh edition of *A Legend of the Wars of Montrose* ed. J. H. Alexander (1995), Chapters 6, 12; 45, 91. For a seventeenth-century text, see J. Forbes, *Cantus, Songs & Fancies* (1666), Song 37; for information, H. Rollins (ed.) *A Pepysian Garland* (1971), 189. For an early nineteenth-century printing, see A. Cunningham, *Ballads and Songs of Scotland* (1825) **1**, 271-73. Once again, Scott has been tinkering with some lines.

35. Also used to less effect in *The Surgeon's Daughter*, Chapter 4. C211; *Minstrelsy*, **3**, 93-104.
36. *The Journal of Sir Walter Scott*, ed. W. E. K. Anderson (1972), **1**, 252.
37. W. Brewer, *Shakespeare's Influence on Sir Walter Scott* (1925), 245.
38. J. Hayden (ed.), *Scott: The Critical Heritage* (1970), 292.
39. *Edinburgh Review*, **36** (October 1821), 53.
40. The significance of the antiquary in this novel is well discussed by Jane Millgate in *Walter Scott: The Making of the Novelist* (1984), 91-96.
41. D. Devlin (ed.), *Modern Judgements: Scott* (1970), 49.
42. For example, J. Buchan, *Sir Walter Scott* (1932), 149.
43. For further discussion, see Brewer, 256-57. Brewer notes twenty-nine uses of Shakespeare in the novel (258).
44. Chapters 38, 30. For Shakespeare references, the Arden edition is used throughout. The relevant passages are *King John*, **3**, 1, 125, and *the Merchant of Venice*, **3**, 1, 112.
45. *Journal*, **1**, 252.
46. J. Bell (ed.), *Rhymes of the Northern Bards* (1812), 258. Scott owned a copy.
47. 'Queen Eleanor's Confession', *Reliques*, **2**, 155.
48. Scott also quoted this in *The Pirate*, Chapter 5. 'Get Up and Bar the Door', or 'John Blunt', *SMM*, **3**, no. 300 and Herd, **2**, 63-65.
49. Percy, **2**, 60, and many other collections.
50. *Minstrelsy*, **2**, 44-50. In 'Lamkin' (C93), a ballad remembered from Scott's childhood, it is the false nurse who is burnt. Hollin and thorn feature in the endings of some versions of these ballads.
51. *Minstrelsy*, **2**, 56-66.
52. *Minstrelsy*, **3**, 247.
53. Herd, **2**, 70. Both Herd and Wilkie saw this as a widespread song; H. Hecht (ed.), *Songs from Herd's Manuscripts* (1904), 192, 312-13; NLS MS 122, 6-9. See also the discussion by C. Lamont in 'The Poetry of the Early Waverley Novels', 11.
54. C163. A sung version can be found on *Lucy Stewart*, collected by K. S. Goldstein, Folkways Records, FG 3519 (1961), **1**, 'Child Ballads'. For a discussion, see D. Buchan, 'History and Harlaw', in *Ballad Studies*, ed. E. B. Lyle (1976), 29-40.
55. Probably recorded just before 1840. See Buchan, 'History and Harlaw', 29, 38, and note 4, above.
56. E. Johnson, **1**, 195.
57. There are relevant discussions in R. K. Gordon, 'Shakespeare's *Henry IV* and the Waverley Novels', *Modern Language Review*, **37**, (1942), 304-16 and Brewer, 357. The theme of the deposition or political murder of a king or other leader is generally appropriate.
58. As hero, Everard speaks Scott's own English and stands up for poetry in the form of Milton at least. C. Worth's paper in *Scott in Carnival* (1993), 380-92, presents a cogent Bakhtinian analysis of competing languages in *Woodstock*.
59. H. Rollins, *Cavalier and Puritan*, 11.
60. *Journal*, **1**, 86, 12 February 1826.
61. *Reliques*, **2**, 143; Ritson, *Ancient Songs* (1829), **2**, 121. This piece is reputed to be by Thomas Deloney but it has analogues in tradition.
62. However, Wildrake claims in Chapter 36 to have invented a song that seems to have survived in tradition. In spite of Scott's note, see A. Williams, *Folk Songs of the Upper Thames* (1912), 296.
63. Chapters 4, 16, 20, 28. Song printed in J. Hogg, *Jacobite Relics*, (1819-21), **1**, 1.
64. For example, by Robin Mayhead, *Walter Scott* (1968), 8.

65.   D. Lodge, *After Bakhtin*, (1990), 33, provides an easily available discussion. Bakhtin's treatment of the topic is in 'Discourse in the Novel', in his *The Dialogic Imagination*, ed. M. Holquist (1981), 320-24.

66.   M. M. Bakhtin, *Problems of Dostoevsky's Poetics*, ed. and trans. Caryl Emerson (1984), 122-37, 157-58.

67.   See Lodge (1990), 46-56, for a discussion of the position of the narrative voice of realist novels.

68.   However, it is far less typical of Scott the poet; see Brewer, 38.

69.   E.g. Scott's 'Saint Monance' sister,/The grey priest kissed her' (*Abbot*, Chapter 16) replaces 'The silly Nunnis keist up thair Bunnis [arses],'And heisit thair Hippis on hie.'

70.   D. Johnson, 18-19. For the history of the tune, see Dick, *Notes*, 29.

71.   The words quoted here are from the following sources: Herd, **2**, 253; *The Whole Book of Psalms: Collected into English Meter* by T. Sternhold and J. Hopkins and others (1649), 72; *SMM*, **2**, no. 106; Thomson, **1**, no. 42; *SMM*, **6**, no. 600, *Jacobite Relics*, **2**, 127; *SMM*, **3**, no. 259; *Jacobite Relics*, **2**, 55; the text given in the novel (for which analogues can be found in C83, 87, 99); C. K. Sharpe's NLS MS 210 f. 18 verso-19 recto; Herd, **1**, 309-10. Scott himself retained a sense of the musical aspect of these songs (E. Johnson, 863). The tunes of the traditional songs are given as an Appendix in the original keys found in the sources stated there. In order to place them together in sequence for singing or playing it is necessary to transpose them into compatible keys. Willie could have done this; Scott, who was not versed in the technicalities of music, though he knew a good tune when he heard one, may well not have realised this. In the Appendix I omit the psalm and one fragment not identified. I am most grateful to Dave Townsend for help with the musical technicalities involved with the preparation of this section.

72.   T. F. Henderson, ed., *The Minstrelsy of the Scottish Border* (1902), **2**, 156-57.

73.   *SMM*, **3**, no. 259; a version mentioned by Sharpe, for which see G. F. Graham, *The Songs of Scotland* (Wood & Co., Edinburgh, n.d. but before 1869), **3**, 115; Wilkie's version in NLS MS 123, 5. Compare the version in Chapter 28 of *Waverley* with his verse 2: 'There's nought in the highlands but lang kale & leeks/And lang legged callants gaun wanting the breeks;/Wantin' the hose, & wantin' the shoon,/But they'll a' get new breeks when Jemmy comes hame.'

74.   For a history of the song, see J. C. Dick, *Notes*, 107, where he says the words of the political version are in *Loyal Songs* (1750), and *Songs*, 474-75. Donaldson dates the political version to just after 1745 (63).

75.   E.g. Herd, **1**, 328-29, **2**, 40-42, *TTM*, 338-39, *SMM*, **5**, no. 478, Sharpe's version in NLS MS 210 ff. 18 verso-19 recto is the one used here.

76.   See Scott's Note 33, 558-60 in Dryburgh edn.

77.   NLS MS 210, f. 31.

78.   There are also versions in Wilkie, NLS MS 122, pp. 37-38 and in Lady John Scott's NLS MS 836 p. 35, which has a tune.

79.   Lady John Scott knew this (NLS MS 836, p. 101) but the words are not so close as those in the printed versions mentioned.

80.   'The Deil Stick the Minister', *Songs and Ballads of Northern England,* collected and arranged by J. Stokoe and S. Reay (n.d. but post 1882), 116-17.

81.   Analogues can be most conveniently found in C4, 15, 16. Elfin knights are dangerous seducers with a touch of the supernatural. C16, which provides the nearest analogue, has an incest motif inappropriate here.

82.   H. Hecht, ed., *Songs from David Herd's Manuscripts* (1904), 204.

83.   W. Chappell, *Old English Popular Music* (1893), **2**, 287-88. There is a tune in NLS MS 836, p. 17.

84. C. G. Zug, 'Sir Walter Scott and the Ballad Forgery', *Studies in Scottish Literature*, **8**, 63.

85. *HM*, 115. Likely immediate sources for this widespread ballad include *Reliques*, **1**, 265-84, and Herd, **1**, 97-107.

86. Herd, **2**, 241; *SMM*, **6**, no. 560. Sharpe wrote a note to Stenhouse arguing that the piece must have been by the first Duke of Argyle. Scott would appear to have changed the place name. The line about 'bannocks of barley' relates this to 'Bannocks of Barley Meal', collected by John Bell, and preserved by Scott in one of the several of Bell's collections in the Library at Abbotsford, Press E, Shelf 1, **2**, no. 24.

3

Scott's contemporaries

Important as Scott was, he was but one of a host of early nineteenth-century prose writers who decided to write historical tales featuring characters from ordinary walks of life or to develop the pastoral. It is worth comparing his work with that of some of his contemporaries. To demonstrate widely differing developments I shall look briefly at the work of James Hogg (1770-1835), John Galt (1779-1839) and Mary Russell Mitford (1787-1855). The first two are Scots, often writing historical novels or romances, and the third English, writing what purports to be contemporary observation but is in fact transparently pastoral. Hogg and Galt are of particular interest in relation to Scott since both of them wrote works about the Covenanters which challenge and revise Scott's *Old Mortality* (1816): *The Brownie of Bodsbeck* (1818) and *Ringan Gilhaize* (1823). Indeed, many readers meet these two authors in the course of comparing the novels.[1]

Galt and Hogg

John Galt offers two contrasting kinds of continuity with Scott: domestic stories and historical tales. The son of a sea-captain, as a sickly child he read ballads and story books such as 'Chevy Chase' and 'Leper the Tailor' (the latter was among the prose chapbooks collected by the young Scott bound up in 1810) and he heard tales and legends from local old women. He, like Scott, is therefore an example of the cultural continuity between working class and middle class in Scotland.[2] According to V. S. Pritchett, his *Annals of the Parish* (1821) was written before *Waverley*, but this account of social change in village life over the latter half of the eighteenth century had to wait twenty years for a publisher until Scott's work kindled interest in Scottish subjects.[3] Galt hoped that this and *The Provost* (1822) would be seen as 'local theoretical history' rather than as novels.[4] *The Entail* (1822) is similar. Erik Frykman points out that 'Galt's factual, sober and humoristic tales of Scottish life were brought out just at the time when Scott had abandoned the more or less contemporary scene in his novels for remoter periods and more romantic themes.'[5]

In these tales, reference to ballads and folk songs is casually used as the common currency of cultural life and as part of the vigorous Scots conversational style. In *The Entail* Claud Walkinshaw's choice of the

pragmatic over the heroic is seen entirely in terms of popular stories and songs:
he

> early preferred the history of Whittington and his Cat to the
> achievements of Sir William Wallace; and 'Tak your auld cloak about
> you,' ever seemed to him a thousand times more sensible than Chevy
> Chase. As for that doleful ditty, the Flowers of the Forest, it was
> worse than the Babes in the Wood; and Gil Morrice more wearisome
> than Death and the Lady.[6]

Nevertheless, Claud begins his rise to worldly prosperity as a pedlar with a
pack of ballads. Leddy Grippy's idiolect is particularly dependent on the
discourse of folk song, often using the same ones as Scott selects, indicating
their quasiproverbial status. There is an elegiac cast to her liveliness, though,
since the novel closes with her death.

Ringan Gilhaize, Galt's favourite novel, is very different. Unlike Scott, Galt
grasps the nettle of trying to make even the most extreme of Covenanters
sympathetic. To dignify his 'raw and undisciplined countrymen',[7] however, he
gives full rein to a quasi-Biblical solemnity of discourse. Vernacular music and
song (anathema to many of the intensely devout, **2**, 53-54) only get a few
passing references. Galt's new earnestness did not go down well with the
novel's few critics. Francis Jeffrey, for example, claimed in the *Edinburgh
Review* in October 1823 that it lacked spirit, and that Galt was better at
'humorous simplicity, intermixed with humble pathos'.[8] In other words, he
was better at what he was up to in *The Entail*, and also what Scott was up to in
large sections of *Old Mortality*, especially those dealing with the Headriggs.

Scott's choice of discourse was more diverse, dependant on his view of the
complexities of the situation, and on his sense of how to construct a social
hierarchy of characters that would be marketable. Songs are used partly to give
colour to the presentation of the lower classes. Thus, trooper Tam Halliday and
Jenny Dennison coquet in verses of a love song with the title (ironically
appropriate to the appearance of Claverhouse in the plot) 'Bonny Dundee'.
The words are fairly open, as the 'poor sodger lad' urges the girl

> To follow me ye weel may be glad
> A share of my supper, a share of my bed.[9]

In a sense this sanitizes and familiarizes Jenny's actions as she tries to seduce
Tam into letting Edith Bellenden see his prisoner, Henry Morton. Halliday,
balked of a kiss, goes on to rebuke Jenny in the words of another song in which
a young man scorns a hoity-toity young woman who asks him for presents.[10]
Tam finally succumbs to financial rather than sexual bribery. Scott has a fine

line to tread between allowing Jenny the sexual latitude conventionally associated with the lower classes, and preserving her integrity sufficiently to allow her to become an appropriate mate for Cuddie Headrigg, Morton's loyal ploughboy sidekick. This may all be rather artificial, but it is a good deal more fun for the reader than the stilted conversation of the two principals as they struggle to retain their stiff upper lips.

On the other hand, Scott maintains the sense that these hard times may require the heroism of stoic acceptance of death, defeat and exile through his ballad references, which are often epigraphs rather than part of the main text. Historically, the most important of these is, of course, 'Bothwell Bridge' (C206), the epigraph to Chapters 27 and 32, and also quoted in a Note. This commemorates the defeat of the Covenanters in 1679 and Scott included it in the *Minstrelsy* (1803, **3**, 209). He also uses a formulaic quatrain as epigraph for Chapter 14, 'Johnnie o' Breadislee' for Chapter 42, and 'Edom o' Gordon' for Chapter 28.[11] Typically, though, Scott displaces the tragic suffering and actual atrocities found in such ballads onto minor characters. The heroism of Morton and most of the other genteel characters consists of bravery in facing up to anticipated rather than actual disaster; it is Evandale who pays the final penalty, not Morton. For example, in Chapter 28, although those in the Castle of Tillietudlem suffer hunger before the siege is lifted by their surrender, the atrocities suggested by the rest of 'Edom o' Gordon', which even in its milder versions run to burning the inmates alive, never happen. Even Cuddie suggests to Morton that they should go and push their fortunes like characters in 'daft auld tales' and then, in formulaic phrase, 'come back to Merry Scotland'.[12] But one of Cuddie's main functions is the traditional role of the hero's lower-class companion, light relief. He also encapsulates his philosophy about the changing fortunes of war in a snippet from a song, 'Tak' turn about mither, quo' Tam o' the Linn'. There are many versions of this farcical song, but the one from which this line comes is an extremely coarse one.[13]

Cuddie's mother is one of the mouthpieces of Covenanting extremism. Her Biblical language, which even extracts a reluctant tribute from Bothwell (Chapter 8, p. 69) has a vehement sonority and energy but, like that of the other Covenanters, its place in the construction of the novel is as a cause of disaster to themselves or others, and not as a justification of the Covenanters' discontent, let alone as a mode of attracting sympathy to their cause.

It was this injustice, as Hogg and Galt saw it, that led each of them to publish their own covenanting tales. James Hogg, the Ettrick Shepherd, really was a shepherd, the son of an unprosperous tenant farmer, and he grew up as a productive part of a living oral tradition; his mother was one of Scott's sources for ballads. Douglas Gifford rightly stresses Hogg's huge debts to 'an oral tradition going back to and beyond the Border legends and Ballads', claiming that 'this Ballad background is the basis of both content and form in the bulk and the best of his fiction.'[14] His poetic work substantially involved writing new ballads and he published two volumes of *Jacobite Relics*, some of which were certainly not bequeathed by the Jacobites, at least in their entirety.[15] His origins, though, were both a help and a hindrance to his ambitions. Cannily marketing himself, and allowing himself to be marketed, as a shrewd peasant, he experienced continuing problems in gauging the reactions of the purchasing public, and his failure to achieve complete cultural amphibiousness got in the way of his relations with mentors and benefactors such as Scott, who found the *Brownie* and other tales 'sadly vulgar'.[16] One important stumbling block was Hogg's continuing attraction to the supernatural, a feature of his oral culture he was not able to mediate successfully for a rationalist Edinburgh audience.[17] It is this that ensures that much of his work definitely falls at the 'romance' end of the realist-romance continuum.

The Brownie of Bodsbeck was actually published in 1818, though there seems to have been an earlier draft; we do not know exactly how much of Hogg's creative impulse was due to reacting to Scott.[18] The title suggests the supernatural interest that is exploited almost throughout; indeed, the main characters are not Covenanters themselves, though they are mistreated as if they were. The eventual explanations—that Watie is the Brownie feared by his wife, and that a deformed Covenanter is the Brownie feared by Watie—are bathetically insufficient for the emotional and narrative effects Hogg generates. At the end he suggests airily that any remaining mysteries could be resolved by reading a pamphlet called 'The Cameronian's Tale' by John Brown (*Brownie*, 168). The reader is unlikely to have this to hand (indeed, I cannot locate a copy.) This is a ploy to make readers delve more deeply into the historical material.   For many contemporary readers, and for modern ones, the supernaturalism sits uncomfortably with the atrocity stories Hogg insisted were drawn not only from tradition but also from historical authorities like Wodrow (105).

The chief vehicle of song is Nanny Elshinder, whose songs are interpolated throughout the text but represent a variety of discourses, from the traditional ballad, such as 'A' the Wild Macraws',[19] to a hymn in standard English (51, 131). Hogg retained a sense of the musical dimension of such intertexts, and in some editions printed music was provided for the hymn, 'O thou who dwellest', since 'without its effect the words are nothing' (131). Nevertheless, the intertexts are in whole or part by Hogg himself. Born into the tradition, he often used his prose as a vehicle for his versatility in a number of poetic modes. This romance feature is at odds with his self-justification in terms of history, whether oral or printed.

The same is true of stories with more remote settings, as in *The Three Perils of Man: War, Women and Witchcraft* (1822).[20] As Douglas Gifford points out in his edition, this is a romance, a 'comic, fantastic and extravagant epic' (vii).

Some of the flavour of the piece can be gauged from the first words of Chapter 1: 'The days of the Stuarts, kings of Scotland, were the days of chivalry and romance;' as Gifford says, 'Hogg's romance *pretends* [my italics] to be based on Border history of the reigns of Robert II of Scotland (1371-90) and Richard II of England (1377-90)' (467). It appears that Hogg is following Scott's example, but this is 'only a matter of seeming' (467). Hogg's intertexts are likewise a matter of seeming. The epigraph to Chapter 1 is noted as an 'Old Song'. As Gifford says, this seems to be a version of 'The Twa Sisters' or 'Binnorie' (C10). The first quatrain originally was, though Hogg has tampered with it to get a focus on the king rather than his daughters; Hogg's king only has one daughter, so the whole point of the ballad's tale of murderous jealousy vanishes. The second quatrain, which contains phrases like 'warlock wight' is almost certainly cobbled together by Hogg and this does not fit the story line of the ballad either. Gifford's notes display a tactful agnosticism about Hogg's use of sources, and summarize the situation with regard to the songs in the main text by saying that they 'are all Hogg's own or his reworking of traditional material' (476). There are examples of his own work throughout. Epigraphs are somewhat closer to oral sources: the one to Chapter 6 is from 'Wandering Willie', which Scott also quotes in *Redgauntlet*. There are two epigraphs to Chapter 5, one from 'Rob Roy', and one attributed to 'Foul Play'. A comparison of the versions of Child 221 (one of which is from the Materials for the *Minstrelsy*) will produce all the lines Hogg uses, though not together. 'Katharine Jaffray' is a ballad cognate with 'Rob Roy' in its theme, the abduction of a bride, and the phrase 'foul play' echoes in the later verses of a number of versions; Hogg is remembering an oral version here. The epigraph from Chapter 25 is 'John Barleycorn'—or at least, the first four lines of the eight lines are; the remainder shows signs of refurbishment by Hogg. The relevance of this tribute to the power of drink is simply that the company get ridiculously drunk in the next few paragraphs. It is difficult to feel that Hogg is forging links between cultures, or capturing the essence of a period with this technique, especially since the time at which the book is set precedes that which gave rise to current forms of the songs used by at least two or three centuries.

The Three Perils of Woman: Love, Leasing and Jealousy (1823) is, as its subtitle 'a series of Scottish tales' implies, rather different.[21] It does not go in for epigraphs, but uses its tradition-type intertexts more sparingly. Some are obvious, for example, 'The sheets were cauld, an' she was away' (346) from 'The Gaberlunzie Man', or 'Ca' the ewes to the knowes' (143), or the reel of Tullochgorum (121) and are used to establish a sense of cultural community.

Hogg's own involvement in continuing tradition, just at the point where print starts to dominate it disruptively, makes him in some ways a metonym for it rather than a chronicler of it. This leads to radical self-division in the marketing of his native culture, a self-division that appears in his narrative strategies, such as the condescension of the framing narrator to Watie's own narration in the *Brownie* ('it may haply be acceptable to the curious, and the lovers of rustic simplicity, to read it in his own words', 18). Paradoxically, therefore, his closeness to tradition in some ways disables him; because he represents it as a sharer in its creative community, he is faced with immense difficulties in *re*-presenting it for an audience whose expectations are at odds with his own.

Mitford

Meanwhile, in England, writers and readers already much more distanced from traditional culture because of urbanisation and a different development of class relations were enjoying a more obvious kind of pastoral. Mitford recounts how a maid, Nancy, read Percy's *Reliques* to her when Mitford was three years old. A possible conduit of oral tradition is already presenting the traditional material as literary. Mitford quickly learned to read the ballads for herself, and recasts the situation thus:

> We, a little child, and a young country maiden, the daughter of a respectable Hampshire farmer, were no bad representatives in point of cultivation of the noble dames and their attendant damsels who had so often listened with delight to wandering minstrels in bower and hall.[22]

Mitford also praises Scott a couple of pages later. She then quotes a feeble and sentimental modern piece from Percy, in an attempt to set up a common culture, as 'the sort of poetry that ought to be popular—to be sung in our concert-rooms, and set to such airs as should be played on barrel-organs throughout our streets' (17).

Writers like Mitford protest their fidelity to the facts but, without displaying the overt propagandist drive of social essayists like Cobbett, use a number of conventional devices to mediate those supposed 'facts'. Mitford's preface to *Our Village* (1824) claims an 'attempt to delineate country scenery and country manners as they exist in a small village in the south of England'.[23] In other words, she is sensible of the social effects of the size, kind and location of a community. She claims to have been faithful to the place and the people even if she has given a 'brighter aspect to her villagers than is usually met with in books' (**1**, v); her assumption is that literature tends to falsify village life by presenting too gloomy a picture. Perhaps she had Cobbett in mind, especially since she knew him. Particularly in the essays solely about Three Mile Cross, this approach produces a result which testifies to the sunniness of Mitford's disposition rather than convincing the sceptical reader that she is properly correcting a fictional bias. Although she gives graphic accounts of agricultural disturbances (for example, the riots of 1830 by the 'misguided peasantry' in 'The Incendiary', **5**, 5-23) and although an early reviewer was suspicious of her identification with 'uneducated society',[24] her own stance is unmistakably one of benign, half uneasy, half self-deceiving assurance. Her work prompted its own revisionary rejoinders, such as Thomas Crofton Croker's *My Village versus 'Our Village'* (1833).[25] Unlike Elizabeth Gaskell or George Eliot, her narrative stance is neither complicated nor redeemed by any attempt at realising the inner life of her characters. The Preface quite plainly sets out her assumptions:

> She has painted, as they appeared to her, their little frailties and their many virtues, under an intense and thankful conviction that in every condition of life goodness and happiness may be found by those who seek them, and never more surely than in the fresh air, the shade, and the sunshine of nature (*Our Village*, **1**, vi)

As she tells us in 'Violeting', her parish is, luckily, unenclosed (**1**, 101). No doubt this mitigated the effects on the villagers and farmers of the agricultural depression which followed the Napoleonic wars, but it can hardly have nullified it. However, in 'A Walk through the Village' she makes her contribution to the myth of rural stability by claiming that the village 'had a trick of standing still, of remaining stationary unchanged and unimproved in this most changeable and improving world' (**2**,1). Consequently she is optimistic, whereas other writers strike a note of at least sporadic elegy for a rural idyll increasingly under threat from that equivocally 'improving world'.

It is interesting to compare Mitford's view with Cobbett's, since they are writing at the same time (the 1820s and 1830s) about the same sort of rural life in the south of England, among farm workers and small farmers. In spite of their radically different aims, class positions, tone and sense of urgency, they have an almost identical sense of the myth of rural community, as in Mitford's portrait of the Allens with their

> thirty or forty acres of arable land which the owner and his sons cultivated themselves, whilst the wife and daughters assisted in the husbandry, and eked out the slender earnings by the produce of the dairy, the poultry yard, and the orchard—an order of cultivators now passing rapidly away, but in which much of the best part of the English character, its industry, its frugality, its sound sense and its kindness might be found (**2**, 204).

The stress on the whole household's contribution to the domestic economy, and on the virtues of hard work, and the chauvinism, are just what are exhibited by

Cobbett in *Rural Rides* (1830). 'There were no fine misses sitting before the piano and mixing the alloy of their new-fangled tinsel with the old sterling metal' might come from the Cobbett who attended a farm sale at Reigate on 20 October 1825, lamenting the change of the family into '*Squire* Charington and the *Miss* Charingtons'[26] but it is in fact Mitford in 'A Great Farm-house' (**1**, 56). Mitford wanted to be independent 'of all questions of policy' (**1**, 48). The decline she laments is caused by 'death and distance' (**1**, 57); she gives no analysis of social relations beyond the family and concentrates on their pets and stock rather than their labourers.

In spite of their common nostalgia for an idealized social past, Cobbett gives an almost unrelieved picture of current distress; Mitford diminishes all problems to the 'little frailties' she mentions in her preface. Her 'intense and thankful convictions' do not lead her to examine the views of her subjects, but her projection of her own wishful thinking onto them is more suspect than Cobbett's condescension because more obviously self-defensive. She exclaims of the Whites in 'Walks in the Country. The First Primrose': 'here they live still, as merrily as ever, with fourteen children of all ages and sizes, from nineteen years to nineteen months ... They are very poor, and I often wish them richer; but I don't know—perhaps it might put them out' (**1**, 76) and she asks of the boy Joe Kirby in 'The Hard Summer' 'but why should I lament the poverty that never troubles him?' (**1**, 206)

It is significant that her prefatory remarks use the dead metaphor of 'painted' for her writing. A letter to Sir William Elford is revealing:

> You, as a great landscape painter, know that in painting a favourite scene you do a little embellish, and can't help it; you avail yourself of happy incidents of atmosphere, and if anything be ugly, you strike it out, or if anything be wanting, you put it in. But still the picture is a likeness.[27]

Always the onlooker ('I cannot say that I ever actually handled the fork or the rake', **5**, 256) her values are coloured by the Romantic picturesque tradition. An added influence is that of reference to realistic genre painting, as found in Scott. Focusing through the lens of canonical art is another safe way of mediating labouring life for genteel consumption, and the layers of reference distance the experience, as in Scott's comparison between Steenie Mucklebackit's fisher's cottage and Wilkie's painting in Chapter 31 of *The Antiquary*.[28] 'The Old Gipsy' gives us a scene 'that might have suited the pen of Salvator Rosa' (**2**, 269) while 'The Young Gipsy' has a face which 'resembled those which Sir Joshua [and readers are expected to be able to supply the surname] has often painted' (**2**, 300) In 'Whitsun-Eve', 'first there is a group suited to Teniers, a cluster of out-of-door customers of the Rose, old benchers of the inn, who sit round a table smoking and drinking in high solemnity to the sound of Timothy's fiddle' (**3**, 149). By making such comparisons Mitford is cementing the idea of continuity in the community through time (Teniers lived from 1610 to 1690) and also placing the reader in the text along with her as a culturally informed observer. The musical experience is subsumed into a prior picturesque one. This kind of allusion is common in nineteenth-century fiction and a number of the other authors discussed (such as Eliot and Hardy) use it; it has received substantial critical attention already.[29]

For some time I have not mentioned song. This is because Mitford's way of dealing with the musical and sung culture of her labourers is to elide it or to conflate it with that of her readers. In 'Walks in the Country. The Cowslip-ball' we are told that 'Shakespeare's Song of Spring bursts irrepressibly from *our* lips [my italics] as we step' (**1**, 138). Hardly anything burst irrepressibly from the lips of her subjects, most of whom have no voices. When characters do burst out in song, it is a song that her genteel readers will recognise. In 'The Shaw', little George Coper comes back from work singing 'Home! sweet Home!' (**4**, 87) and in 'Whitsun-Eve' Jem Tanner whistles 'cherry-ripe' while his sweetheart Mabel Green walks with the lame mantua-maker who, as the couple meet, hums lines from Burns (**3**, 151). This is improbable but not impossible. 'Home! sweet Home!' was written by J. H. Payne and Sir Henry Bishop and first performed in 1823[30] and was certainly printed on broadsides which could have contributed to the repertoire of singers like this and, as we have seen, Burns was common property for all classes. But the choice of songs is meant to reassure the reader that s/he and the characters do share a sentimental taste, that the latter have glimmerings of genteel sensibility, and such scenes are usually the subject of blatant social moralising. Little George's response to the words of 'Home! sweet Home!' is conjectured at thus:

> looking as if he felt their full import, ploughboy though he be. And so he does; for he is one of a large, an honest, a kind, and an industrious family ... oh, to be as cheaply and as thoroughly contented as George Coper! (**4**, 87)

The dance in 'Our Maying' is used to suggest an ideal social order:

> an honest country dance ... with ladies and gentlemen at the top, and country lads and lasses at the bottom; a happy mixture of cordial kindness on the one hand, and pleased respect on the other (**3**, 206).

Presumably the common movement known as 'casting off' did not occur in this dance or was excised. In casting off the dancers would have performed the dangerously levelling action of moving from the top of the set to the bottom! The way in which the author distances herself from participation is made literal in the paragraph of 'The Shaw' that follows the description of Jem Tanner and Mabel Green as she listens to the crying of Harvest Home in a chorus; her reaction to the 'pleasant noise' is 'to get away from it' (**4**, 88). The nervous mistrust this implies is to be echoed in later writing.

Endnotes

1.   For critical discussions, see M. Elphinstone, 'John Galt's *Ringan Gilhaize*: A Historical Novel', in S. R. McKenna (ed.), *Selected Essays on Scottish Language and Literature* (1992), 177-93, M. Elphinstone, *'The Brownie of Bodsbeck*: History or Fantasy?' in *Studies in Hogg and his World*, **2** (1991), 81-90. E. Frykman, *John Galt's Scottish Stories 1820-1823* (1959), 168-78; F. R. Hart, *The Scottish Novel* (1978), 49-50; D. Mack, 'The Rage of Fanaticism in Former Days', in *Nineteenth-century Scottish Fiction*, ed. I. Campbell (1979), 37-50; C. Swann, 'Past into Present: Scott, Galt and the Historical Novel', *Literature and History*, **3** (1976), 65-82; P. Wilson, '*Ringan Gilhaize*: a Neglected Masterpiece?' in *John Galt 1779-1979*, ed. C. A. Whatley (1979), 120-50.

2.   R. K. Gordon, *John Galt* (1920), 10-11.

3.   V. S. Pritchett, *The Living Novel* (1966), 39.

4.   For a concise and useful analysis of Galt's provincial fiction in the *Annals*, see G. Kelly, *English Fiction of the Romantic Period* (1989), 209-12.

5.   Frykman, op. cit., 85.

6.   John Galt, *The Entail or the Lairds of Grippy*, ed. I. A. Gordon (1970), 4.

7.   John Galt, *Ringan Gilhaize: or the Covenanters*, ed. D. S. Meldrum & W. Roughead, 2 vols (1936), **2**, 176.

8.   Excerpted in edition cited, **2**, 342.

9.   This textually complex song appears in Thomas D'Urfey's *Pills to Purge Melancholy*, **5**, 17, but in a very different form, without these words, and in various later compilations, usually in shorter versions. For a history of the song, see Dick, *Songs*, 388-89.

10. 'My Joe Janet'. Widespread; a girl asks a reluctant lover for presents, Ramsay, *TTM*, Johnson would not let Burns include a verse implying impotence in *SMM*, no. 111.

11. *The Tale of Old Mortality*, ed. D. S. Mack (1993). This edition uses the chapter divisions within volumes, but the continuous numbering is used in running heads, so I have used this for the benefit of those who do not yet have access to this edition. Page references are to this edition. 'Bothwell Brig' is quoted on pages 214 and 255. The epigraph to Chapter 14 (**2**, Chapter 1, 119) 'My hounds may all run masterless' is in the *Minstrelsy* version of 'Jamie Telfer of the Fair Dodhead' (**1**, 97-110) and it also appears in Lady John Scott's version (NLS MS 837, p. 59) but it is more usual in 'Young Beichan' (C53; see notes). For two versions of the latter contemporary with Scott, see Kinloch, 262, and Jamieson, **2**, 119. 'Johnnie o' Breadislee' (327) has a plot in which Johnnie offends his mother by going out hunting; apart from the theme of an old woman advising a young man going into danger, it is not particularly appropriate to what follows. Scot was the first to publish a complete version of this ballad (C114). Scott's most likely source for the widespread 'Edom o' Gordon' (C178) is Herd, **1**, 38-44.

12. *OM*, 125, Chapter 14.

13. Scott liked this song and even sang it (E. Johnson, op. cit., 1142). He presumably didn't sing this version in polite company, since it opens 'Tom o' Lin and his wife, and his good mother They gaed a' to the midden together; Some sh—t thick, and some sh— t thin. Fye for a spoon, quo' Tom o' Lin' (Sharpe MS 210, f. 34). Sharpe prints two verses in his *Ballad Book* and Scott's notes, printed in the 1880 edition, 138, have the line used in the novel. The verse in question refers to Tam and his mother rolling over in the fire.

14. D. Gifford, *James Hogg* (1976), 11.

15. Harker, *Fakesong*, 73.

16. For accounts of Hogg's reception, see Gifford, 22-28, 72, 84, 124, 134, 197, 220-21, 116-31; L. Simpson, *James Hogg: A Critical Study* (1962), 21-25; D. S. Mack's introduction to Hogg's *Memoirs of the Author's Life* and *Familiar Anecdotes of Sir Walter Scott* (1972).

17. Gifford, 16, 20, 196.

18. J. Hogg, *The Brownie of Bodsbeck*, ed. D. Mack (1976), xiii-xvii.

19. This is included in the *Jacobite Relics of Scotland*, **1**, 151-53 but is also recorded earlier, e.g. Herd **1** 179-80, *SMM*, no. 572. Scott quotes a snippet in Chapter 30 of *Waverley*.

20. J. Hogg, *The Three Perils of Man: War, Women and Witchcraft*, ed. D. Gifford (1972).

21. J. Hogg, *The Three Perils of Woman: Love, Leasing and Jealousy*, ed. D. Groves, A. Hasler & D. S. Mack (1995).

22. M. R. Mitford, *Notes of a Literary Life* (1857), **1**, 4.

23. M. R. Mitford, *Our Village* (1824-32), **1**, v.

24. W. J. Keith, *The Rural Tradition* (1975), 90.

25. T. Crofton Croker, *My Village versus 'Our Village'* (1833). Disappointingly, Croker turns out to be almost equally conventional; he is only debunking Mitford's optimism about general human nature, not her social analysis. In terms of the mark made on the literary world, Mitford wins hands down, though John Britton, the topographer born a labourer, distrusted her 'glowing colours' and said his own village was a different world (Keith, *Rural Tradition*, 92).

26. W. Cobbett, *Rural Rides*, ed. G. Woodcock (1967), 227.

27. Quoted in Keith, 91.

28. See M. Praz, *The Hero in Eclipse in Victorian Fiction* (1956), 1-33.

29. E.g. H. Witemeyer, *George Eliot and the Visual Arts* (1979) and J. Grundy, op. cit.

30. R. Palmer, *A Ballad History of England from 1588 to the Present Day* (1979), 111. 'Cherry Ripe' and 'Home, Sweet Home!' were sung by street glee-singers in London according to Henry Mayhew (*London Labour and the London Poor*, **3**, 194). However, they are not found in rural tradition.

4

Scott's Legacy, and Three Muscular Christians

Mid Nineteenth-century Novelists

The debt Victorian novelists owe to Scott is a heavy one, as has frequently been recognised.[1] However, the ways in which they develop his techniques of multiple discourses vary, as the emphases of their developments of the novel vary. Some continue along the paths of Romance, whether contemporary or historical, while others develop a new and grimmer realist concern with the depiction of the lives of the poor, especially the new urban proletariat, as an uneasy social conscience aligns itself with the instinct for self-preservation. Writing at either the romance or the realist end of the continuum might be supported by the apparatus of references and notes. As well as notes there are quotes, put to the same multifarious uses as we find in Scott, whichever class the novel focuses on. There was still a thriving trade in self-penned false intertexts. The most important of the emphases to which allusion to folk song and popular culture contribute are these:

1. a Romantic sense of the alienation of the individual,
2. pastoral nostalgia, often tinged with a socially conservative Wordsworthianism,
3. mediaevalist nostalgia, with similar implications,
4. the historian's impulse to record the past,
5. the evangelical social worker's concern to inform about the present,
6. the provision of a socially subversive subtext,
7. the manipulation or invention of 'intertexts' to suppress subversive implications.

The flavour of different novels of the period can be partially defined by analysing the proportions in which these interests are manifested in them. Thus, for example, George Eliot's *Adam Bede* (1859) and Elizabeth Gaskell's *Sylvia's Lovers* (1863) are both set around the turn of the eighteenth century. Both authors extenuate the limitations of their characters by giving a clear picture of the historical and social constraints under which they operate. Both display a susceptibility towards the charms of a life of rural simplicity which to some extent they have imagined rather than recaptured. The pastoralism of someone like Mitford has played its part here, though both novelists use the pastoral past to illuminate the nature of moral choice in the present. Gaskell gives more of a sense of trying to recreate a little-known community, Eliot of trying to recreate a remembered idyll against whose warmth the actual cruelty and selfishness of real people stands out in relief.

Before examining writers who investigate new areas of experience I would like to discuss briefly some of those operating in more established ways. From here onwards, the discussion will concentrate almost wholly on the work of English fiction and essay writers, though the assumption of a more unified culture still operates in Scottish writers up to the end of the century. A good example would be Robert Louis Stevenson's *The Master of Ballantrae* (1889), set in the decades following the 1745 Jacobite rising. This has a few deeply significant uses of folk song as well as a scene set with a few lines of constructed 'tradition'.[2] The Master himself manipulates people through his masterly performance of 'Shule Aroon', trying to seduce his sister-in-law's affections back to himself as a political martyr lost to the Jacobite cause, and presenting himself (in a phrase borrowed from Scott) as a 'hero of romance' (102). One verse is quoted (95) but the audience is obviously expected to be familiar with the tone and sentiment of this well-known Irish song.[3]

In England, one of Scott's early followers was G. Harrison Ainsworth (1805-82). Son of a solicitor, he was a voracious reader of Scott and of Gothic fiction.[4] He was a good friend of Thomas Hughes's grandmother, who also knew Scott well and was a great collector of ballads and tales.[5] Ainsworth developed the historical romance side of Scott. Only the terminally naive would look for anthropological authenticity in a novel which opens with a man snatching the hand from his mother's corpse because the wedding ring it bears is evidence of his disputed legitimacy. Such is *Rookwood*, published in 1834. The Dick Turpin part of the plot makes it a 'Newgate Novel' of the type fashionable in the 1820s and 1830s, purporting to give an account of low-life society among the criminal classes.[6] This is partly Gothicised sensation, partly a continuation of an eighteenth-century novel interest in vicarious slumming, and partly a continuation of the street literature of criminal lives and ballad 'goodnights', i.e. farewells from the gallows. Ainsworth makes it quite clear in his Preface that the songs he inserts in thieves' cant are his own attempt to remedy what he regards as the curious absence of 'any slang songs of merit' (5-6). This is hardly surprising, since the point of a specialist vocabulary is its protective incomprehensibility (Ainsworth has to add comprehensive footnotes to his songs). This militates against written publication, and also against purchase.

There are some cant broadside songs, but little evidence of their entering oral tradition.[7] The songs about criminals that have been preserved, both from the time the novel is set and from the time of writing, are usually severely moral broadsides such as 'The Wild and Wicked Youth' or 'The Flying Cloud', where the message is almost always spelled out: 'He was a wild and wicked youth' or 'Young men, a warning by me take/And shun all piracy.'[8] Even where the verses are mostly celebratory of the criminal's exploits, as in 'Bold Turpin',[9] the last verse makes the point dramatically by marking the hero's fate at the hands of the law. Turpin plays a prominent part in Ainsworth's novel, and is made to say 'I trust, whenever the chanter-culls and last-speech scribblers get hold of me, they'll at least put no cursed nonsense into my mouth' (319). Ainsworth is well aware that 'goodnight' ballads supposedly spoken from the scaffold were almost always faked, since they had to be composed and printed before the day of execution in order to gain a greater sale to the crowds assembled for it. Nevertheless, he is not concerned to imitate their rather gloomy conventional morality, choosing instead to create a factitious jolliness likely to appeal to an audience likely neither to encounter highwaymen nor to join their ranks. It is notable that in both his introduction and his *envoi* (5-6, 393) he mentions songs attributed to named authors, including the notorious 'The Night Before Larry Was Stretched', which he greatly admires and which became popular but rather as a piece *sui generis* as an eccentric piece of Irishry.[10]

English historical romance, though declining in popularity, continued throughout the nineteenth century on familiar lines. A mid-Victorian example would be R. D. Blackmore's *Lorna Doone* (1869). It has some perfunctory bits of local colour such as carol-singing (Chapter 13) but Lorna's 'ancient song' in Chapter 16 or the 'Exmoor Harvest-Song' from Chapter 29, supposedly as sung at the end of the seventeenth century, are thorough-going pieces of Victoriana, not even pastiche.

Novelists looking for something more apparently authentic looked in some odd places. In Chapter 9 of *Wuthering Heights*, Nelly Dean sings a lullaby to Hareton in what appears to be Yorkshire dialect:

> It was far in the night, and the bairnies grat,
> The mither beneath the mools heard that.

She does tell Lockwood that she has read more than he might expect, but Jamieson's translations of Danish ballads seem to be pushing the point too far, especially as they were not published until several decades after this episode is meant to take place.[11] It is most likely that the immediate source for Emily Bronte is Scott's Note 49, which he added later to *The Lady of the Lake* (1810), quoting these lines.[12]

One would not say that any of these novelists was deliberately focusing on the lower ranks of a society with clear class distinctions. George Eliot, though, is anxious to justify the commitment of her attention to ordinary people of humble rank in her early novels *Adam Bede* (1859), *The Mill on the Floss* (1860) and *Silas Marner* (1861). Her principles are apparent even earlier, in her critical work, where she argued in favour of replacing the idyllic pictures of painters and writers with something more accurate. Thus, in 'The Natural History of German Life' (1856) she makes a case for realism: 'How little the real characteristics of the working-classes are known to those who are outside them'.[13] Unlike opera, 'our social novels profess to represent the people as they are, and the unreality of their representations is a grave evil', so Scott and Kingsley are praised for trying to redress the balance and for 'linking the higher classes with the lower' (270).

Eliot felt well-qualified to try this herself. As Henry Auster points out, she boasted of having a wide range of social experience; she had 'a father who was well acquainted with all ranks of his neighbours' and the advantages of 'daily fellowship and observation'.[14] Though many of Eliot's characters in these early novels are farmers, tradesmen or even gentry, they are less exalted than the characters of later novels, and their world is one of whole rural or small-town communities with large numbers of labouring-class characters from the poorest to the upwardly-mobile artisans like Adam Bede. She also mentions the value of local songs in understanding community life, though only with reference to the Continent (*Essays*, 275). An interest in British folk song is implied by the presence of several collections of ballads and songs (including the *Reliques*) in the library she and Lewes shared.[15]

For all these reasons, one might have expected a more radical and accurate view of village culture than we actually get. For all her theoretical political correctness, Eliot seems to have held back from involvement in community life: 'though I saw a great deal of the Poor in my early youth, I have been for so many years aloof from all practical experience in relation to them.'[16] No doubt this was in part due to the difficulties of her equivocal position with Lewes, and it is noticeable that her subjects move away from homely village life as her art develops. Nevertheless, the judgmental severity of her early attitudes can hardly have been conducive to an intimate participation in the lives of the poor: 'the only realm of fancy and imagination for the English clown exists at the bottom of the third quart pot' (*Essays*, 269). In German peasant society she was unable to find any individuality: 'the cultured man acts more as an individual; the peasant, more as one of a group ... many thousands of men are as like each other in thoughts and habits as so many sheep or oysters' (*Essays*, 274).

This did not stop her creating highly individualised characters from the labouring classes. (English farm workers were not, of course, peasants, however much nineteenth-century commentators liked to use the term.) However, a problem for her, as for contemporaries like Kingsley and later writers like Jefferies, was that she could not argue both that the working man's individuality and his creative and spiritual faculties were depressed by his economic conditions *and* that he had an active and lively culture. (In part she evades the issue by setting her novels in the past, whereas the matter was more urgent for the other two writers.) Eliot had a lively interest in high culture music which has been extensively discussed.[17] However, her interest in the culture of oral tradition was equivocal and the greatness of her presentation of rural life in her early fiction does not lie in her handling of this area.

For Eliot, village music was religious in the Latinate sense; it was a force that bound people together, and therein, rather than in its intrinsic interest, lay its value. *Scenes of Clerical Life* (1857) has a debate about church bands and the loss of the old church music as a loss of community that foreshadows Hardy in *Under the Greenwood Tree* (1871) but Eliot makes fun of the musical style and standard rather than recognizing the simple nature of the bass parts, writing of an 'anthem in which the key-bugles always ran away at a great pace, while the bassoon every now and then boomed a flying shot after them'.[18] This debate also appears in *Adam Bede* (101, 225). This novel, *The Mill on the Floss* and *Silas Marner* all mention carol singing. *Adam Bede* and *Silas Marner* both have set pieces of village music-making. In Chapter 25 of *Adam Bede* Eliot describes a variety of country pursuits in the course of the celebrations for Arthur Donnithorne's coming of age, including the fiddling of Joshua Rann and the solo hornpipe of Ben Cranage. Eliot admits the skill of musicians and singers like Rann here and elsewhere (a gentleman may sing woefully out of tune, while 'some narrow-browed fellow, trolling a ballad in the corner of a pot-house, shall be as true to his intervals as a bird').[19] She compares a 'real English rustic' with the stage imitation (324). Yet she insists on treating Rann and Cranage from a position of amused condescension. Wiry Ben looks 'as serious as a dancing monkey' (324), not perceiving that his dancing is a source of amusement to a genteel audience. Some of the ladies of the party, such as Anne Irwine, are so feebly constituted that they can't even get this far; her brother leads her out on the grounds that 'that fiddle-scraping is too much for you' (323).

One of Eliot's most famous pronouncements about realism is in Chapter 17 of this novel, where she justifies her work in terms of the truthfulness of 'many Dutch paintings, which lofty-minded people despise' (223). Their celebration of humble vernacular life is, of course, a great achievement, yet in seeing her characters through the lens of genre art Eliot is already tacitly admitting the power of convention to shape the way the world is represented into something acceptably consumable. This narratorial recommendation has a fatal complicity with Arthur's pretence of treating Hetty as an art-object in Chapter 7, and with his recommendation that his aunt and the Miss Irwines should view the tenants as a feature of the picturesque, worth a brief viewing: 'they were afraid of the noise of the toasts, but it would be a shame for them not to see you at table' (316).

These attitudes are repeated in the set-piece of the Harvest Supper in Chapter 53, where Eliot quotes extensively from an authentic Harvest Home song. This was available in J. H. Dixon's *Ballads and Songs of the Peasantry of England* (1846). Eliot owned the later Robert Bell edition of this, so she may not have been reproducing it from direct observation, though it is fairly standard form, and her version differs slightly from his.[20] She surrounds the song with an apparatus of ponderous irony and comic placement, beginning with a disquisition into the origins of folk-song which de-naturalizes what follows. She continues with an insistence on the connection between singing and drinking, and then introduces attempts at songs by individuals in the terminology of genteel music-making ('there appeared to be a general desire for solo music after the choral', 565). After more drinking, some songs are forthcoming, though 'My Love's a Rose without a Thorn' and 'Three Merry Mowers' are not songs recoverable from tradition. Eliot describes the performance of the labourers comically by imposing one song over the other and making the singing style ludicrous:

> old Kester ... suddenly set up a quavering treble,— as if he had been an alarum, and the time was come for him to go off.
>
>   The company at Alick's end of the table took this form of vocal entertainment very much as a matter of course, being free from musical prejudices; but Bartle Massey laid down his pipe and put his fingers in his ears (570).

Joshua Rann's counterpart in *Silas Marner* is Solomon Macey, and the set-piece is the New Year's Eve dance in Chapter 11. Macey plays tunes adopted into tradition and appropriate to the setting: 'The Flaxen-headed Ploughboy', 'Over the Hills and Far Away' and 'Sir Roger de Coverley'.[21] Later (Chapter 13) Bob Cass dances a solo hornpipe. However, a good deal of the chapter is occupied with Nancy Lammeter's musings about Godfrey. Eliot gets some fun out of the rural chorus discussing the dancers. There is a similar scene of frank bucolic cheer earlier, in Chapter 6, where the conversation of the regulars at the Rainbow inn foreshadows Hardy's similar scenes in *Far From the Madding Crowd*. In passing, Eliot mentions the prowess of Solomon's brother as a singer. The Squire used to invite him in just to sing the 'Red Rovier' (98). What Eliot had in mind here is unclear. Beryl Gray suggests three songs prompted by Fennimore Cooper's novel *The Red Rover* (1827), noting that all postdate the time the novel is meant to be set. These would provide 'an innocent contrast between the sung experience of a romantically piratical rover and the honest Raveloe-centred life.'[22] Equally anachronistically, I suspect

Eliot may have been thinking of R. E. Egerton Warburton's hunting song 'The Little Red Rover', first published in 1834 but with a continued popularity throughout the nineteenth century. Whichever it was, it was not an English folk song.[23] This is part of Eliot's nostalgia for a rural past always at vanishing point; Macey laments comfortably 'our family's been known for musicianers as far back as anybody can tell. But them things are dying out ... there's no voices like what there used to be, and nobody remembers what we remember' (99). The novel redoubles this effect by showing that the seven year-old Aaron Winthrop can tune his voice to 'God Rest You Merry, Gentlemen' (Chapter 10) yet the novel constantly reminds us that this healthy tradition is the condition of an England half a century ago. In spite of her perceptive suspicions of pastoral as a genre, Eliot is herself drawn to it. More like Mitford than Scott, she emphasizes those aspects of culture which characters of all classes, and readers, supposedly have in common, thus demonstrating that one does not need to use false intertexts to misrepresent. The singers' repertoires are falsified by omission rather than commission. Like both Mitford and Scott, she implies a subject position for the reader as auditor of traditional singing and music, whether secular or sacred, not as generator of it, an effect emphasized by the weight of her narrative authority.

Borrow

As first-person, semi-autobiographical picaresque novels with only the sketchiest kind of closure, George Borrow's *Lavengro* (1851) and *The Romany Rye* (1857) are hardly mainline realism, yet they do display realist intention, as in the description of the conditions for French Napoleonic prisoners-of-war that opens Chapter 4 of *Lavengro*. In spite of the irritable reservations he had about Scott, which he expresses in Chapter 40 of *The Romany Rye*, Borrow had 'always entertained the most intense admiration' for his genius.[24] He certainly shared with him and with Disraeli a Gothic fascination with the charismatic stranger; in Borrow's case, though, this alienated individual is given the narrator's role as well as cropping up as sundry wandering Jews, Armenians, Hungarians, gipsies, etc. Borrow had little time for the 'peasantry' of his own country, whom he found 'in speech ... slow and uncouth, and in manner dogged and brutal'.[25] However, he admired ancient English and Scottish ballads, and still more, Danish ones, of which he brought out a translation in 1826.[26]

Mostly, though, his interest lay with the gipsies. One reason he distrusted Scott was that he felt Scott had misrepresented their language and culture. Scott had created some memorable gipsies, such as Meg Merrilies, but he did not know much about them and was not interested in the remnants of their verbal culture. Borrow accuses him (rightly) of making them speak thieves' cant, with which they were familiar, but which was not Romany.[27] Like Scott,

Borrow uses these people as repositories of arcane lore and quasi-supernatural powers, such as Mrs Herne's prophetic dream of her own end.[28]   Also like Scott, he equips them with a distinctive rhetoric, one based more upon knowledge than Scott's was, but hardly one more accessible to verification by the reader. Anglo-Romany word order, and much of the grammar, was by this period like English, but the vocabulary was very different. Travelling people were until very recently (i.e. up to the last third of the twentieth century) repositories of traditional music and song extinct elsewhere, but Borrow's construction of the gipsies seems more designed to impress the reader with his arcane narratorial authority than to recreate an historical culture.   He does sometimes provide partial translations of the Romany phrases he employs (for example, two versions of Leonora's song in Chapters 70 and 71 of *Lavengro*) but he enjoys the power this gives him and the element of mystification that remains.

Borrow was unique as a novelist in actually possessing a working knowledge of Romany, as well as of a large number of other languages. He would have claimed mastery ('lav-engro' means 'language master'). Remarkable as he was as a linguist, he was not quite as remarkable as he said he was.   His knowledge of English Romany language and culture has been questioned by some with good authority as critics, such as Isaac Heron, who had met Borrow and was the son of the woman who taught him Romany, but 'was no admirer of this Lavengro's linguistic powers or his knowledge of the Gipsy tongue'.[29]

There is little work available on Anglo-Romany songs in the nineteenth century, and W. J. Ibbetson points out that what little there is in Borrow himself, Leland, and Groome.[30]   F. Hinde Groome says, however, in his edition of *Lavengro*, that Borrow's 'knowledge of the strange history of the Gypsies was very elementary, of their manners almost more so, and of their folk-lore practically *nil*.'[31]   In his own book *In Gipsy Tents* (1881) Groome gives fragments of Gipsy song, but much more obviously English than Romany, and he claims that 'the Anglo-Romani muse is dead, if indeed she ever lived' and that Borrow, though his vocabulary is trustworthy, is led astray by his 'love of effect'.[32]

Leland has a higher opinion of Borrow, saying that *Lavengro* and *The Romany Rye* are the only novels in English 'in which the writer has shown familiarity with the *real* life, habits, or language of the vast majority of ... the itinerants of the roads'.[33]   Leland is a more scholarly and reliable collector than Borrow and his book *English-Gipsy Songs* (1875) contains a few authentic examples, and one, 'Mullo Balor' about a plot to poison a pig, though the resemblances to Borrow's 'Poisoning the Porker' in *Romany Rye* Chapter 7 are largely those of situation and vocabulary.[34]   However, though he records that gipsies sing a good deal he finds the words 'wanting in metre and rhyme' and almost tuneless (v). Not finding what he wanted, the idea came to him 'that poetry, impressed with the true Gipsy spirit, and perfectly idiomatic, might be written and honestly [!] classed as Rommany [sic], even though not composed by dwellers in tents and caravans' (vi). The majority of songs in the book are of this kind. If other contemporary collectors found themselves driven by lack of material and/or frustrated expectation to such shifts of invention, it is perhaps hardly surprising that Borrow, as a novelist, should also have felt the need to contribute work of his own as evidence of gipsy culture.

Borrow does have a nostalgia for an idealised past of a peculiar Young-Englandish kind, which mixes admiration of rude physical fortitude, expressed in fighting and bloodsports, with a pugnacious patriotism and Protestantism. Although this is not a link commonly made, he does clearly have a lot in common with Kingsley and Hughes, discussed later in this chapter. This is apparent at the beginning of *Lavengro*, when the narrator recalls the days of his youth during the Napoleonic wars. He regrets the 'bygone time, when loyalty was in vogue, and smiling content lay like a sunbeam on the land.'[35] On the whole, though, Borrow's tone is not one of lament. The most important spokesman against the decline of Romany culture is Mrs Herne, Jasper Petulengro's mother-in-law, and since one of her few ascertainable pursuits is poisoning people and animals, including the narrator, the reader's sense of loss at her suicide is slight. Jasper and his tribe appear to prosper as well as any of the other mysterious figures in the two novels who enhance the mystery of the narrator, Lavengro, by reflection and analogy.[36]

Although it was published in 1851, *Lavengro* is set in the world of the 1820s, as is made obvious from the references to Cobbett, the return of Byron's remains, and the debate over Catholic emancipation. In no way is it an historian's record, though. The period is merely a background across which pass those Romantic outcasts and social oddities, beginning with the wandering Jew of the first chapter who testifies to Lavengro's mysterious force even as a child ('forced to speak to it') and to his destiny as a traveller alienated from his own society ('has all the look of one of our people's children'). He introduces the theme of arcane language, seeing 'holy letters' in the illiterate child's 'strange lines in the dust' (7-8). Lavengro's natural affinities with vipers give him an entree to the most important of the figures whose power and situation parallel his own, the gipsy Jasper Petulengro and his Romany culture.

Song itself, of which the gipsies are the most conspicuous users, is in this novel indicative of separation from the mass. It belongs to the coherence of a different and venerable tradition, as in the passage at the end of Chapter 83 where Lavengro blends his singing with a description of the traditional gipsy trade of horseshoe making couched in Romany terms.

Other uses of song and ballad in the book have less cultural coherence but a similar function as a mode of moving beyond the commonplace. Hence

Lavengro's fascination with Danish ballads, in which, significantly, the society in which he is trying to earn a living will take no interest. They represent the heroic world of the past which he had originally encountered through the Danish skulls of Chapter 2: 'deeds of knights and champions, and men of huge stature; ballads which from time immemorial had been sung in the North' (145). The common appeal of these very different kinds of song appears first in Lavengro's description of his travels north as a child, and his encounter with

> songs upon the river from the fisher barks; and occasionally a chorus, plaintive and wild, such as I had never heard before, the words of which I did not understand, but which, at the present time, down the long avenue of years, seem in memory's ear to sound like 'Horam, coram, dago' (42).

No reader of Wordsworth's 'The Solitary Reaper' could miss the similarities of feeling: 'the music in my heart I bore/Long after it was heard no more'. His influence also appears in the idea of an inward ear parallel to the inward eye of 'I wandered lonely as a cloud', in Borrow's response to 'the loveliness of nature, and ... the happiness and handiworks of ... fellow-creatures' (42) and the melancholy in the listener in response to the suggestions of an unknown tongue. ('Iorram' is a Gaelic word for a song; Jeanie Deans hears a 'woeful jorram' in crossing to Roseneath [*Heart of Midlothian*, 468] and words like these crop up in songs in English as nonsense choruses.)[37] Borrow adds to these his sense of an intuitive perception of the supernatural, the 'sorcery' of Elvir Hill, which he links with the Danes.

Borrow's use of song allusion, then, is quite opposed to any impulse to provide a simple historical or anthropological record; it is not descriptive but suggestive, and in this way provides thematic links throughout the book. Such links are especially important given the looseness of Borrow's overall picaresque form. The message of the book is coherent, even if the structure is not; the man who is divorced from the usual constraints of social intercourse finds repeated access to considerations which challenge and enrich his perception of the world, though by the end of *Lavengro* the hero has not succeeded in forging from them any doctrine that will allow him to overcome his existential depression. Though some of this access to a different world is through texts and figures which cannot be related to this discussion (figures like the Armenian merchant or the Welsh preacher) Borrow's use of song and ballad at crucial junctures is certainly an important guide to the way we interpret a complex and confusing book.

The sequel to *Lavengro*, *The Romany Rye* and its lengthy polemical appendix, manifest a discrepancy between Borrow's declared aim and his actual achievement. In the first chapter of the Appendix he defends *Lavengro* for the philological information it contains and declares that 'it is particularly

minute with regard to the ways, manners and speech of the English section of
the most extraordinary and mysterious clan or tribe of people to be found in the
whole world—the children of Roma'.[38]   However, he also claims to have
introduced deliberate philological errors in order to catch out the critics, who
failed to notice them.   Such a practice, whether intentional or not, renders any
information conveyed suspect.   Although it is difficult to ascertain the exact
proportions of Borrow's invention compared to his observation he does seem to
have worked up the versions of gipsy songs in his novels rather than simply
using ones taken down from genuine originals.[39]   Some of the songs collected
by him and published in *Romano Lavo-Lil* (1874) have parallels in the work of
other collectors, such as Leland, Laura A. Smith and A. E. Gillington[40] but I
have not traced any significant correspondences with the songs in his novels.
His work is sometimes republished along with that of other (and worse)
imitators such as Leland and Smith as 'gipsy song'.   On occasion he selects
material which can be shown to be inappropriate.   According to Angus Fraser
the Romany verses he puts into the mouth of Captain Bosvile in *Wild Wales*
Chapter 98 were ones he picked up in Transylvania in 1844.[41]   Knapp's notes to
The Romany Rye discuss the building up of 'Poisoning the Porker' in Chapter 7
'from a very slender prose draft', through two verse drafts, one of which has
more correct spelling of the Romany than the printed text (380-81).

If these songs were built up by Borrow they reveal an equivocal attitude to
his subject.   His defence of *Lavengro* stresses his aloofness, his retention of a
scholarly interest in what he observes rather than a whole-hearted commitment
to it.   *The Romany Rye* and the Appendix show Borrow trying to substitute his
literary gipsy world for the more fashionable Scottish one.   However, his
comparisons have the effect of degrading both rather than elevating the gipsies.
To a straw opponent who thinks gipsyism 'is particularly low' he responds by
ridiculing the Scotch (359).   Scots songs are mentioned only in disparaging
contexts.

The most extensive treatment of this theme in the novel is in Chapter 7,
which describes the festivities in honour of Ursula's wedding.   Since Jasper
describes her own song as 'somewhat of an old song, and ... sung ... as a
warning at our solemn festivals' (58) we can presumably take this to be an
occasion on which the gipsies' celebration is intended to represent the integrity
of their culture.   Borrow presents the two songs 'Poisoning the Porker' and
'The Song of the Broken Chastity' as items with which the narrator is already
familiar, having translated them for a lady's album, thus implying that the
songs have a safely traditional status and that the narrator is well-versed in
Romany culture while retaining links with a more genteel one.   The repetitions
and varying verse lengths of 'Poisoning the Porker' do suggest a song in the
process of being corrupted by uncertain oral transmission.   The section of
discussion between Jasper and the narrator claims that they are 'remarkable

songs, strongly expressive of the manners and peculiarities of a remarkable people'.[42] Whether Borrow composed or merely collected these songs, or, as is most probable, mixed the two methods, it seems odd that he should use these examples to make this point. Admittedly the finer points of the metrics (if there are any) are inaccessible to the reader, who can detect only the rhyme, but the content seems oddly prosaic and bald. As is obvious from the translation Borrow gives, the first song is about poisoning a farmer's pig in order to gain a free meal. The second song, that of the Broken Chastity, is not translated, though a summary is given later (66). Presumably this was to avoid offending the audience;[43] the readers of the first edition did not have the advantage of the word list provided in later ones. The gipsy girl says to her mother, 'My dear mother, I am pregnant' ('cambri', the key word of the song, and the one that provides the rhyme). Her mother enquires who is responsible, and on finding out that it is a non-gipsy, a gentleman who rides upon a stallion, calls her daughter a vile little harlot and tells her to get out of her tent. The narrator comments to Jasper:

> At your merry meetings you sing songs upon the compulsatory deeds of your people, alias, their villainous actions; and, after all, what would the stirring poetry of any nation be, but for its compulsatory deeds? Look at the poetry of Scotland, the heroic part, founded almost entirely on the villainous deeds of the Scotch nation; cow-stealing, for example, which is very little better than drabbing baulor, whilst the softer part is mostly about the slips of its females among the broom, so that no upholder of Scotch poetry could censure Ursula's song as indelicate, even if he understood it (43).

It would be possible to argue that Borrow is skilfully maintaining the moral disengagement of the narrative persona here, in order to question the moral values of his audience. In view of Borrow's own vehement inconsistencies on the subject of the Scots in the Appendix, however, this seems too generous. Whose are the standards of villainy and delicacy? If the reduction to the trivial and brutal of the songs appropriate to this festival is intentional, what does it do to our sense of the role of the gipsies in the rest of the book? Nor is this the only example. In Chapter 9 the narrator justifies the gipsies' existence with the following irony:

> You are certainly a picturesque people, and in many respects an ornament both to town and country; painting and lil [book] writing too are under great obligations to you. What pretty pictures are made out of your campings and regroupings, and what pretty pictures have been written in which gypsies, or at least creatures intended to represent gypsies, have been the principal figures (55).

Admittedly he is using considerations introduced into the conversation by Jasper, but they then move on to questions of religion, leaving the reader with a sense of inadequacy in the argument.

Borrow has two motives. In one sense he is using the gipsies, like his other eccentrics, originals and wanderers, as ornaments. At the same time, his protest against Scott's portrayal of them in Chapter 40 through the figure of the Hungarian is justified. Borrow's Romany may not have been perfect, but it was recognisably Romany. The vocabulary of his gipsy characters may have a wistful completeness about it, but it is not the thieves' cant that he complains about in Scott. On the other hand, the lines he claims he heard from a party of harvesters in Lincolnshire (*Romany Rye*, 177) sound like a complete fabrication, and he must have cast rather a blight over their festivities by performing his own translation of 'Sivord and the Horse Grayman'. His impulse to record is at odds with his pastoralism, and both are shaped by his desire to assert his essential apartness even from the culture to which he seems most sympathetic.

Kingsley

The two writers I wish to discuss next were friends with common political ends. The first is most notable for trying to engage with the culture of the new urban proletariat, and the second for mingling the work of a collector with two tales descriptive of rural life. Charles Kingsley (1819-75) is fairly well-known as a versatile author whose works include historical and condition-of-England novels, and poems including song and ballad pastiches like 'Airly Beacon' and 'The Sands of Dee'; two of his earliest poems are imitation ballads.[44] He met Thomas Hughes (1822-96) in 1848, and with him, F. D. Maurice and J. M. Ludlow formed the basis of a Christian Socialist Group.[45] With their mutual stress on physical prowess in sport and even violence, Kingsley and Hughes are so-called 'muscular Christians', and, politically, Tory Radicals. Kingsley claimed that the real battle of the time was between 'the Church, the gentleman, and the workman, against the shopkeepers and the Manchester school'.[46]

In his sympathy for the urban workman Kingsley was one of a new breed of novelists. He gave him a voice in the first-person eponymous narrator of *Alton Locke* (1851). However, it was a very atypical voice. The Victorian working class continued to have a variety of forms of verbal and musical culture, some still maintained in a withering oral tradition bolstered by cheap printing, as noted in the Introduction. The street broadsides were augmented by songs from the early music-halls, which by 1850 were a dominant influence on popular song even at the street level. By the 1860s tuppenny and threepenny songbooks including music hall hits were more popular than broadsides.[47] *Alton Locke*, set in the 1840s, would coincide with this time of change. It also coincides with the latter end of a working-class movement to colonize the middle class by imitating a rather outmoded model of high-culture verse and allusion.[48] Initially, in the eighteenth century, most of these aspirants (for example, Bloomfield and Yearsley) were rural, as Burns had been and Hogg was. In the early decades of the nineteenth century many workers from textile and other manufacturing industries joined their ranks, and this phenomenon is further discussed in relation to Elizabeth Gaskell. Both she and Kingsley focused on the working-class poet as proof of common humanity, but only Kingsley created a working-class poet who would be presented as writing his own verse within the novel. Thus, as Brian Maidment points out,

> Alton Locke, as poet ... became part of a literary culture, based on the journals of popular progress, where class differences could be partially submerged in common cultural and literary interests. Such locales, even havens, constructed within fiction for the purpose of sustaining discussion across and between class are, of course, a crucial requirement in the meliorist programme of the naturalistic novel of social concern.[49]

This verse may be given a musical setting, but it is primarily designed to be read and it is a very different thing from the actual songs which Kingsley quotes copiously in his novels.

For Kingsley, the idea of a communal song tradition was important as a hegemonic instrument: 'the man who makes the people's songs is a true popular preacher.'[50] No doubt the knowledge that none of the adult labouring population of his Eversley parish could read reinforced this imperative.[51] He attributed the death of effective peasant song to changing social conditions, and was concerned lest negative emotions should 'fret and canker within' the currently 'utterly dumb English peasant'.[52] Kingsley was familiar with a wide range of ballads as available in literary collections such as Percy's *Reliques* and was suspicious of most modern imitations.[53] Like many Victorians, he believed that the old ballads were some of the 'early writing of the Middle Ages', whereas modern scholars would be aware that the linguistic and poetic forms in which most ballads have been preserved are characteristic of the Renaissance or later.[54] However, he was also aware that the power of a song lies in its performance, and regarded the true test of a song as its going to music.[55] The gaps between Kingsley's construction of folk song and the still-living reality can, however, be seen in his dislike of negro workers' songs in the West Indies, and of what appears to be a real traditional ballad sung by the steersman on a trip back from Lundy; Kingsley selects the verb 'moaning out' to describe the rendering.[56] As we shall see, he was similarly unsympathetic to street songs.

Although Kingsley's historical novels post-date his more socially concerned fiction I shall deal with them first since their techniques seem less innovatory. Like Scott, he mingles real and false intertexts; the latter are common but not particularly novel; they almost all act as reinforcements of local and/or national patriotism. He uses literary ballad references copiously in his historical novels *Westward Ho!* (1855) and *Hereward the Wake* (1865). The distance in time and choice of heroes dictate a largely rural, and in the case of *Westward Ho!*, even exotic setting. Like Scott before him, Kingsley sets out to establish the heroic nature of his characters and their times by evoking a galaxy of by now, for him, literary ballads. Sometimes these will be entirely appropriate. One example would be the epigraph to Chapter 12 (2, 104) of *Westward Ho!* from 'The Dowie Dens of Yarrow' (*Minstrelsy*, 3, 72-79) where the original is about a battle over a lady and the following chapter deals with Cary's challenge to Guzman over Rose. Another would be the Elizabethan ballad of 'Mary Ambree' (*Reliques*, 2, 219-23) which forms the epigraph to Chapter 26 (3, 141). Mary Ambree was a warlike woman who fought in memory of her lover and refused to be the mistress of the Prince of Parma; the subsequent chapter has two female warriors, the slave Tita, who murders the Spanish intendant on board the great galleon, and Ayacanora, who saves Amyas from the captain and whom Amyas himself calls 'Mary Ambree with a dark skin'.[57]

On the other hand, Kingsley may quote with a blithe lack of concern for either anachronism, or the appropriateness of many of the intertexts beyond the immediate one of the lines actually quoted. In *Westward Ho!* the setting is at least Elizabethan, so it does make sense to use songs of the period such as 'Brave Lord Willoughby' (Chapter 9; 2, 1), though there does not seem to be much point in quoting 'The Wife of Usher's Well (*Minstrelsy*, 2, 122-27) as the epigraph to Chapter 28 (3, 214), when Mrs Leigh's longings are nothing like the impiety of the wife in the ballad, only one son comes home, and he is not a revenant ghost who will have to return to the grave. In *Hereward the Wake* the anachronism is more obvious. As well as using standard ballad quotations[58] and mock-Viking chants, Kingsley makes Hereward advise his young followers to learn 'to plough and to sow,/And to reap and to mow,/And to be a farmer's boy' in the lines of a song untraceable before 1832.[59] Kingsley also relies crucially on ballads of Robin Hood and other outlaws, all rolled into a kind of *ur*-outlaw which includes Hereward himself. At one point Robin Hood is imagined singing ballads about Hereward, about 'how Hereward played the potter' (2, 169)— as Robin Hood himself did, according to a ballad.[60] Robin Hood, let alone Hereward, might have been surprised to learn that their spirit 'makes, to this day, the life and marrow of an English public school' (2, 252).

This is game, not history. The principle behind the action can be projected forward into the mid-nineteenth century by the reader reflecting on the causes of social discontent. However, the use of a dehistoricised ballad tradition lays bare the mythologising nature of both Kingsley's history and his politics. As Michael Young points out,

> social rebellion on a historical scale, with its specific grievances and a particular cause, is naturalized and generalized, reduced to the dimensions of a transient phase stripped of all its serious threat.[61]

The two works I wish to concentrate on are novels of nineteenth-century life, one with a largely urban setting, *Alton Locke* (1850), and one with a rural one, *Yeast* (1848/1851). Alton Locke is a Chartist tailor poet, working class in manner of living if not in his origins and connections. Various originals have been suggested for Locke, including the poet agitator Thomas Cooper, a Chartist tailor, Walter Cooper, and the working class writer John Bethune.[62] Outside the novel, Kingsley had a low opinion of artisan writers. He disapproved of the verse of the Corn Law Rhymer Ebenezer Elliot and was very grudging about that of Thomas Cooper and Bethune.[63] Within the novel he was more sympathetic. Locke himself has a number of working-class poets in mind as role models and quotes two of them at length.[64] Since Kingsley read *Mary Barton* while the novel was germinating, he may have had Gaskell in mind as a model.[65] Gaskell's selective principles in quoting the work of artisan poets are discussed below. Kingsley's main concern is to stress the poetic success of their work, which bolsters Locke's ambitions and presages possible disaster. Thus, the quotation from Bethune is from a conventionally poetic bit of pastoral, while the quotation from Mackay is more to the point as a voice of protest, but Kingsley's stress is more on the manner than the matter. The three pieces given as Locke's resemble the work of such poets; they have some merit, but only one is a song ('The Sands of Dee') and that was designed specifically for Lillian and her piano.

In *Alton Locke* Kingsley uses two kinds of intertextual allusion to popular song. The first occurs in Chapter 2 where Alton tries to create a community of cultural interest between himself and any middle class readers he may have by denying the aesthetic value of the popular song tradition among the tailors. Those mentioned include 'Oh! no, we never mention her' and 'The Poor Man's Beer' (a song Hughes took a more positive view of).[66] There are also three other fragments I take to be Kingsley's invention. The idea is to imply vulgarity, and Locke apologizes to his readers 'for introducing all this ribaldry' (27). None is ribald. Later Mike Kelly quotes 'Love Farewell', a traditional song made more alien by its displacement onto a Celtic singer and the use of stage-Irish dialect features.[67]

The 'pure' tradition is displaced onto a Scottish character, Sandy Mackaye, and is exemplified by a number of songs of the tradition-based Scottish type by various writers, especially Burns. (In such a case, the dialect is acceptable as a form of Doric pastoral sanctified by a hundred and fifty years of convention.) Examples include 'Little Dunkeld', 'Aye Waukin, O', 'The Bush aboon Traquair', 'The Land o'the Leal', 'The Broom o'the Cowdenknowes', and even 'The Lyke Wake Dirge', most of which occur in a splurge of sentimental and improbably operatic excess on the part of the dying Mackaye.[68] Continuity is assured by Sandy's claim to have knelt at the deathbed of Burns and his quoting these songs on his own deathbed. Burns's radical side is featured in the prominent use of 'A Man's a Man for A'That' and in Sandy's revisionary use of an English song adapted by Burns, 'John Barleycorn', to suggest the possibilities of revolution: 'John Barleycorn got up again/And sore surprised them all.'[69] One of the implications of Sandy's death is that, like the song tradition, a comparatively pure ideal of moral commitment may die with him, though the last song allusion in the novel is in fact to a modern song, the Chartist standard 'There's a Good Time Coming'.[70]

The songs of the country people in *Yeast* are either saccharine, or far more sanguinary than those he criticises. Kingsley strikes a false note in the rick-burning song by having the representative labourer's voice threaten 'you and your stock may roast./Vor aught us poor chaps care.'[71] They are also different from what survives of protest song of the period without literary aspirations; those in revolt against their masters might threaten to burn property, but not horses. Apart from the improbability of really revolutionary songs surviving, given the power of magistrates to seize inflammatory material, it seems that rural workers had a different perspective. One glimpse of this is available in James Hawker's journal, *A Victorian Poacher*; Hawker was born in 1836, and worked in the fields in the 1840s. His hatred of 'the Class' would not have appealed to Kingsley in his attempt to forge closer links between the top and bottom of society.[72] Kingsley mentions poaching songs at the revel but gives no authentic ones. Traditional songs about poaching are common, but they fall into two main camps. The cheerful ones rejoice in having got away with it and cock a snook at the authorities, or even acquiesce ruefully in the punishment and resolve to carry on as before. The dismal ones focus on the horrors of transportation, which could indeed be imposed on poachers, though it was supposed by this time to be reserved for aggravated offences. The offence itself and harsh punishment were both common, and left an enduring memory, even though the proportion of poachers transported in songs exceeds that of those transported in actuality.[73] The trouble was that the working classes, both rural and urban, just did not demonstrate the kind of political consciousness that earnest middle-class radicals wanted them to. Indeed, they sometimes complained of this; William Howitt protested in 1846 that labouring men had been 'a thousand times too patient' with the poor conditions they were forced to endure.[74]

Yeast is notable in this context of intertextual allusion for its grand set piece of a village revel in Chapter 13. Here Kingsley's concern is to disabuse his audience of any vision they may have of the country as rosy idyll. The hero, Lancelot (!) Smith, is a middle-class 'innocent eye' who has to attend this revel with his class disguised, and he expects 'something of pastoral sentiment, and of genial frolicsome humour' (262)—a Mitford picture, perhaps, though Kingsley doesn't explicitly say so.[75] Kingsley's intention of *constructing* a voice of protest might well be deduced from his use in Chapter 9 (without any mention of a source) of three verses of an outlaw ballad, beginning with an implied criticism of Victorian poaching laws: 'The forest-laws were sharp and stern.' This is part of one of Kingsley's own poems, 'A New Forest Ballad', written in 1847.[76] The plot might be taken as traditional, and so might the versification and grammar, but the vocabulary, range of lyric description and apostrophe mark the pastiche. In Chapter 11 Kingsley's own powerful poem 'The Bad Squire' is put into the mouth of Tregarva, the preternaturally articulate gamekeeper who is Lancelot's guide to the evils of modern country life. As with Walter Scott, however, neither the presence nor the absence of a poem in the writer's poetical works is proof positive of authorship, and a similar exercise of judgement on some of the pieces sung at the revel leads to the conclusion that Kingsley is sometimes pastiching working class songs to create false intertexts.

That this is not merely an insignificant sideline to the main business of the book is shown by the review in the *Spectator*. This noted that 'the form of the work is subordinate to the object of the author', which was to expose social problems, including 'The brutish abject spirit but angry discontent pervading the mass, at least of the agricultural labourers.' It focuses on the Feast, with a column and a half of excerpts, largely the two verses and chorus of the rick-burning song, and the contrasted 'poetry' of 'A Rough Rhyme on a Rough Matter', which gets Tregarva the sack. Without making any comment on the authenticity of these two pieces, which are quoted entire, the magazine is obviously taking them both seriously as voices from the 'peasantry'.[77]

Three songs are actually 'quoted' in 'The Village Revel', and two of these are rendered in dialect. Traditional singers did not think of themselves as singing in dialect, and printed versions do not reflect local pronunciation; this is a device that deliberately distances the performers from the reader.[78] The first piece is a two-line fragment that might be traditional, although I do not know of its occurrence in any traditional song, and Kingsley heaps ridicule on the performer, 'a huge hulking farm-boy' and on his performance: 'ursine howls', 'roaring, dolefully ... with a punctuation of his own invention' (245). The other dialect piece is the ferocious song in favour of rick-burning, although

Lancelot has already been struck by a 'dread of violence' in the assembled labourers (244). This and the second song are sung melodiously and movingly, but the power of music is displaced from the community proper onto a wandering alien figure, a gipsy boy. Both appear to come from Kingsley's own pen, though the love ballad of a soldier's return incorporates a traditional floater as its conclusion. We are told a dozen different songs in which 'the same case of lawless love was embodied' are sung, but we are not shown another, nor any of the poaching songs or any 'of the lowest flash London school—filth and all' (247).

What is Kingsley up to here? The point of his novel is to offer his readers 'yeast' to get their minds working. His main theme in this chapter is the degeneracy and appalling poverty of the rural poor, a challenge to those who see the country as a haven from the vice and poverty of the town. The social situation is carefully explained to the readers by Tregarva, an improbably skilled analyst who even tries his hand with a Machereyan gap:

'There seems very little here to see.' . . .
'I think sir . . . that very thing is what's most worth seeing.' (237)

Lancelot even finds it difficult to understand the brand of English spoken by those around him. It is not Kingsley's purpose here to articulate nostalgia, and he dismisses one old man's attempt to do so. Kingsley wants to expose the sexual laxity of the rural poor, and a discontent liable to erupt into attacks on property such as rick-burning. Unlike Hughes, he wasn't particularly familiar with songs current in sung tradition from which he might select. In truth, Kingsley has painted himself into an ideological corner here. If worsening social conditions have caused the death of the working class muse, whether peasant or proletarian, this social class cannot be allowed a voice through contemporary verbal art, and it has to be constructed for them, or coped with by some sort of displacement. The best way to make his points fast was to encapsulate them in compositions which spoke *for* a supposedly inarticulate mass. There is no escaping the contradiction here. Lancelot interprets these songs as evidence that 'in these poor creatures, too, lay the genius of pathos, taste, melody, soft and noble affections' (262). But if the songs are presented to the audience as representing a real expressive capability in terms of popular verbal art, his point about the degeneracy caused by social exploitation falls to the ground. Thus, his argument becomes contradictory whether or not the songs are genuine, and he certainly can't afford to offer them in a context which champions their efficacy as art.

Hughes

Hughes was also quite capable of creating what he wanted to find, but his more openly idyllic work paradoxically embodies a comparatively more honest record of rural tradition. Hughes was the son of a country gentleman, and as a child he met Scott, who was a friend of his grandmother, and whose works remained favourites with him. As a boy he was a receptive audience, rather like Scott, for the culture of his social inferiors. The family knew a London coachman who had a fund of songs and stories. He spent most of his early life at Uffington, near the White Horse on the Berkshire Downs, playing with the village children and learning the local ballads. Later in life he went to harvest suppers.[79] He was also inoculated with Scots songs in the usual Victorian manner. The exact nature of his variety of repertoires is not now recoverable, but he had sufficient experience to justify a claim that he recognised the existence of an active *sung* tradition, and to suggest that he was at least capable of producing authentic examples.

Hughes is, of course, most famous for *Tom Brown's Schooldays* (1857). I don't propose to discuss this in detail, but it is worth mentioning that in it he alludes to several songs he also uses in the almost exactly contemporaneous *Scouring of the White Horse* (1859), and that the hero is fond of songs genuinely part of the rural singing tradition ('The Leathern Bottel', 'The Lincolnshire Poacher', 'Billy Taylor') while other boys sing more modern pieces which made their way into oral tradition, 'Chesapeake and Shannon' and 'The Poor Man's Beer' as well as other British standards.[80] The songs mentioned are metonymic symbols of the living spirit of Britain in the microcosmic community of the school. Hughes regrets the tendency of 'Young England' to travel abroad rather than getting to know their own country, and 'all the country folk, and their ways and songs and stories' (5). In Chapter 2 Hughes quotes the idiosyncratic dialect piece 'George Ridler's Oven' (13), describes a village revel, and commends the traditional life-style of the paternalistic Squire Brown with its cyclic celebrations such as Christmas mummers and village feasts. The latter have degenerated, as is shown by *Yeast*, Hughes explains (32). He attributes this to the fact that 'the gentlefolk and farmers have left off joining or taking an interest in them' (23). The fact that he as narrator admits that he has not been to one for twenty years does not seem to be taken into account in this censure (33). In this passage Hughes sounds rather like Cobbett, who was making similar remarks in rather than about the 1830s, thus demonstrating a long-standing reversion to images of the past to locate a myth of rural stability.

The *Scouring* and *The Ashen Faggot* set out to provide a more programmatic image of community. In some ways they resemble the 'dreams of Maypole dancing and athletic games' derided by Kingsley in Chapter 13 of

Yeast. However, both texts betray an anxiety of class distinction which precludes the full enjoyment of tradition in a communal sense. *The Scouring of the White Horse* is about one of the last traditional festivals to accompany the weeding of the open chalk out of which the design of the Uffington White Horse is cut. The narrative persona is that of a rather priggish London clerk on a long vacation ramble, gathering up scraps of local tradition. Chapter 7 is about local songs, performed in a supper booth. The clerk's companions are two Oxford scholars and a doctor. The short scholar is cheerful but blunt and ignorant; his companion is better informed, with an antiquarian bent.

Hughes's aim appears to be to give a comprehensive range of kinds of song—'specimens of patriotic, legendary and sentimental ditties' and drinking songs.[81] However, the songs presented seem to show a variety of linguistic features and apparent provenance which somewhat undercuts his message. We do know that in January 1858 the writing of the *Scouring* was hanging fire rather, so Hughes went down to Berkshire for more materials, but did not get what he wanted.[82] He may, therefore, have filled in the gaps as best he could.

In the 1889 preface to the two stories Hughes fears that 'that old time and old life [have] passed away' but he hopes there is 'a growing sense of fellowship and brotherhood amongst our people, which may well bind all classes together in the future in a truer and deeper national life'.[83] In seeing the commemoration of local legends, customs, etc. as likely to achieve this, he sounds very like early folk song revivalists, such as Cecil Sharp, converting their antiquarian interests into social engineering.[84] In Chapter 3 he actually quotes the antiquary Francis Wise, who, after a visit in 1738, praised the celebratory games in spite of 'the abuse of them to riot and debauchery' (55). They are 'proper intervals of recreation' for 'the common people', especially because of their 'manlike games', which are a bulwark against 'the general luxury and dissoluteness of the age' (55-56). Wise's words expose the way in which the social nostalgia of Hughes and Kingsley (and to some extent of Cobbett, a generation before them, and Richard Jefferies a generation after) utilises the same pattern. Both attempt to contain the subversive carnival elements of such popular ceremonies by rationalising them as the 'abuses' of a custom which is then redefined in the service of the interests of the dominant class. The repetition of this pattern betrays the hegemonic and formulaic nature of what purports to be historical observation.

Part of this mythologising is seen in the verse interventions in Hughes's text. Several of these are in 'dialect'. Again, it is not possible to prove whether these are all Hughes's composition, especially since one of the basic reference sources for local songs, Alfred Williams's *Folk Songs of the Upper Thames* (1923) and the still unpublished parts of his collection in Swindon Public Library, so much post-dates Hughes. It is possible that Hughes's work actually fed into the tradition from which Williams collected;[85] certainly Hughes's work has been taken as recording authentic folk song, by Jefferies, for instance. However, Hughes does sometimes give introductions that hint at the potential falsity of the intertext, for example, with the 'Ballad of the Scouring of the White Horse' in Chapter 4. The narrator claims to have received this, and 'The Lay of the Hunted Pig' (Chapter 6; 156-57) from the tall scholar but isn't quite sure 'whether he wasn't cutting his jokes upon' him (79). These two pieces are so apt to Hughes's purposes in describing the games and history that they must fall under suspicion of being his own invention in spite of the fact that the genre of songs commemorating and praising traditional gatherings is a genuinely popular one.[86]   Certainly I have not found them in tradition or in other printed sources, and Hughes even adds footnotes to 'The Lay of the Hunted Pig', which suggests an exercise.

However, most of the songs in Chapter 7 are a different matter. They take place in the specific context of a discussion of song composition and its social changes which articulates the standard binary contrast between town and country and also the hackneyed complaint about the English not being a musical nation:

> We have ceased to be a singing nation. The people have lost the good old ballads, and have got nothing in their place ... those [songs] in the Robin Hood Garland, for instance ... Songs written for the people, about their heroes, and, I believe, by the people ... the popular songs now are written by *litterateurs* in London (151-52).

The Doctor reassures the tall scholar that there are 'plenty of ballads sung about which you never hear' and these are 'real modern ballads, written by some of the masses, in this century' (172) and he persuades one of the locals to sing 'The Death of Lord Nelson'. Hughes's version has Berkshirized the words a little, but this is a widespread song traceable in broadside versions (and indeed probably a town production).[87]

Then the Doctor sings 'The Vicar of Bray'. This satirical song about a political turncoat, as indicated by the singer, is a literary rather than a popular one (and is quoted by Scott's Richard Waverley.)[88] This prompts 'The Barkshire Tragedy', a version of 'The Bonnie Mill Dams of Binnorie'. This is indeed the real thing, although it is a strangely comic version of what survived in oral tradition. Hughes told Francis James Child he learned it from his father.[89] It prompts another (patchwork) version from the tall scholar which preserves the original element of crafting the body of the dead girl into a magic fiddle. A young carter then responds with the fairly well-known but quite authentic 'Cupid's Garden', again, turned into 'dialect', although this is not the way in which it appears in its numerous print versions.[90] The Doctor adds to the list of love songs with 'The Bonny Labouring Boy', widespread in Southern

England and on broadsides.[91] The shorter scholar points out that drinking songs are missing, and someone on the lower tables sings 'Tovey's Tap', which is not traditional—nor, in fact, a drinking song, but a comic ballad, in 'dialect'. The short scholar knows the rather more modern production known to Tom Brown, 'The Poor Man's Beer'. The prize piece is produced by an old farmer, who sings one of the very few songs that does seem to have been regarded and sung as a dialect song in the area, 'George Ridler's Oven', renowned as a 'famous old Gloucestershire Song'. Hughes had already used it in the first chapter of *Tom Brown's Schooldays*. Some of the latter part of this is also found (in a different 'dialect', of course) in the Scots song 'Todlen Hame' quoted by Scott in *The Fair Maid of Perth* (Chapter 16), and we know from manuscript evidence that Scott knew of it as a Gloucestershire song, and of its shouted opening 'The stuones'.[92] Williams printed it, in 'dialect' (*FSUT*, 291-92). The narrator curtails his record with just one more song out of several, this seemingly a great favourite, 'Buttermilk Jack', a variant of the comic ballad 'Begging Buttermilk' recorded by Williams (*FSUT*, 40). An appendix to the *Scouring* includes two local pieces on shepherds: verses by a local man, Job Cork, and a more widespread 'Shepherd's Song' also found in Williams (241-42).

In provenance, therefore, most of these seem fairly respectable, but their presentation is revealing. Hughes has tended to select or even create Berkshire 'dialect' versions of songs. However, this stress on regionalism disguises the fluid and errant possibilities of the orally transmitted song. Moreover, its 'quaintness' sets up a barrier between the likely readers and the supposed communal nature of the experience. This is reinforced by the description of most of the singers and the paralinguistic comments. The singer of 'The Death of Lord Nelson' is referred to as 'a quaint old grisly party'. The short scholar finds the 'rumbling bass' rendering of this piece, which is entirely tragic in intention, supremely comic in effect. He may be acting as a spokesman for the embarrassment of the reading audience here. The two scholars act out a potential conflict of responses in the reader. 'The Vicar of Bray' has the correct invigorating effect on the Doctor's working class listeners:

> It was hailed with rapturous applause by the lower tables, though *you* [my italics] would have said, to look at them, that scarcely a man of the audience ... could have appreciated it. People don't perhaps always like best what they understand (178).

The sense of communality induced by this process provokes 'The Barkshire Tragedy', whose singer casts his eyes up to the tent top and drones this 'mournful ditty' through his nose. Features of oral performance are presented as ground for amusement. The Doctor actually has to rebuke the short scholar for treating 'Cupid's Garden' as comic, but even he laughs at the thought of interpreting the phrase 'increasing nature's prospects' in 'The Bonny Labouring Boy' (165). Since this clearly means 'having children', the middle classes are deriding a working-class song for its very attempt to come up to the standards of linguistic gentility usually demanded by the doctor's and scholars' class. The farmer who sings 'George Ridler's Oven' is introduced as 'the best master in all his neighbourhood', who will help the parson 'keep up the wages in the winter, and never let a man go to the house who will work' (168-69). However, he knows his place relative to doctor and scholars (and the clerk). When he begins, the tall scholar claims not to recognize what language he is using, and narrator's shorthand breaks down, though the final verse involves most of the company singing. We are told there is no merit in Job Cork's lines beyond quaintness (226; the modern reader might agree, but that isn't the point) and that the composer of the 'Shepherd's Song' was a poet in a rough sort of way (227; the modern singer might still feel he knew how to write a song better than Hughes.)

The Ashen Faggot is a story originally issued in *Macmillans Magazine* in 1862 and has similar intentions in presenting a society unified across class lines by the enjoyment of traditional pastimes, including songs, carols and a mummers' play, held in the servants' hall 'when the Kendricks made entertainment for their vassals' (310). Again, there is a fairly generous recording of texts such as a reasonably coherent though dialecticised shepherd's song. Two of the family sing traditional songs, 'The Twelve Days of Christmas' and 'Parra Marra Dictum', which in spite of its nonsense-Latin chorus is a nursery rhyme. These two pieces are rendered in standard English and without disparaging comments, though they are both, significantly, children's songs.[93] However, the mummers' play shows 'queer attempts at costume' (there is no understanding of the ritual disguise), 'queer nasal sing-song', the 'ridiculous figure' of the doctor and 'much more ridiculous doggerel', absorbing only to 'the younger portion of the audience' (314). The performance is valued as a social symbol only, and the mummers receive their *accustomed* [my italics] gratuity' (314). The school children sing the carol. The various working men of the parish are seated at table in a socially-stratified order and the carpenter sings a dialect rendering of a genuine harvest home health to the master and mistress (319; also used in *Adam Bede*).

In conclusion, then, Kingsley and Hughes have similar political aims with regard to forging an alliance between traditional power holders and ordinary people but manipulate tradition in rather different ways. Both denigrate modern popular street songs. Kingsley sites value in literarily respectable traditional ballads and Scottish songs, and appears to invent most of what he needs to illustrate contemporary English labouring class culture. Hughes, with a deeper knowledge of oral tradition, tries to offer more in the way of a record, but mediates his material in ways that turn it into a consumer item, a cultural cul-de-sac for condescending colonisation by readers with a different background. But perhaps what Maidment calls 'a Baedeker guide to artisan culture for the concerned (or apprehensive) middle classes' was better than none at all.[94]

Endnotes

1. For example, the essays by W. Baker and F. Jordan, in *Scott in Carnival*, 523-29, 543-55; A. Cruse, *The Victorians and their Books* (1935); J. T. Hillhouse, *The Waverley Novels and their Critics* (1936); J. H. Raleigh, 'What Scott Meant to the Victorians', *Victorian Studies*, **7** (1963-64), 7-34; J. Shaw, 'Scott's Influence on the Childhood of the Victorians', *Scottish Literary Journal* (1980), **7:1**, 51-64; J. Wilt, 'Steamboat Surfacing: Scott and the English Novelists', *Nineteenth-Century Fiction*, **35** (March 1981), 459-86.

2. *The Master of Ballantrae*, ed. E. Letley (1983), 9-10.

3. Widespread all over the British Isles and America. See K. Dallas, *The Cruel Wars* (1972), 12-13.

4. W. H. Ainsworth, *Rookwood*, ed. F. Swinnerton (1954), vii-viii.

5. S. M. Ellis, *William Harrison Ainsworth and his Friends* (1911), **1**, 281.

6. For a brief account of the Newgate Novel, see G. Kelly, *English Fiction of the Romantic Period 1789-1830*, 220-30.

7. Ellis discusses their history, op. cit., **1**, 249-54. Some of Ainsworth's were set to music and became popular as songs (**1**, 280). For examples, see J. Holloway & J. Black (eds), *Later English Broadside Ballads* (1979), **1**, nos 9, 33, 67; **2**, nos 22, 127, and J. S. Farmer (ed.), *Musa Pedestris. Three Centuries of Canting Songs and Slang Rhymes (1536-1896)* (1896).

8. Both in D. Milner and P. Kaplan, *The Bonnie Bunch of Roses* (1983), 72-73, 96-97. A version of the former in the Cecil Sharp Broadside Collection 2061 (198) has a properly moral title, but the last line is more celebratory—'He was a wild and undaunted youth'. (This collection is located in the Vaughan Williams Memorial Library, the Library and Archive of the English Folk Dance and Song Society.)

9. See R. Palmer (ed.), *Everyman's Book of English Country Songs* (1979), 89-90.

10. Farmer, op. cit., 79-81, 220. The authorship is debated. It has some oral currency, mostly Irish.

11. The translation is by Jamieson, though there are some verbal differences, but this ballad was not included in his first set of translations, in his *Popular Ballads and Songs from Tradition* (1806).

12. Ian Jack, note in World's Classics edition (1981), 346. See Scott's note to *The Lady of the Lake* (1810), lxxxiv.

13. T. Pinney, ed., *George Eliot: Essays* (1963), 268.

14. See H. Auster, *Local Habitations: Regionalism in the Early Novels of George Eliot*, (1970), 25, for quote and discussion.

15. W. Baker, *The Libraries of George Eliot and George Henry Lewes*, (1981), 20, 56, 97.

16. May 1874; quoted in Auster, op. cit., 30.

17. E.g. B. Gray, *George Eliot and Music* (1989).

18. *Scenes of Clerical Life*, ed. D. Lodge (1973), 43.

19. *Adam Bede*, ed. S. Gill (1980), 246. This edition will be used for page references. The tension between secular and sacred music implicit here, and the tensions between various kinds of sacred music are found elsewhere in the book too: 52, 104.

20. Baker, op. cit., 56. See J. Dixon (ed.), *Ancient Poems, Ballads, and Songs of the Peasantry of England* (1846), 190, or 170 in the 1857 Bell edition of this. Eliot comments on the repetition of a line; the Dixon/Bell version does not have this, but a more religiously oriented line.

21. *Silas Marner*, ed. Q. D. Leavis (1967), 156-57. The first two are associated with songs; the third is a dance tune; see *The Edinburgh Musical Miscellany* (1804), 192-94; *Pills to Purge Melancholy*, **5** , 319 and L. Winstock (ed.) *Songs and Music of the Redcoats 1642-1902* (1970), 36-38; T. Wilson, *Companion to the Ballroom* (1816), 182-85.

22. B. Gray, 'The Listening Faculty: Studies in George Eliot's Use of Music, Voice, and Natural Sound' (Ph. D., 1986), 359-60. This information is not in her book (see note 17) which concentrates on the later novels.

23. R. E. Egerton Warburton, *Hunting Songs, Ballads etc.* (1834), 24-25. There is a Scottish variant of 'Captain Ward and the Rainbow' (C287) called 'Wallace and the Red Reiver' in *The Greig-Duncan Folk Song Collection*, ed. P. Shuldham-Shaw & E. B. Lyle (1981 onwards), **1**, 88, and an American variant of 'Little Musgrave' (C81) called 'The Red Rover' in Bronson, version 60.

24. G. Borrow, *Romano Lavo-Lil* (1874), last sentence.

25. G. Borrow, *The Zincali* (1841),18.

26. G. Borrow, *Romantic Ballads* (1826).

27. Though Meg Merrilies is often speaking to criminals, so Scott might be excused.

28. *Lavengro*, ed. W. I. Knapp (1900), 388-89. Page references will be to this edition. For other uses of the gipsy in Victorian times, see J. R. Reed, *Victorian Conventions*, 1975.

29. D. Yates, *My Gipsy Days* (1953), 29.

30. W. Ibbetson, *Notes & Queries*, series 7 (1887), **4**, 397.

31. *Lavengro*, ed. F. Hinde Groome (1901), xxiii.

32. F. Hinde Groome, *In Gipsy Tents* (1881), 146, 324.

33. Leland, *The English Gipsies and their Language* (1873), 5.

34. C. Leland, E. H. Palmer & J. Tuckey, *English-Gipsy Songs in Rommany with Metrical English Translations* (1875), 130-31.

35. Quoted by Keith (*The Rural Tradition*, 110) who provides further discussion of Borrow's use of the past in Chapter 6, especially page 112.

36. These figures are discussed in Keith, Chapter 6.

37. E.g. chorus of 'Sir John Malcolm', *SMM*, **5**, no. 455; Dick, *Songs*, 479; P. Buck (ed.), *The Oxford Song Book*, **1**, no. 3.

38. G. Borrow, *The Romany Rye*, ed. W. I. Knapp, (1900), 303. Future page references in text will be to this edition.

39. On the other hand, the liberties he took with the Danish ballads he translated were noticeable but not drastic, according to S. B. Hustvedt, 'George Borrow and his Danish Ballads', *Journal of English and Germanic Philology*, **22** (1923), 262-70.

40. L. A. Smith, *Through Romany Songland* (1889), 107-56, but note Smith's uncritical acceptance of Borrow, and, later, of Scott (177-78); A. E. Gillington, *Songs of the Open Road* (1911), 23-29.

41. Angus Fraser, pers. comm., March 11, 1984.

42. 43. These words are in the manuscript, but not in the first edition, though the sentiment is the same.

43. A letter from Murray of January 27, 1855, worries about the songs that 'border on the indelicate'. D. Williams, *A World of His Own* (1982), 157.

44. *Poems of Charles Kingsley* (1913), 289, 294.

45. E. C. Mack and W. H. G. Armitage, *Thomas Hughes* (1952), 52-57.

46.   B. Colloms, *Charles Kingsley* (1975), 148.

47.   M. Vicinus, *The Industrial Muse* (1974), 19; *Victorian Lancashire*, ed. S. P. Bell (1974), 172-77.

48.   E.g. Thomas Cooper, *Purgatory of Suicides* (1845), and his note 9, 'the practical joke of Diogenes upon Plato's definition of a Man will be remembered by almost every reader' (255).

49.   B. Maidment, 'Magazines of Popular Progress and the Artisans', *Victorian Periodicals Review* (Fall 1984), **17:3**, 86.

50.   'Burns and his School', *Literary and General Lectures and Essays* (1890), 180.

51.   S. Chitty, *The Beast and the Monk* (1974), 96.

52.   *Literary and General Lectures and Essays*, 148-49, 154.

53.   *Literary and General Lectures and Essays*, 111; letter to J. M. Ludlow, June 1852, *Charles Kingsley: his Letters and Memories of his Life* ed. F. Kingsley 1877, **1**, 346.

54.   *Literary and General Lectures and Essays*, 253-54.

55.   *Literary and General Lectures and Essays*, 145.

56.   Chitty, op. cit., 260; 'North Devon', *Prose Idylls* (1891), 292. Since the ballad of a female smuggler that Kingsley heard was a long one it was likely to be traditional; parodies tended to be shorter. For a possible text, see D. Dugaw, *Warrior Women and Popular Balladry* (1989), 77-82.

57.   *Westward Ho!* (1855), **3**, 163. As editions of the novel are legion, I have used continuous chapter numbering, but the page references are to the first edition, in 3 vols.

58.   Page references are to the first edition of 1866. 'Young Beichan' (C53), **1**, 72; 'Lord Thomas and Fair Annet' (C73), **1**, 270; 'Glasgerion' (C67), **1**, 348; various Robin Hood ballads (C117-54 for corpus), Chapter 34 (**2**, 249-54, 284); 'Chevy Chace' (C161), **2**, 322; 'Adam Bell, Clym of the Cleugh, and William of Cloudeslee' (C116), **2**, 394.

59.   *Hereward the Wake*, **1**, 51. R. Palmer, *Everyman's Book of English Country Songs*, 42-43. This song seems to have been absolutely standardized by print. It has the tone of false bucolic cheer found in pieces of urban origin; unfortunately for political theorists, it is sung with enthusiasm in the current oral tradition. For a wry comment on it by a real farmer's boy, see J. Hawker, *A Victorian Poacher* (1978), 70.

60.   **2**, 169; (C121).

61.   'History as Myth: Charles Kingsley's *Hereward the Wake*', *Studies in the Novel* **17:2** (Summer 1985), 181-82.

62.   R. B. Martin, *The Dust of Combat* (1959), 112-13; B. Maidment, *The Poorhouse Fugitives*, 138.

63.   *Literary and General Lectures and Essays*, 154-6, 174.

64.   *Alton Locke*, ed. E. A. Cripps, 1983. This World's Classics edition will be used for page references. Kingsley mentions Thomas Cooper (whom he had met) 22, 83, 243, 273; Bethune 32, 82; William Thom, 78; J. C. Prince, 83; Charles Mackay, 95; Elliott, 243.

65.   Martin, op. cit., 108.

66.   The first is actually a popular song by T. H. Bayly and H. Bishop, written while the former was a student at Oxford; see *English Minstrelsie*, ed. S. Baring Gould (1895), **4**, vii, 66-67. It was issued as a broadside by Pitts, and collected by Alfred Williams early this century; it is Mi 655 in the Alfred Williams Collection of Folk Songs in the Wiltshire and Swindon County Record Office in Trowbridge (Catalogue no. 2598). The second is quoted by Hughes in *The Scouring of the White Horse*, Chapter 7 and *Tom Brown's Schooldays*, Chapter 6, and used semi-proverbially by Jefferies in *World's End* (1877), **2**, 265. For a text, see *The Red White and Blue Monster Song Book*, 80.

67.   *Alton Locke*, 309. L. Winstock, op. cit., 116-17.

68. *Alton Locke*, 38, 316-19. Sources: J. Maidment (ed.), *A North Country Garland* (1824), 54; J. C. Dick, *Songs*, 133, 401; A. Moffat (ed.), *The Minstrelsy of Scotland* (1896), 85 (probably by Caroline Nairne rather than Burns); there are versions of the last two in Scott's *Minstrelsy*, **3**, 280; **1**, 250.

69. Dick, *Songs,* 314, 487.

70. 389, by Charles Mackay (note name). Widely available on broadsides; for a text, see P. S. Foner (ed.), *American Labor Songs of the Nineteenth Century* (1975), 150. Hughes mentions this in *The Scouring of the White Horse*, Chapter 7.

71. *Yeast: a Problem* (1851), the first revised version of the 1848 text, 248. Louis James makes a similar point: lower-class poets are 'sincere, with little or none of the cynical vindictiveness Kingsley portrays in the Chartist poetry of Alton Locke and his friends' (*Fiction for the Working Man* [1974], 206).

72. J. Hawker, op. cit., 95. For a record of continuity of tradition in later Victorian performance of songs registering rural discontent, see A. Williams, *In a Wiltshire Village* (1981), 87-88; although the two quoted may be traceable as titles, I can find no complete texts of them.

73. R. Palmer (ed.), *The Sound of History* (1988), 47-49, and *The Painful Plough* (1973), 36-38; H. Hopkins, *The Long Affray: The Poaching Wars 1760-1914* (1986), especially 305-6 for summary of legislation.

74. *The People's Journal*, ed. J. Saunders (1846), **1**, 319. Compare W. Tomlinson, *Papers of the Manchester Literary Club* (1886) 306-7, complaining about the singing of ' A New Political ABC'.

75. Kingsley wrote a sonnet to Mitford in 1855, praising her aim as his own: 'To knit in loving knowledge rich and poor', *Poems*, 321.

76. *Poems*, 289.

77. *The Spectator*, 22 March, 1851, **24**, 281-82.

78. Songs were composed and printed in non-Scots dialects at this period but their heyday was later, and they were more usually northern. See Maidment, *The Poorhouse Fugitives* (1987), 355-59, B. Hollingworth (ed.), *Songs of the People* (1982), 1-7. For a labourer's surprise at seeing dialect written, see A. Somerville, *The Autobiography of a Working Man* (1848), 87 and A. Williams, *Folk Songs of the Upper Thames*, 13.

79. Mack & Armytage, op. cit., 9-11, 13, 37, 39.

80. *Tom Brown's Schooldays*, 6th edn. (1889; this is the most frequently reprinted and accessible). Most of the singing is in Chapter 6, 98-105; see also 163, 255. For texts of Tom's songs, see A. Williams, *Folk Songs of the Upper Thames* (1923), 244-45; 175 (as well as many earlier collections); Chapter 5, note 25, below. For 'Chesapeake and Shannon', see R. Palmer (ed.), *The Oxford Book of Sea Songs* (1986) 181-83 for text, tune and history of this song commemorating a British victory of 1813, and for others, note 66, above.

81. *The Scouring of the White Horse* (1859), 165.

82. Mack & Armytage, op. cit., 109.

83. *The Scouring of the White Horse and The Ashen Faggot: A Tale for Christmas* (1889), xi.

84. D. Harker, *Fakesong*, Chapter 8.

85. A. Williams, *Folk Songs of the Upper Thames* (1923), hereafter *FSUT*. Williams was collecting in 1914-16 and the early 1920s. His manuscript collection includes 'The Lay of the Hunted Pig' (Wiltshire 478), possibly copied from Hughes, but this was not Williams' immediate source; Williams may have decided not to publish it because he felt it was not a folk song; I would agree.

86.   E.g. R. Palmer (ed.), *A Touch On the Times* (1974), part 2, and *Room for Company* (1971), 42-43. Such songs tend to have a rather limited distribution unless they are sufficiently general for other place names to be substituted.

87.   V. de Sola Pinto (ed.), *The Common Muse* (1965), 132, 611.

88.   *Waverley*, 5. Text, W. Chappell, *Popular Music of the Olden Time*, **2**, 652-54.

89.   C10. See notes to versions R and L. It is not clear whether Hughes's father knew both; Hughes's scholar admits his version is 'a patchwork'. See also *Notes & Queries* Series 1, **6**, 102; most of the traditional versions of this variant are American.

90.   W. Chappell, *A Collection of National English Airs* (1840), **1**, 55. Discussed further in Chapter 8 in relation to Hardy.

91.   For example, D220, D 874 in the Hammond manuscript collection, and the Lucy Broadwood Ballad Sheet Collection, 4, 134, both in the Vaughan Williams Memorial Library, the Library and Archive of the EFDSS.

92.   NLS MS 893, f. 43. Kingsley also admired this song, and quotes it twice in *Two Years Ago*, Chapter 21, and Hughes commends it in the first chapter of *Tom Brown's Schooldays*.

93.   For texts, see I. & P. Opie (eds) *The Oxford Dictionary of Nursery Rhymes* (1952), 119-24, 386-88.

94.   B. Maidment, 'Magazines of Popular Progress', *VPR*, **17:3**, 83.

Gaskell

The first chapter of *Mary Barton* is preceded by an epigraph said to be from a 'Manchester Song'. It isn't. As far as we know, snippets with this attribution—there's another one as epigraph to Chapter 6—are the work of William Gaskell, who was quite a lively and competent versifier.[1] These lines might therefore be deemed to come from Manchester, but are not songs in the sense of being complete pieces composed for music. Still less are they what the attribution seems to imply, the locally produced voice of an urban working class. In using such epigraphs, and in making allusion to or actually quoting songs from a variety of popular sources, Elizabeth Gaskell too is following in the Scott tradition. Like Scott, she is not averse to creating the occasional false intertext; here, it seems to have been created by her husband.[2] Gaskell uses common forms of attribution for this sort of epigraph such as 'old song', 'old play', the adjective being used to stress the continuity of tradition or literary wisdom implied in the act of quotation. Popular material such as folk song or nursery rhymes may be included, but it is deracinated from its original sung context.

More like Mitford than Scott, or, later, Hardy, Mrs Gaskell was never either part of the working-class culture she describes or a sharer in it through a living interest in song as performance. For her, folk song and ballad text are overwhelmingly verbal, and part of an established literary context. In discussing 'Modern Greek Songs' she compares them with ballads about Adam Bell, Clyne o'the Clough and Robin Hood. She feels free to alter ballad texts playfully, as part of an established consensual canon; for example, in 'Company Manners' she adapts the tragic ballad 'The Douglas Tragedy' to describe a gourmet diet.[3] This kind of usage is now typical of Victorian writers for and from the middle classes. Harriet Martineau and Margaret Oliphant testify to the changes of fashion which first see ballad tradition as outmoded and then resurrect it as quaint.[4] The heroine of Mrs Craik's *The Woman's Kingdom* (1869) seems to have been typical; her fantasies of serving the man she loves include doing him 'good in any way; ay, in the pathetic way of some ballad heroine she had *read* [my italics] of—making the house ready for his bride, and helping to rear and cherish his children.'[5] As Gaskell puts it, in 'Modern Greek Songs', '*reading* [my italics] any good ballad is like eating game; almost every thing else seems poor and tasteless after it.'[6]

The dislocation of such material from Gaskell's own musical milieu is suggested by a consideration of her own teenage manuscript music books, compiled during the years 1825-27. These are now in the Gaskell Collection at Manchester Central Reference Library. They contain a variety of pieces, some with words. A few are religious, a number are foreign. English folk songs of any sort, lyric or ballad, are conspicuous by their absence, though the tradition-influenced Scots songs so beloved of middle-class English parlour society are plentiful, for example, 'The Blue Bells of Scotland', 'Auld Robin Gray', 'Caller Herring'.[7] Revived ballads were later popular in Mrs Gaskell's set—the Winkworths sang them in 1854, to the delight of Charlotte Brontë—but her early music books don't include them.[8] There is no overlap between the traditional pieces alluded to by Gaskell and her own youthful favourites. Even 'Lizzie Lindsay', mentioned in *North and South* (166) and praised in her letters, is not included.[9]

Like so many of her predecessors and contemporaries, Gaskell shared the belief that the English were deficient in national music.[10] In thinking of her daughters' education, she bemoaned this lack: 'it is so difficult to meet with *good* English songs' (*Letters*, 160). One of the reasons for this difficulty was an unspoken effect of the class barrier. Songs visibly sung by the working classes were not for imitation by the genteel, though they could be mentally accommodated by taking an antiquarian interest in them as relics of a tradition now defunct.

Another problem was a more forthright attitude to sex than was comfortable for a Victorian middle-class audience. Gaskell writes that she has heard that 'Jess McFarlane' is improper, though she cannot see why (*Letters*, 286). From the versions she seems to have known, neither could we, though the answer probably lies in its links with the rather more forthright 'Aye Waukin O' associated with Burns, where it is the girl who admits to lying awake all night thinking of her lover. 'Jess MacFarlane' was issued as a song sheet in 1793, and, interestingly, it also occurs in the music books of other genteel young women of the early nineteenth century, such as Lady John Scott and Harriett Ann Bisshopp, in an anglicised version, as well as in a printed collection, R. A. Smith's *The Scotish Minstrel* (1821-24).[11]

However, Gaskell certainly did take an interest in traditional song. In May 1852 she thanks Lord Hatherton for obtaining a 'Cornish ballad' and tells him that one of her servants says she knew a much longer version in her youth. Mrs Gaskell has also received a copy of this song ('Shall Trelawney Die' or 'The Song of the Western Men') from an old miner (*Letters*, p. 190). Since the only words we now have for this are those by the Reverend R. S. Hawker, expanding on a traditional fragment in 1825, Gaskell may have come tantalisingly close to recording a now lost traditional ballad.[12] It is worth noting that she does not despise her servant as a source of knowledge of tradition. Nursery rhymes and songs were part of the tradition that she did participate in—she quotes several, such as 'Polly Put the Kettle On' (*MB*, epigraph to Chapter 2)—although of course relegating it to the nursery is another way of marginalising it. (Scott had argued that ballads were a feature of 'the childhood of society'.)[13]

We know her continuing interest stemmed from both aesthetic and antiquarian impulses, from some of her earliest writing, as in her letter to Mary Howitt of 18 August, 1838. In this letter she describes various Cheshire customs, including the verses for sanding the ground for a wedding which she later put into the mouth of Kester in *Sylvia's Lovers* (*Letters*, 29; Chapter 30). This was later recorded by Henry Green in *Knutsford, its Traditions and History*,[14] and although Green and she knew each other his source seems to have been tradition rather than her. She recommends 'Jess MacFarlane' to Forster (*Letters*, 286) as well as mentioning it in *Sylvia's Lovers* (81), 'French Life and Letters' and 'Mr. Harrison's Confessions'. She wanted to write and thank Francis James Child for his ballads, which she delighted in (*Letters*, 488).[15]

Regrettably we do not have any extensive information about Mrs Gaskell's library and early reading. This can be reconstructed to a limited extent through the selections she made for a commonplace book at the age of twenty-one, which included many ballads, and through information about the sale of the Gaskell family library and the catalogues of libraries from which Elizabeth may have borrowed books, through her husband if not in person. Unfortunately the sale catalogue for the Gaskell library gives insufficient detail about some of the ballad collections she may have known, though we do know these included Scott's *Minstrelsy of the Scottish Border*, Allan Cunningham's *Songs of Scotland*, and Percy's *Reliques*.[16]

For Elizabeth Gaskell, though, ballads were ancient and respectably literary. Performed pieces were displaced into Scottish or other non-English traditions. English sung traditions might be quaint but not exactly art. In her long letter about local customs to Mary Howitt she writes: 'about Knutsford we have Christmas carols, such a pretty custom ... with their old words of bygone times!' On All Souls Day, on the other hand,

> parties of children go from house to house singing:
>> An apple, a pear, a plum or a cherry,
>> Or any good thing to make us merry.
>> One for Peter and one for Paul,
>> And one for Him who saved us all.
> This is sung over and over again to a very monotonous tune. (30-31)

Gaskell's fictional rural or small-town singers, like Sally in *Ruth* (Chapter 18), are also represented as unaccomplished. Traditional singing style did not appeal to an ear trained as hers had been. Other observers shared Gaskell's prejudice about traditional musical styles, for example, Thomas Hughes or Richard Jefferies.[17]   And in the case of the tune for the souling song one might have some sympathy for her judgement.[18]   That it is a prejudice, however, can be argued by looking at the musical sophistication of traditional songs collected by people like F. D. Hammond and George Gardiner which I discuss later in relation to Hardy.

Gaskell's position as an outsider is best seen in her essay 'Cumberland Sheep Shearers' (1853).   This very deliberately constructed pastoral is reminiscent of Mary Mitford in its distancing from the details of popular celebration. The community is seen through the eyes of middle-class observers with no liking for rum butter, and is placed by quotations from Marvell, Austen and Wordsworth. Entirely onlookers, the visitors voice a sentimental envy of a shepherd's life, which 'must be a pleasant employment'.[19]   All shepherds are lumped together, Cumberland, Greek and Chaldean, and allusions are made to 'shepherds keeping watch by night', Poussin and Cooper (3, 470).   The moment the fiddler arrives for the shearing celebrations is the moment the visitors depart.

Much of Gaskell's writing, of course, is about the life of her own class, and quite naturally and properly reflects their tastes.   For example, the only reference to popular song in *Wives and Daughters* is to Molly's being 'as tall and as straight as a poplar tree, as in the "old song"' (466). This is 'The Maid of the Mill', sometimes found on broadsides and nowadays preserved as a vocal element in a Morris dance.[20]   In *Cranford*, Miss Jessie sings 'Jock o'Hazeldean', with its words by Scott based on a traditional fragment (Chapter 1; 8), and Miss Pole remembers 'poor dear Captain Brown's song "Tibbie Fowler"', a piece adapted by Burns about a young lady with a multiplicity of wooers (114). Chapter titles and epigraphs in *North and South* are drawn from this literary and/or Scottish area. Mr Hale quotes from 'Chevy Chase' (Chapter 10; 81) and Margaret is compared to Lizzie Lindsay (who was swept off her feet by a northern wooer) in Chapter 21 (166).

Ruth's musical sensibility is symbolic, and unspecific.   She invites the audience's sympathy for her orphaned state by humming a brooding song she remembered from her mother, when plagued by Farquhar's attentions (Chapter 25; 316).   One of her talents as a nurse is singing. While dying she sings continually, but *what* is not specified, other than childish ditties. Since she is said to suffer from 'a sweet child-like insanity', the effect is reminiscent of Ophelia (Chapter 35; 448).

Gaskell was given to indicating picturesque fidelity in servants by putting into their mouths a scrap of traditional song or verse. Kester gets the sanding verses in *Sylvia's Lovers* (Chapter 30). In *Ruth*, the Bensons' servant, Sally, gives an account of her rejection of Jerry Dixon, with reference to the likelihood of his dying like Jemmy Gray, the rejected lover in the well-known ballad 'Barbara Allen' (Chapter 16; 169).[21] In the kitchen Sally is always singing 'The Derby Ram'—a jolly and slightly coarse song well-represented in tradition. It was not, as early as 1853, common in print, though it had been rewritten as a glee by John Wall Callcott (1766-1821).[22] Ironically, many versions display a hostility to dissenters. However, the content of these songs relates to the main text in an oblique or contrastive way rather than directly. Unlike Jemmy, Jerry does not die, but, comically, marries someone else within three weeks. And Gaskell's interest in Sally's singing is for its symbolic rather than artistic value: 'if music is a necessary element in a song, perhaps I had better call it by some other name' (191). What is noticeable is Gaskell's refusal to take Sally's singing seriously in a cultural context. The tragic young Jemmy Gray of the ballad becomes the comic Jerry Dixon, 'a stout, middle-aged man, ruddy-complexioned, with a wart on his left cheek'. This can be compared with the way in which Hardy treats his rural chorus at the shearing supper in *Far From the Madding Crowd* (Chapter 23).

Sylvia's Lovers is the only one of Gaskell's full-length novels to deal extensively with a rural community. Moreover, because of its historical setting, the town characters are much closer culturally to the farmers than was the case later and the class divisions are less culturally marked. Jennifer Uglow claims that the first volume of *Sylvia's Lovers* is 'the world of the ballad, the hornpipe and the sailor's yarn', 'part of a "natural" organic culture' (Uglow, 512-13). I would agree, though one would have to add that Gaskell's skill in depicting such a world is sketchy compared with that of Scott or Hardy. However, unlike them, she represents this world as still vitally capable of reproduction. Charley Kinraid is the dancer of hornpipes, the implied hero of the novel's theme song, 'The Keel Row'. This is a song associated with Tyneside—only about 60 miles from Whitby, and, as Alan Myers points out, it is appropriate to Charley's origin in Cullercoats.[23] It is well-known and widespread in northern England and Scotland. There is also a song based on it called 'The New Keel Row' by Thomas Thompson (1773-1816). In the absence of any evidence that Gaskell knew it we cannot claim that she had this in mind, but it was published by Robert Bell in *Northern Rhymes* in 1812 and both songs are usefully reproduced in Andrew Sanders' edition of the novel. Its hero sounds just like Charley Kinraid, a noted dancer, a success with the girls, not over-learned, and one who fought with Nelson. The song expresses a hatred for the press-gang. At any rate, a comparison shows how Gaskell caught the flavour of the time and locality. The original is a simple expression of good wishes for the welfare of the girl's sailor boyfriend, with a brief affectionate description of his appearance:

> As I cam thro' Sandgate, thro' Sandgate, thro' Sandgate,
> As I cam thro' Sandgate, I heard a lassie sing,

Weel may the keel row, the keel row, the keel row,
  Weel may the keel row, that my laddie's in.

He wears a blue bonnet, blue bonnet, blue bonnet,
  He wears a blue bonnet, a dimple on his chin,
  And weel may the keel row, [etc.][24]

The press-gang, too, though, are rooted in this culture; as Charley is being carried off, one of them jeers that he wants his sweetheart to come and serve on board ship like Billy Taylor's (218).[25]

Even Philip is not above thinking about Sylvia in the terms of 'Jess MacFarlane': 'I sent my love a letter/But, alas, she cannot read/And I lo'e her all the better' (Chapter 8). But he is no dancer or singer, and the song, as noted earlier, is one used in a literary context in 'French Life and Letters' (7, 665) and part of Gaskell's own genteel mental repertoire. Philip and Kinraid are contrasted on page 165. Sylvia herself sings at her work (111) just as their servant Dolly Reid does (193) but she is set apart from her peers by her own demureness and by her mother's social anxiety. Mrs Robson is alarmed at the idea of Sylvia's demeaning herself by dancing and marlocking with the fair folk (Chapter 11; 124). In fact she did not do so, yet she hankers after the rude communal energy represented in Kinraid, and her life is soured by her failure to commit herself to the traditional community of lasses who sing 'The Keel Row' while waiting for the ship to come to harbour in Chapter 2. It is this song that Kinraid sings at Acre, and his men take it up. Like Hardy, Gaskell sees Sylvia's choices as difficult and ambivalent, but every reader sees the loss forced on her. So much for Gaskell's use of song in a rural or small town context, but her use of allusion to working-class culture is fuller and more original in a novel where she combines her interest in working-class discourses with a local and almost contemporary setting in Manchester, *Mary Barton*. Here the word 'song' stands for two very different kinds of discourse. One is the mixed art of actual song, sometimes using the dialect of the urban working class, composed as part of a living sung tradition. One is the more purely verbal art, called 'song' metaphorically, and representing the voice of a newly literate labouring proletariat, or what was taken to be such. It is this latter voice that is imitated in the otherwise unidentified 'Manchester Song' lines.

In turning to novels with a predominantly urban subject matter we have seen a shift in the kinds of popular material alluded to. In part, though *only* in part, this reflects a real change in the nature of popular verbal art, and the northern mill and manufacturing towns developed quite distinctive kinds of local poetry as well as acting as centres for the kind of broadside publishers found across the country. This shift from a largely oral to a print-dominated culture went hand-in-hand with the development of an industrialised urban proletariat. As

Martha Vicinus puts it, street ballads, though still 'an integral part of popular culture', 'were sold to passers-by, and were not part of a shared, communal art, as were the songs of an oral tradition.'[26]

The female characters in *Mary Barton*, even the younger generation, are still in touch with the old ballads as part of their musical culture. Coral Lansbury argues that Mary, Alice and Margaret are shown to have a more vital and deep-rooted culture than the vapid middle-class Carson girls.[27] Mary sings 'Barbara Allen', at least when she is cheerful (164). Alice remembers 'The Demon Lover' (35). This leads Michael Wheeler to claim that 'balladry is the special province of the female working-class characters in *Mary Barton*, who compare themselves to the familiar victim figures of the traditional ballad' (Wheeler, 46) The first claim is certainly true; women are the bearers of song tradition in the novel. However, the characters are not conscious of any allusive appropriateness in their relation to these songs. It is the reader who has to make the connection between the love-triangle of Mary, Jem Wilson and Harry Carson, and 'The Demon Lover', where the heroine, having married a decent and (in most cases) working-class man, is seduced into deserting him by a fiend in the shape of a former lover offering riches. In case the audience's ballad repertoire isn't quite equal to this level of allusion, Gaskell makes Alice give a plot summary: 'something about ... a lover that should hae been no lover'.[28] When Harry Carson appears later, it is we who apply this to Mary's situation, not Mary, and anyway, the original heroine is not so much a victim as someone punished for deserting her husband and children.

Traditional song is used here to reinforce the theme of the early part of the novel, well developed in this chapter, of the contrast between an idyllic rural past and a deprived urban present, acted out by Alice's own shift from country to town. To do this, the ballad itself is cast back into the past. Alice remembers her mother singing it, rather than singing it herself.

The other two songs Wheeler mentions at this point are 'The Siller Crown' and 'Barbara Allen'. These are sung by the girls. But Margaret's 'Siller Crown' is more lyric than ballad, and though influenced by tradition is probably the work of Susan Blamires (1747-94).[29] Mary certainly applies it to herself, for she says she never quite liked the part about thinking o' Donald mair (110). Revealingly, she misquotes; the original line four says '*nor* [my italics] think o' Donald mair'; Mary deletes the negative. Margaret, on the other hand, is applying it to her own wryly-perceived ambitions, and the prospect of her being a professional singer presenting songs from widely different cultural milieux marks her out as someone with a new kind of class mobility.[30] 'Barbara Allen', which Mary sings, does not use the choice of lovers theme, and the heroine, again, is hardly a victim, since she first causes a young man to die for love of her and is then hoist by her own petard. These allusions, therefore, seem to present Mary as more culpable than victimised.

Gaskell continued to use references to ballad and nursery rhymes in a minimal way throughout her career. However, *Mary Barton* attempts a range of allusion not repeated elsewhere in its recognition of the shift whereby an increasingly literate and diversified working class was rapidly developing aspirations of its own towards entering into the dominant literary culture. As we have seen in relation to Kingsley, the trickle of working-class poets became a flood by the third and fourth decades of the nineteenth century. Burns was the hero of such aspirants, and always commented on by critics, but those following his example were less and less poets based in the countryside—not that this stopped them writing about it. Some commentators saw the development of poetry by self-taught writers from an urban industrial background 'as a sudden new symptom of major changes in the cultural aspirations of the lower orders'; W. J. Fox (the father of 'Tottie' Fox) dated this movement to the first publication of Ebenezer Elliott's work in volume form in 1834.[31] Some of these writers were specifically aligned to the cause of Chartism, as Brian Maidment explains in *The Poorhouse Fugitives*. One and all were determined to display their literary credentials by attempting complex forms in elaborate language in deference to the literary expectations they had internalised from their cultural 'superiors'.

To some extent Gaskell's own early publishing milieu was that of these working-class poets in so far as they sought an audience wider than that of their own locality. This could be done through journals designed specifically for artisan readers in the provinces but produced in London or Edinburgh, and edited by (and largely written by) members of the middle classes. Such journals were characteristic of the 1830s and 1840s, for example, the *People's Journal* (1846-49), and *Howitt's* (1847-48), amalgamated as the *People's & Howitt's Journal* (1849-51).[32] The tone can be gauged from the introductory address from the editors of *Howitt's Journal of Literature and Popular Progress* (volume 1, January 1847, 1). They say they are 'bound to no class' but claim 'the people' are grateful for support and manifest 'delightful confidence' 'in our humble endeavours on their behalf'.

Gaskell was well-acquainted with William and Mary Howitt. They were members of a radical writers' group in Nottinghamshire, the Sherwood Foresters. Indeed, Gaskell's first published fiction, 'Libby Marsh's Three Eras', appeared in the June 1847 issue of *Howitt's* under the title 'Life in Manchester'. Some of her writing had appeared in print as an account of Clopton Hall in the Howitts' 1840 *Visits to Remarkable Places*, and the notes on Christmas customs already mentioned were used in William Howitt's *Rural Life of England* (second edition, 1839). The Howitts read the manuscript of *Mary Barton* before publication, and helped Mrs Gaskell with arrangements.

The circles in which the Howitts moved were much more habitually radical than Gaskell's own.[33] Even so, they and other editors of similar journals intervened directly in working-class writing through their patronage in editing and introducing it. Sometimes they changed, or put pressure on contributors to change, their sentiments and language (*Poorhouse Fugitives*, 283-86). Elliott features quite prominently as a contributor to the *People's Journal*, but his tone is less fierce here than in his work as whole. The processes of mediation at work in the editing of working-class voices for these journals are also found at work in Gaskell's use of such poets. By including lines from a writer like Ebenezer Elliott as epigraphs she implicitly endorses his claims for admission to a world of genteel literature. At the same time, the inclusion of his voice serves to validate the truth of Gaskell's attempt to speak for the ordinary people of Manchester. However, the passages she selects from him, from Samuel Bamford, and from the discourse of urban song are all subtly mediated in ways that accommodate them to Gaskell's own class position, as I hope to show in the following discussion.

In *Mary Barton*, presented quite explicitly in its subtitle as 'a Tale of Manchester Life', Gaskell uses four quotations from Elliott, and a couple of set piece quotations supposedly representing the voice of the workers, one from Samuel Bamford, and one from the local song 'The Oldham Weaver'.

Ebenezer Elliott (1781-1849) was a convenient bridge between the discourse of those Gaskell chose for her subject matter and her intended audience. According to Maidment, as 'easily the best known "radical" self-taught poet of the early Victorian period[,] Elliott was the first self-taught writer to make any impression on middle-class consciousness' (*Poorhouse Fugitives*, 48). Much of his renown rested on his implacable resistance to the Corn Laws, a cause he shared with manufacturers who would have found it to their advantage for their workers to be able to buy their staple food item, bread, more cheaply than the protectionist trade and import regulations allowed. Elliott was known and praised as the Corn-Law Rhymer by such critics as Carlyle. His *Poetical Works* had been published in 1840, a date entirely appropriate to that section of *Mary Barton* dealing with Chartism. Since Elliott's place of origin was Sheffield, a town associated with metal working rather than with the textile industry, he could hardly be taken as speaking specifically to or from the circumstances of the average Mancunian, but he was often seen as the representative of the average Northern industrial worker, for example, by Carlyle in 1832.[34]

This image was not entirely consonant with the facts, as Elliott himself pointed out.[35] In later life, Elliott established an iron foundry and retired with £3,000 (Vicinus, 97). Although an early supporter of Chartism, after 1839 he denounced it. Nor would Elliott's poetry support attempts at pigeonholing. Like many other self-educated poets, his aim was to storm the citadels of conventional culture by excelling in the forms acceptable to the dominant classes, and publishing in ways suited to their income. His *Poetical Works* demonstrate a variety of forms. The first portion of the book consists mostly of medium-length narratives in blank verse, couplets, or skilfully crafted intricate rhyme schemes. Elliott's handling of rhyme and rhythm is fluent and accomplished. The moving force of these poems is some extreme, even Gothic, emotion; the actual plot may be veiled in a grandiloquent mistiness that makes it difficult to follow. Major influences are Milton, Byron and Crabbe, to all of whom he pays tribute (*Poetical Works*, 50, 55). This mixture of styles can be most successful, as, for example, in 'Withered Wild-flowers'. Senena has just drowned her illegitimate child and contemplates suicide:

> Hopeless, she longed to mount th'unhallow'd bark,
> And sail the deep irremeable dark. (45)

The latinate 'irremeable', meaning 'admitting of no return', is borrowed from Pope. Its punning overtones of 'irremediable' combine with a classically-tinged metaphor for death in a condensed and effective image, but this is hardly the language of the average Sheffield steel worker.

Elliott's best known work, the *Corn-Law Rhymes*, came out in volume form in 1830 after earlier piecemeal publication. These are all shorter pieces, often lyrics. Five of them are supposedly written to specified tunes such as 'Robin Adair' and 'Scots Wha Hae', and more are called 'songs'. These lyrics are very plain-spoken; for example, 'The Jacobin's Prayer', which opens Miltonically with 'Avenge the plunder'd poor, O Lord', wishes appropriate punishments on those who support the Corn Laws:

> Lord, let his hollow rental fail,
> And lice instruct him in a jail! (*Poetical Works*, 113)

It also punningly attacks the perpetrators of the Peterloo outrages:

> He back'd his war-horse through the panes
> Of quiet people who had brains. (*Poetical Works*, 113)

Nor are the extensive notes more moderate: 'whoever does not oppose the Corn-Law, is a patron of want, national immorality, bankruptcy, child-murder, incendiary fires, midnight assassination, and anarchy.' (119)

Some of Elliott's later work displays softening. The Preface to *Miscellaneous Poems* is noticeably more religious in tone, and a number of these poems are written as hymns, including a batch entitled 'Corn-Law Hymns'. An example of a rather more quietist position may be found in 'Win-hill':

So bad men frown! but can their frowns compel
  The cowslip to remain beneath the sod?
Can they prevent the mosses of the dell
  From lifting up their tiny hands to God? (*Poetical Works,* 129)

Mrs Gaskell did not cite either of these Corn-Law collections in *Mary Barton*, though Corn-Law Hymn 8 seems in its sentiments and structure to anticipate John Barton's famous protest in Chapter 6. 'They never heard their children's grim despair' (*Poetical Works*, 170) is an obvious parallel to 'Han they ever seen a child o' their'n die for want o' food?' (*MB*, 74) and to the 'Manchester Song' motto for this chapter: '*He* never heard that maddening cry,/"Daddy, a bit of bread!"'[36] Equally worth comparison is the ending of the hand-loom weaver William Thom's 'The Food-rioter Banished':

Well, patience is a silly word,
  So meaningless and dead,
To him who hears the sickening cry,
  'Oh, father, give us bread.'

This poem—in Scots English, and with a rural story—appeared in *Tait's Magazine* in 1847.[37] Whoever was actually responsible for the words of 'Manchester Song' was clearly using the discourse of protest both for and from urban and rural labourers but nevertheless not actually quoting them.

    The extracts Gaskell actually selects from Elliott are chosen for their general applicability to the chapter that follows, sometimes without regard for their original context. They come from the milder or more literary side of his writing. As the motto for Chapter 34, which deals with the repentance of the dying John Barton and his reluctance to face his daughter, Gaskell chooses an extract from Elliott's *Kerhonah*. This is a sub-Shakespearian drama set in seventeenth-century America. The dialogue quoted is between Dixwell, supposed to be the executioner of a social superior—Charles I—and his daughter Mary, as his guilt prompts him to pray for forgiveness even in his sleep (*Poetical Works*, 93). The main theme of the drama, relations between white men and the native tribes they have antagonised, might also be considered tangentially relevant, since the tensions of the drama rest on the struggle between a desire for revenge and one for reconciliation.

    The five lines from 'Withered Wild Flowers' which form the motto for Chapter 4 represent a hope for quiet contentment alien to most of the poem in spite of its innocuous title:

To envy nought beneath the ample sky;
To mourn no evil deed, no hour misspent;

And, like a living violet, silently
Return in sweets to heaven what goodness lent,
Then bend beneath the chastening shower content. (*Poetical Works*, 42)

On a purely local level they are highly appropriate to Alice Wilson. The bulk of the chapter is taken up with a description of tea at Alice's, and Mary's first meeting with Margaret; this includes Alice's reminiscences of missing her own mother. Here, Elliott is lamenting his teacher. The grief of the main story moves in the opposite direction; Senena mourns the loss of the child she has murdered—about as different a character from Alice as could well be imagined, even though 'her long-lost mother to her thought arose' (*Poetical Works*, 46). However, as in much of Elliott's work, and as with this chapter, the bitterness of loss is mediated by the relief offered by passages of rich pastoral description. This palliative use of Elliott is particularly interesting given that this is a chapter in which Gaskell quotes from a well known ancient ballad, 'The Demon Lover' and a more recent dialect piece.

Chapter 5 also takes its motto from Elliott to provide a further authority for Gaskell's portrait of that well-attested figure, the working-class natural historian.[38] Of the three important features of this chapter, namely, the introduction of Job Legh, Margaret's coming blindness, and the Carson factory fire, this extract from *The Splendid Village* is, of course, only relevant to the first:

Learned he was: nor bird nor insect flew
But he its leafy home and history knew;
Nor wild-flower deck'd the rock nor moss the well
But he its name and qualities could tell. (*Poetical Works,* 85)

The Wanderer figure who is the poem's narrator is lamenting the changes in the village. Here he commemorates the humble man who treated the villagers' ailments. This quotation is flanked by the speaker's indignation that his subject's cottage has been converted into 'six large styes for thirty human swine'—again, a theme relevant to the novel, but not what Gaskell has chosen to focus on.

Gaskell's other Elliott motto is one for Chapter 10:

My heart, once soft as woman's tear, is gnarl'd
With gloating on the ills I cannot cure. (*Poetical Works,* 63)

The twin themes of the chapter are the increasing poverty of the Barton household, and John Barton's growing resentment at this, and Mary's moral danger in encouraging Harry Carson rather than Jem. The latter is exemplified in the reappearance of Esther at the end of the chapter and is introduced by the second of the chapter's two mottoes, four anonymous lines. The speaker of Elliott's lines in *The Village Patriarch* is the anonymous poet observer who provides the main point of view of the poem, and descants on the ills that surround Enoch Wray (the patriarch of the title) and his village. Here Gaskell obviously has picked up the overt voice of criticism, though Elliott's comments are even more critical. For example, he claims in the introduction to the poem that the landowners have 'rendered revolution in this country inevitable' (*Poetical Works,* 56). He reserves some especially savage satire for the parson: 'no wretch is tried for want, but he is there'; 'he shoots, and hunts;/Then whips, or jails, the wo that cannot pay' (71). If the context of the quotation were to be brought to the fore, this would resurrect John Barton's authority as an analyst of social evils, which would unbalance Gaskell's attempts to moderate the voice of protest. As she said in November 1848, 'I never can ascertain what I am in politics; and veer about from extreme Right,—no, I don't think I ever go as far as the extreme Left' (*Letters*, 60).

Gaskell also used Elliott for three epigraphs in her other Manchester novel, *North and South.* Chapter 21 is prefixed with: 'on earth is known to none/The smile that is not sister to a tear.' This generalised sentiment about the interchange between pleasure and suffering in human life precedes a chapter dealing mainly with Mrs Hale's illness. It comes from *The Exile*, a poem about a Royalist refugee in America. The hero's beloved arrives as a convict slave, and he rescues her from the slave-driver's whip. She tells the tale of her suffering as an unmarried mother forced by want into theft. She also tells the story of her son's decline and death. Then she dies too. These lines come from an introductory invocation which Elliott later dropped.[39]

Chapter 22 deals with the riot at Thornton's mill, and its epigraph is entirely appropriate, since Thornton has indeed imported Irish workers to break the strike:

> But work grew scarce, while bread grew dear,
>   And wages lessen'd, too;
> For Irish hordes were bidders here,
>   Our half-paid work to do. (*Poetical Works*, 107)

This actually does come from one of the Corn-Law Rhymes, 'The Death Feast', which tells of a family of four orphans who die off one by one. The speaker and her brother James celebrate only the anniversary of her other brother's death. This poem does represent the voice of the dispossessed, though not Elliott's own experience. The narrative point of view in this chapter, though, is that of Margaret and the Thornton family rather than the strikers, with Margaret acting as the mediator who urges Thornton to speak to the rioters. The verse quotation provides a more rational statement of the rioters' case than do the violent animal images that follow in the novel text.

Chapter 43 is about Margaret leaving Milton and asking for a memento of Bessy. She is given her cup. Book 9, section 4, of *The Village Patriarch*, from which the lines of the epigraph come, is about a projected view of England in twenty years' time through a series of sarcastic rhetorical questions relating to the present state of England. Enoch Wray is dying, and taking leave of all the little details of his life:

> The meanest thing to which we bid adieu,
> Loses its meanness in the parting hour. (*Poetical Works*, 76)

Like Margaret, he makes a kind of local tour bidding farewell to the neighbourhood. The section ends with lines of defiant anti-Corn-Law rhetoric that sound much more like the rebellious voice of Higgins than this piece of sentiment does.

We may conclude, therefore, that in her other full-length Manchester novel Gaskell is still eager to use Elliott's voice as one of her significant intertexts, but that, again, in two cases out of three, her selection downplays the radical implications of that voice.

Nor is Elliott the only writer treated in this way in *Mary Barton*. However, the quotation Gaskell makes in Chapter 9 from Samuel Bamford operates somewhat differently, since it is both entire (and reasonably accurate), and included in the main body of the text.[40]   Samuel Bamford (1788-1872) achieved some notoriety as a radical just after the Napoleonic Wars and was several times imprisoned. His poetry dates mainly from the early decades of the century and is particularly associated with the Peterloo massacre in 1819, at which he was one of the non-violent protesters, though he was later arrested for the part he took. To get the flavour of Bamford's verse it is worth reading a piece like 'The Fray of Stockport' (a title presumably based on 'The Fray of Suport' in Walter Scott's *Minstrelsy of the Scottish Border*) which has tinges of dialect and is supportive of, and spoken by one of, the protesters at Stockport who stoned and attacked the yeomanry.[41] 'Touch Him! Or, Verses occasioned by the Outrage committed upon Mr HUNT, and his Friends, at the Theatre, Manchester, on the evening of Friday, January 22, 1819, by Lord Uxbridge, Captain Frazer, George Torr, and twenty or thirty other "gemmen" of the same stamp' is a revealing title to a poem in which Bamford wishes that the gentry had only stayed around long enough to get beaten up properly by Hunt's supporters (*Miscellaneous Poetry*, 100-02). Bamford also wrote a few dialect poems, such as 'A Dialogue Betwixt Peter Spinthreed, a Cotton Manufacturer, and Zekil Lithewetur, a Hand Loom Weaver'. This dialogue concerns the political power balance. It ends with Peter's family patronising Zekil:

When forth coom Miss, all don'd i' silk,
  Enoof to captivate us,
Hoo gan poor Zeke some buttermilk,
  An' a plate o'cowd potatoes.[42]

His 1821 poems were reprinted, with additions, in 1843 and 1864, so although his radicalism was typically associated with an earlier generation it was obviously still seen as relevant. Bamford was a weaver, and marketed his poems as such, and some of his work bears traces of an oral straightforwardness of phrasing or of being written to be sung to traditional tunes (*Hours in the Bowers*, 10, 68) but he was still overwhelmingly a literary author issuing verse in a format designed for the reader who could afford a volume costing half a crown—cheap, but beyond the average worker's pocket.

Impeccable as were Bamford's origins as a working-class radical, he was also susceptible to mediation for a socially-responsible but more timid middle-class readership. The temptations to such an enterprise are obvious in the publisher's preface to *Miscellaneous Poetry* (1821). This stresses that Bamford is 'unlettered' (obviously untrue by the time of publication!) and tries to create a pastoral image: 'he sings to the motion of his loom ... or tunes his simple reed along the sedgy margin of the distant river.'

However, having painted a picture of sublime rural objects, he then says Bamford 'has not ventured to sing them' (also untrue). Moreover, after Bamford became a correspondent for a London paper in 1826 his old weaver acquaintances began to be suspicious of his class allegiances (*Homely Rhymes*, 9). He rejected the violence of physical-force Chartism. In 1839 he published a translation of 'La Lyonnaise', which deals with a weavers' rising in Lyons in 1834 in which 7,000 are said to have been killed. An endnote warns Englishmen, especially Chartists, not to attempt armed insurrection and expresses a conciliatory hope of mutual education: 'all ranks have been in error as it respects their relative obligations; and prejudice has kept them strangers and apart' (*Homely Rhymes*, 244).

This later Bamford has obvious links with Gaskell's habits of mind. Bamford was associated with Manchester, because he retired there, and Mrs Gaskell had a personal respect for him, even conspiring with Forster to get Tennyson to send Bamford a copy of his poems (*Letters*, 84-85). In turn, Bamford wrote to congratulate Gaskell on *Mary Barton*, even though he was a bit dubious about the dialect (Uglow, 218).

In Chapter 9 Gaskell takes the unusual step of quoting all 65 lines of Bamford's poem 'God Help the Poor'. Through the medium of Job Legh the text is attempting to preach to John Barton, and others of the disaffected poor beyond the text, in the words of a poet who was a weaver like themselves. The footnote actually says Bamford 'illustrates his order, and shows what nobility may be had in a cottage' (127). It must be said that the quietism of this piece is untypical of Bamford's work as a whole, in that the responsibility for helping the poor seems to be landed squarely on the shoulders of God without specifying any human responsibility for assisting Him. The victims whose plight Bamford evokes are typically those of the tradition of Sentiment: the victim of seduction, the starving mother, the child alone, the forlorn old man. Some generalised workers appear in the last stanza, but the effect of pretty well ending the chapter with this poem is to undercut the force of John Barton's disappointment at the beginning that 'Parliament had refused to listen to the working men' (112). Barton's reliance on God is born of desperation at man's refusal to accept the Chartist case: 'we mun speak to our God to hear us, for man will not hearken; no, not now, when we weep tears o' blood' (113). Most of Bamford's work sounds more like John Barton's voice than that of Job Legh.

The last text I want to discuss is the dialect piece 'The Oldham Weaver'. This was composed just after the Napoleonic War. It was somewhat atypical for its time, but Brian Maidment points out that dialect writing was already self-conscious and conventionalized by the 1830s. It was predominantly an oral mode until the 1860s, when the fashion for dialect reached its height (*Poorhouse Fugitives*, 355-56). 'The Oldham Weaver' was still being printed at this period and was of interest to middle-class antiquarians who saw dialect as a significant relict of an older tongue (as did William Gaskell, who, of course, provided notes on the dialect of *Mary Barton* and used the piece to make a point about pronouns.)

This piece is one of the 'Jone o'Grinfilt' series commenting on social conditions through the first person persona of a Lancashire workman. Because of its continued popularity, and because early printed versions usually bear no date and sometimes no imprint, it is not easy to say which versions of the song were current at the time *Mary Barton* is set, or even at the time Gaskell was writing the novel. For, as has been pointed by Martha Vicinus and Brian Hollingworth, Gaskell's version is less radical than the standard ones, which probably date from the 1860s.[43] For this reason, there is a special interest in looking at earlier versions. I wish to compare Gaskell's version with two of an apparently early date, probably no later than the time of writing, one printed by the Manchester printer Wheeler and one by John Harkness of Preston, each of ten stanzas.[44] Gaskell recognises that the musical dimension of the piece would be available to only a small proportion of her audience. It is also worth noting that she comments on it in the terms of the musical culture likely to be more familiar to that audience, describing the air as 'a kind of droning recitative' (39).

The main points of difference are these: the content of verse 2, and the speaker to whom the message of quietism is attributed, the omission of three stanzas, and the toning down of Marget's final resolution. In Gaskell's version, the purveyor of the quietist message of verse 2 is 'Owd Dicky o' Billy's'. This man is presumably more prosperous, and not a weaver—'he never wur clemmed, /An' he ne'er picked ower i' his loife'—but the familiar dialect form of his name places him as one not too far removed from the speaker's sense of community, as with the shopman 'Owd Billy o' Dans' in stanza 4. Other versions suggest that the recommendation just to endure and hold one's tongue comes from those at a greater social remove, and arguably with a greater interest in repressing radical murmurings. The usual villain is 'our church parson'. As the wife of a Unitarian, Elizabeth Gaskell is capable of taking a jaundiced view of the established church, but as the wife of a minister she was not likely to endorse the cynical view of the parson's mode of getting a living: 'I know he lives weel by backbiting the deel.' A less common villain has an even more naked class interest:

> Our cotton mesters kept telling me long
> We should hav better times if I'd but h[o]ld my tongue.

Starvation appears in Gaskell's version as unavoidable—'Oi'se soon clem to deeath'; in the other versions it is the result of malignant intention: 'they mean t' clam me to death.'

After her verse 5 Gaskell omits a verse. In other renderings the callousness of the bailiffs is intensified, and attributed to frustration:

> They would'n a cared had they broken our necks
> They'n mad at owl Bent he'd [t]a'en goods for rent,
> They was ready to flee us alive.

Gaskell's other omission, of two verses after her verse 6, also softens the song's stress on class distinction and exploitation. Although intimidated by his master, the weaver is determined to defend himself, and break away from the vicious circle of providing labour to earn the capitalists profit:

> Then I geet up my piece an took it em back,
> I scarcely dare speak mester looked so black.
> He sed you were o'er paid the last time ye coom,
> I sed if I was 'twere for weavi[n]g bout loom.
>   In the mind as I m in, I'll ne'er pick o'er again
>   For I've woven mysel to th' far end.

Then I coom out of th' house an left him t' chew that,

> When I thought at it again I was vex'd till I sweat
> To think ot I mun warch to keep him an aw th set
> All the days my life an still be in ther debt
>   So I'll give over trade and work with a spode.
>   Or go an break stones upo th' road.

The last verse shows signs of a similar softening. Gaskell's Marget is prepared just to lie down and die: 'hoo's fully resolved t'sew up meawth an' eend.' However, other variants are more violent and aggressive: 'hoo swears hoo would fieht blood up to the een.'

We cannot be certain whether Gaskell knew more than one version of the song, and perhaps chose the most pacific, nor how much she altered what she knew. Tantalisingly, she sent three verses to Chapman in 1848 (*Letters*, 56) but these verses are no longer extant with the letter.[45] It is quite possible her own variant existed as a broadside, but it has not been traced, whereas multiple copies of other renderings exist, and those available in print are certainly more outspoken than she is. Interestingly, the song has survived in tradition in a much shorter version collected in 1947 from a man of nearly 80 who learned it from his Chartist handloom-weaver father. Much is omitted, but not the declaration of fighting 'wi' blood up t' th'een'.[46] The case is not absolutely proven here, but the probability is that in taking this spectacular and very rare course of quoting a dialect broadside so fully Gaskell is following her usual course of mediating a working-class view by letting the account of human suffering speak for itself, but softening the note of rebelliousness. She is taking liberties of compression and omission beyond those she employed with writers of fixed literary texts like Bamford. Given her audience and her own sensibilities this was perhaps inevitable. At least she had more courage than Kingsley in letting some of the weavers' own popular voices come through, rather than constructing a voice on their behalf, however movingly.

Endnotes

1.   For examples of William Gaskell's work, see *Temperance Rhymes* (1839), especially 'Ah! The Change', with its first and last line 'Bread for my children—bread!' 39-42.

2.   Page references for the novels and some stories are to the 'World's Classics' editions. *Mary Barton*, ed. Edgar Wright (1987). Wright repeats this conclusion in his notes, 475-76.

3.   Page references for the non-fiction essays and some stories are to the Knutsford edition (8 vols, 1906). This remark is **3**, 498. 'The Douglas Tragedy' is C7, and in the *Minstrelsy*, **3**, 247.

4.   Harriet Martineau, *Deerbrook*, (1839), **1**, 170-71 (Chapter 9). An elderly lady sings 'the shrill, quavering notes of the monotonous air' of the tragic ballad of 'Giles Collins'; the company go on to sing parlour songs such as 'Fair Enslaver'. Margaret Oliphant, *Chronicles of Carlingford: Miss Marjoribanks*, (1866), **1**, 107 (Chapter 8); the heroine

'sang them a ballad out of one of those treasures of resuscitated ballads which the new generation had then begun to dig out of the bowels of the earth. There was not, to tell the truth, a great deal of music in it.'

5. Dinah Maria Craik, *The Woman's Kingdom*, (1869), **1**, 275. For the sort of ballad referred to, see C63.

6. Knutsford edn, intro. A. W. Ward, (1906), **3**, 490.

7. For the older version of 'The Bluebells of Scotland', see *SMM*, **6**, no. 548; this was superseded by a playhouse tune and words by Mrs Grant of Laggan (Chappell, *Popular Music of the Olden Time*, **2**, 739-40. 'Auld Robin Gray' is by Anne Lindsay, c. 1790, *SMM*, **3**, no. 247. 'Caller Herring', Caroline Nairne; R. A. Smith, *The Scotish Minstrel*, 4th edn, **5**, 18.

8. J. Uglow, *Elizabeth Gaskell: A Habit of Stories* (1993), 346. The literary commonplace book she compiled at twenty-one did include ballads; see J. G. Sharps, *Mrs Gaskell's Observation and Invention* (1970), 26.

9. *The Letters of Mrs Gaskell*, ed. J. A. V. Chapple & A. Pollard (1966), 57; note that my references are page numbers, not letter numbers. Originally a ballad (C226), this was boiled down by tradition, perhaps with some help from Burns, into a lyric. For a text, see *SMM*, **5**, no. 434.

10. For similar views in publications Gaskell was sympathetic to, see W. J. Fox in *The People's Journal*, ed. John Saunders (1846), **1**, 201.

11. Mentioned by Gaskell, *SL*, Chapter 8, 'French Life and Letters' (**7**, 665). In NLS MS 835, p. 155, and Bodleian collection Mus 2 c. 99 (20). R. A. Smith, *The Scotish Minstrel*, **2**, 104. For notes on the history, see *The Songs of Robert Burns*, ed. J. C. Dick, 401-2.

12. For a text and discussion, see R. S. Hawker, *Cornish Ballads and Other Poems* (1869), 1-2, and H. B. Wheatley's introduction to the 1886 edition of the *Reliques*, **1**, xlv. Dixon took it to be traditional in 1846 (232). Three versions based on Hawker, with tunes, in R. Dunstan (ed.), *The Cornish Song Book* (1929), 12, 17-19.

13. 'Introductory Remarks on Popular Poetry', *Minstrelsy* (1902 edn), **1**, 6.

14. H. Green, *Knutsford, its Traditions and History* (1859), 85-87.

15. Mrs Gaskell had encountered Child's earlier collection, *English and Scottish Ballads* (1857-59), then in the process of publication, the forerunner to *English and Scottish Popular Ballads*.

16. M. Wheeler, 'Mrs Gaskell's Reading and the Gaskell Sale Catalogue in Manchester Central Library', *Notes & Queries*, n.s. **24** (1977), 25-30.

17. For a supposedly more objective account of rural singing, see W. Tomlinson, *Papers of the Manchester Literary Club*, **5** (1886), 307-9. Tomlinson recollects an old Warwickshire shepherd heard in his youth who sang all kinds of songs 'with an entire absence of inflection, and at the slowest possible of paces'; another old singer performed 'in a low, monotonous, and lugubrious tone, a song which for length and duration is perfectly fearful'.

18. See L. Broadwood, *English County Songs* (1893), 30-31.

19. Knutsford edn, *Ruth, and Other Tales, etc.*, **3**, 455-70.

20. According to the note in the World's Classics edition, this is from Act 1 of a comic opera, *Rosina*, by F. Brooke (words) and W. Shield (music) which appeared in 1782. This, then, would be an example of a song moving downwards through broadside publication to be preserved in oral tradition. For the Morris song, see *Journal of the English Folk Dance and Song Society*, **8** (1956), 8, or G. Deacon, *John Clare and the Folk Tradition* (1983), 180.

21. Percy, **3**, 124 is a likely source.

22. An early printed traditional version is 'The Ram of Diram', G. R. Kinloch, *The Ballad Book*, (1827), no. 26, reproduced in *Choice Old Scottish Ballads*, ed. T. G. Stevenson (1868, repr. 1976). For the Callcott version (without the anti-dissenter verse), see *A Collection of Glees, Canons, and Catches*, ed. W. Horsley (1824), **3**, 88-93; the earliest sheet copy I have traced is 1800.

23. A. Myers, *Myers's Literary Guide: the North East* (1995), 33-34.

24. This version is quoted in the World's Classics edition and comes from J. Bell (ed.), *Rhymes of the Northern Bards* (1812).

25. The earliest texts of this ballad with a transvestite heroine 'seem to come from comic playhouse pantomimes of the 1790s', but it was probably originally a non-parodic street ballad; D. Dugaw, *Warrior Women and Popular Balladry 1650-1850* (1989), 73-75.

26. M. Vicinus, *The Industrial Muse* (1974), 21.

27. C. Lansbury, *Elizabeth Gaskell: The Novel of Social Crisis* (1975), 46.

28. *MB*, 35; C243. Gaskell's line is closer to the Minstrelsy version than to many others (1902 edn, **3**, 246-52).

29. *SMM*, **3**, no. 240. Unlike the heroine of the song, Mary is neither betrothed to her poor lover, nor consciously faithful to him in thought.

30. Gaskell herself compares her to Deborah Travers (properly Travis) on p. 39. For a brief note on her career, see p. 478 of the World's Classics edition.

31. B. Maidment, *The Poorhouse Fugitives* (1987), 281, 49. The *Corn-Law Rhymes* were in fact first published as a group in 1830.

32. B. Maidment, 'Essayists and Artisans—the Making of Nineteenth-century Self-taught Poets', *Literature and History*, **9:1** (Spring 1983), 74-91.

33. J. Uglow, *Elizabeth Gaskell: A Habit of Stories*, 170.

34. 'Corn-Law Rhymes', *Edinburgh Review*, vol. **55**, no. **110** (1832), 338-61. Excerpted in *Poorhouse Fugitives*, 297-99.

35. Ebenezer Elliott, *Poetical Works* (1840), 100-1, 124.

36. Graham Handley discusses Gaskell's use of Elliott in 'Mrs Gaskell's Reading', *Durham University Journal*, **59** (June 1967), 136-38. He compares this 'Manchester Song' with Corn-Law Rhyme 2, 'Child, is thy father dead?' but I would read the Elliott poem more ironically.

37. For an annotated text, see *Poorhouse Fugitives*, 32-36, 63-65

38. E.g. Samuel Bamford, *Homely Rhymes, Poems, and Reminiscences* (1864), 130-32.

39. For the text, see *Peter Faultless and his Brother Simon*, issued anonymously in 1820, 50, and A. Easson's note, *N&S*, 442.

40. Even here Gaskell makes a few softening changes in the last verse. The version she knew was probably that in *Manchester Poetry*, ed. James Wheeler (1838), 152-54. This volume also includes two poems by William Gaskell.

41. Samuel Bamford, *Miscellaneous Poetry* (1821), 49-51.

42. Samuel Bamford, *Hours in the Bowers* (1834), 67.

43. Vicinus, 58; *Songs of the People*, ed. Brian Hollingworth (1982), 128.

44. I use the version printed by Wheeler in the Cecil Sharp Broadside Collection 2062, no. 10, in the Vaughan Williams Memorial Library, the Library and Archive of the EFDSS, to whom I am indebted for permission to quote. Wheeler also issued at least one other version, mentioning the parson in verse 2.

45. The letter is in the Pierpoint Morgan Library in New York and I am indebted to the Librarian for confirming that the verses are no longer with it.

46. *The Singing Island*, ed. Peggy Seeger and Ewan MacColl (1960), 38.

6

Dickens and Thackeray

Some New Contexts

In turning to Dickens and Thackeray we move away entirely from the worlds of the classic ballad or the surviving oral traditions of time-honoured songs. As with Gaskell and Kingsley, this is partly because of the switch from a rural subject matter to an urban one, but it is not this alone that makes the difference.

Even more than other cities, London was the base of new kinds of popular entertainment for a variety of audiences. As Britain's only really large city at the beginning of the nineteenth century, London had a population with a high proportion of people born and bred to an urban environment rather than first-generation incomers.[1] It was the base for some of the most productive of broadside publishers, such as Pitts and Catnach.[2] These encouraged the composition of new songs at very cheap rates[3] as well as the reproduction of popular stage pieces, hits from Vauxhall and other pleasure gardens, and, increasingly, songs from the new song-and-supper rooms such as Evans's in Covent Garden, the rather less respectable Coal Hole (which had women singers) and the Cider Cellars. Such establishments arose in the 1830s as convivial venues for men out on the town. They were the precursors of music-halls (and favourite pieces from these also rapidly found their way into broadsides and song sheets.) Drink and food were available in the song-and-supper rooms along with sung entertainment. This was led by paid singers such as the improvisatore Charles Sloman or W. G. Ross, with contributions from members of the audience, sometimes of a ribald character. Up till the midnight watershed, the performance of both amateurs and professionals might be augmented by a boys' choir, whose ears would be protected from the bawdier offerings. The standard musical fare was glees, i.e. simple, unaccompanied English songs arranged for male rather than female voices, and to suit the capacities of amateurs.[4] Dickens, Thackeray, Jerrold, Mayhew and Sala all visited the strictly male Evans's, and Thackeray frequented others such as the Cider Cellars as well.[5] Increasingly, in the later 1840s and 1850s, the entertainment became more sedate, and more controlled by the managers and restricted to paid choirs, groups, and star individual performers. Sala and Thackeray both describe the raunchier past with affection and note the increase in respectability with ambivalently regretful approval.[6]

Contemporary evidence of London life at various stages in the careers of Dickens (1812-70) and Thackeray (1811-63) stresses the dominance of popular song (rather than traditional folk song) in oral culture. This chapter will examine, first, Dickens's focus on street song, with an audience from the poor and lower middle class, through the figure of Silas Wegg in *Our Mutual Friend*, and secondly, Thackeray's use of the popular songs of the song-and-supper clubs, with their mixed clientele from lower middle class to the aristocracy slumming, in *The Newcomes*. There was a considerable overlap in repertoires, in spite of the differences in milieux.

Mayhew investigates the world of street song in detail in *London Labour and the London Poor* (1851-52). He reported that there were 1,000 street musicians and 250 ballad singers in London, mostly musically illiterate; some were musical, some survived by getting people to pay them to go away.[7] One of them explained the workings of oral tradition to him (196). The songs, like some of the singers, had come down in the world. He had started street-singing over twenty years ago performing glees such as 'The Wolf' and 'The Red Cross Knight' (both mentioned by Thackeray; Sloman specialized in the former.)[8] Ballad singing paid better, but by then (1850s) the 'ballads' were popular songs like Haynes Bayly's 'Isle of Beauty'.[9] Comic songs were very popular; they were not indecent, but often political (196). Mayhew notes a tendency to parody the sentimental—'I'd be a butterfly, born in a bower/Making apple dumplings without any flour.'[10] This parodic tendency is also apparent in the 'patter' songs with their spoken commentary; the *Red, White and Blue Monster Songbook* contains at least 49 of these. John Ashton confirms that in the 1880s street ballad vendors like Wegg still survived, but that they mostly sold reproductions of songs from the music halls.[11]

Dickens: a withdrawal from narrative commitment

At first glance both authors look likely to sympathize with at least some forms of popular culture, though at different social levels. Dickens is the more obvious candidate because of his deeper involvement with society's underdogs. His upbringing brought him into contact with a variety of forms of popular culture. Harry Stone argues that folk and fairy tales took over his imagination and were a major influence on the structure of his fiction.[12] Fairy tales were published in chapbooks rather than as respectable children's literature as late as the 1850s (Stone, 22-23) and Dickens developed a taste for them fostered by his nurse, Mary Weller, and his grandmother (33-34). As a child he used to sing comic songs in pubs, and he bought sensational penny magazines on his way back from working in the blacking warehouse (Stone, 46, 63). Dickens himself wrote songs like 'The Ivy Green' which passed into the popular repertoire.[13]

However, Dickens's use of popular song allusions in his fiction—whatever the social level he is writing about—is decidedly equivocal. His relish for popular forms of entertainment was characteristically a relish for their innocent absurdity, and he was capable of regarding them as a nuisance, and of adopting the position of an aloof middle-class arbiter, especially in early and non-fictional work before he established his narratorial persona. In 'Vauxhall Gardens by Day' he makes fun of the Vauxhall singers, and he mocks equestrian shows in 'Astley's'.[14] Popular theatre came in for parodic summary in 'The Amusements of the People II' (*Household Words*, 1850), though Dickens also notes the resemblances in plot motifs between these plays and Italian Opera.[15] Magisterially, he intends to open up this unknown world for his audience:

> the upper half of the world neither knows nor greatly cares how the lower
> half amuses itself. Believing that it does not care, mainly because it does
> not know, we purpose occasionally recording a few facts on the subject.[16]

He defends the right of the people to be amused but would be quite prepared to interfere with their current diversions: 'We had far better apply ourselves to improving the character of their amusement' rather than try to suppress it.[17] In the same year, though, *Household Words* was also complaining of the noise of street music.[18]

There might be three reasons why Dickens should distance himself in this way. The first is that early experience of popular culture may be a formative experience without being a positive one. If 'Nurse's Stories' is to be read autobiographically, then he was quite terrified by the tales his nurse related to him, apparently maliciously, before he was six.[19] Secondly, Dickens's parodic eye made him see all art as ridiculous, whether high culture or low, because of the gap between reality and representation.[20] Thirdly, as with so much of his knowledge of the life of the poor, his own childhood fear of sinking irretrievably into their ranks created equivocal sympathies in his narrative persona. Always ready to explain, to warn and to pity, Dickens is reluctant to write in any way that aligns his viewpoint with that of his working-class characters, who are allowed occasional speeches but not free indirect discourse or first-person control of the narration.

On the whole, Dickens remains broadly in favour of current popular amusements, especially if someone is trying to stop them on the basis of some discourse unable to see beyond the work ethic and the cash nexus. Stone's thesis that Dickens's art feeds off popular forms is a compelling one and he certainly incorporates some popular song discourse into his own narrative presentation. Early in *Martin Chuzzlewit* (1843), for example, he uses a joke about the Chuzzlewits' descent from the Lord Nozoo, which can be found in a popular song of the day.[21] One of the major characters in *Our Mutual Friend* (1865), Noddy Boffin the Golden Dustman, must be based not only on the real-life example of Henry Dodd but on a song which Dickens could have heard sung about the streets from the 1830s onwards, 'The Literary Dustman'.[22] Dickens's most famously partisan defence of a broad spectrum of popular culture is in *Hard Times* (1856), where its various manifestations have a heavy symbolic burden to bear as the repositories of the 'Fancy' needed to save the world from arid Utilitarianism. Dickens mimics the voice of a disapproving Benthamite complainant that the people

> *would* resort to low haunts, hidden from the public eye, where they heard low singing and saw low dancing, and mayhap joined in.[23]

This voice cites 'the old nursery fable' to confirm (ironically) the notion that the poor are 'eternally dissatisfied':

> There was an old woman, and what do you think?
> She lived upon nothing but victuals and drink;
> Victuals and drink were the whole of her diet,
> And yet this old woman would NEVER be quiet.[24]

Significantly, though, Dickens presents this as a *nursery* rhyme. The innocence and fancy of the circus world are associated with a Romantic view of childhood, and it is important that we are introduced to its chief representative, Sissy, as a child. Dickens never offers us much sense of what this adult world of 'low singing' and 'low dancing' was like; it is a symbol of known community, but, except for the Circus, not a community known to the audience.[25]

Dickens's sympathy for popular culture focused largely on theatrical events (in the widest sense, including Astley's equestrian spectacles). He maintains this sympathy in general terms in *Our Mutual Friend*, as in his ironically phrased description of a musical evening at a pub and a fair:

> All this was a vicious spectacle as any poor idea of amusement on the part of the rougher hewers of wood and drawers of water in this land of England ever is and shall be. They *must not* vary the rheumatism with amusement. They may vary it with fever and ague, or with as many rheumatic variations as they have joints; but positively not with entertainment after their own manner.[26]

He also refers to nursery rhymes and fairy tales in a positive manner throughout the novel. When it comes to focusing on one of the bearers of popular oral tradition in *Our Mutual Friend*, however, Dickens is not so generous. Indeed, the ballad seller Wegg is one of the villains of the lower-class side of the novel. Instead of fancy, he stands for ignorance and debasement. Even his wooden leg—ballad-sellers were often disabled—is the focus of comedy rather than pity. As far as we can tell from Mayhew and Ashton, Wegg is a realistic figure, even with regard to his passing his ballads on orally (92) but Dickens turns him into a comic nuisance. He exploits the traditional mode of introduction Wegg uses (the personalisation of a song, whereby he claims that 'The Soldier's Tear' was written to commemorate his elder brother's enlistment) to make Wegg seem a charlatan.[27] This is not just a matter of the introductions. Wegg habitually reshapes the songs he introduces into his discourse as 'poetry'. He improvises to include personal and topical considerations (and completely shatter metrical ones):

> I'll tell thee how the maiden wept, Mrs Boffin,
> When her true love was slain, ma'am,
> And how her broken spirit slept, Mrs Boffin,
> And never woke again, ma'am.
> I'll tell thee (if agreeable to Mr. Boffin) how the steed drew nigh,
> And left his lord afar;
> And if my tale (which I hope Mr. Boffin might excuse) should make you sigh,
> I'll strike the light guitar.[28]

These interventions parallel the parodic spoken commentary found in many Victorian music-hall songs, and, indeed, sung by Sloppy (882). In these, of course, the comic intent is that of the performer, whereas Wegg is trying to impress and we are laughing at him, not with him. Even when the improvisation is metrical, Wegg appears incompetent because of failing memory: 'A stranger to something and what's his name joy/Behold little Edmund the poor Peasant boy.'[29]

Wegg's choice of song can be wildly inappropriate, as when he uses Thomas Moore's seduction song 'Eveleen's Bower' to hint darkly at a sense of guilt he wants to instil into the Boffins in order to extract more money from them:

> Weep for the hour,
> When to Boffinses bower,
> The Lord of the valley with offers came;
> Neither does the moon hide her light
> From the heavens to-night
> And weep behind her clouds o'er any individual in the present
> Company's shame.[30]

Perhaps his most macabre transformation lies in fitting 'Home, Sweet Home' to the establishment of Mr Venus, the taxidermist and articulator of skeletons:

> An exile from home splendour dazzles in vain,

O give you your lowly Preparations again,
The birds stuffed so sweetly that can't be expected to come at your call,
Give you these with the peace of mind dearer than all.
Home, Home, Home, sweet Home (562).

To some extent, of course, Dickens is having fun here; 'Home, Sweet Home' does richly deserve parody, and so do some of the other songs Wegg sings or alludes to; the others are: the naval song on page 356, 'My Ain Fireside' (538), 'Auld Lang Syne' (539), 'The Sentry' (555), 'Drink to Me Only' (644), 'When the Heart of Man is Depressed with Cares' (647), 'Come to the Bower' (719), 'The Death of Nelson' (727).[31] However, the travesties also redound on Wegg, who is, after all, trying to disrupt the comfort of the Boffins and others for his own pernicious ends.

Wegg is not the only singer in the novel. Jenny says or sings three lines about a hypothetical soldier lover.[32] Eugene sings, especially hunting songs which imply Headstone is his quarry.[33] Mr Wilfer gets his nickname from 'the beginning of a social chorus' (76). Dickens himself as narrator uses little odds and ends of song, sometimes sardonically, as in a reference to 'the Miller of questionable jollity in the song' 'The Miller of Dee',[34] sometimes with a cosy conclusiveness, as when Bella marries and the chapter ends with the 'bright old song "Oh 'tis love, 'tis love that makes the world go round".[35]

What is more, the middle-class characters and Wegg share a repertoire of popular songs—all Wegg's are respectable parlour ditties, and some of them are ones noted by Thackeray as being performed by and for a largely middle-class clientele. They are also the kind of songs familiar to the shabby-genteel Dick Swiveller in *The Old Curiosity Shop* (1841). Dick is the chairman of a song club, the 'Glorious Apollers'.[36] He specializes in the anacreontic and mildly amatory, being particularly fond of Thomas Moore, T. H. Bayly and John Gay, and his repertoire overlaps with that of Eugene Wrayburn.[37] So intimately acquainted is he with these songs that his own discourse is shaped by their words. Dickens reproduces whole verses without lineation in Dick's conversation, and Dick himself ruefully manipulates their cosier and more sentimental clichés: 'I never nursed a dear Gazelle, to glad me with its soft black eye, but when it came to know me well, and love me, it was sure to marry a market gardener' (Chapter 56).[38] This feature of his speech contributes greatly to Dick's raffish charm and implies its author's and audience's indulgent enjoyment, but this indulgence is contingent on Dick's being a sort of gentleman really. Wegg is not. Dickens's audience would probably have recognized all Wegg's pieces, but would have found their associations with him and the contexts of their performances disruptive.

There may well be a satiric subtext to all this, but Wegg is the only singer to end up in such a symbolically condemnatory posture—in a cartload of muck.

(Incidentally, this idea is used as a simile at the end of a comic ballad, 'Timothy Briggs the Barber' though I know of no evidence that Dickens was familiar with it.)[39] Since Wegg is the active conduit of street song, Dickens's disgust for him is transferred to the version of popular culture he represents, and this undermines some of Dickens's more generalized pronouncements of support for popular amusement. He appears deeply suspicious of a working-class attempt to colonize middle-class song.

Thackeray, Popular Song and Gender Politics

The class position of the young Thackeray was higher and much more assured than that of Dickens. The son of a civil servant, born in India and soon sent to an unhappy but privileged school life at Charterhouse, Thackeray shared much of Dickens's 'keen interest in children's literature—fables, fairy tales, nursery rhymes, *The Arabian Nights*'[40] though he did not associate them as strongly with working-class channels or manifestations. He had a faculty for metrical imitation that made him a good parodist and pastiche writer and he wrote lively (non-musical) ballads for *Punch*.[41] He also composed election ballads, which were sung, one for an election campaign in Liskeard in 1832 and 'A Rare New Ballad of Malbrook' (a parody of the 'Fine Old English Gentleman', using traditional material) which was part of the opposition to the Duke of Marlborough's election campaign on behalf of his son, at Woodstock, in May 1844.[42] His parody of a shipwreck ballad, 'Little Billee' was one of the pieces he sang himself in smoking rooms and it gained wide, even oral, popularity.[43]

As J. K. Law points out, though, Thackeray's real interest was opera. In his work, 'references to specific pieces of music often function as poetic allusion, providing momentary local illumination by bringing the whole of the operatic text to bear on Thackeray's real text.'[44] This is what I have argued that some writers, especially Scott, do with allusions to ballads and folk song. Thackeray does not attempt to use folk song in this way, nor is he given to using the texts of specific popular songs either, at least in *The Newcomes*, though his use of art song is significant and has been widely discussed.[45] However, he does use certain types of context for the performance of popular songs as a structural device.

Thackeray had a sympathetic nostalgia for the men-only diversions of his youth and chronicles these in various essays, such as 'A Dinner in the City' (1847) and 'Mr Brown the Elder takes Mr Brown the Younger to a Club' (1849). One of his most extensive accounts is a *Punch* contribution of 1848, 'A Night's Pleasure', in which he records the changes and continuities in the song-and-supper rooms over a generation, with some regret for their less reputable side: 'all the songs are quite modest now, not like the ribald old ditties which they used to sing in former days.'[46] He offers his own parodic versions of various types of song, 'the battle-song and the sentimental ballad', but refuses even to attempt to imitate 'the folly of the comic country song' although he describes the content in some detail. Those 'ribald old ditties' are conspicuous by their absence both from the present repertoire and from Thackeray's description, and this absence is also notable in the fictionalized episode with which *The Newcomes* opens. As early as *Pickwick Papers* (1836-37) Dickens also seems to be refusing to write such a scene, when, in Chapter 20, Pickwick goes to the Magpie and Stump in search of a lawyer and nothing happens. Pickwick's (too innocent?) presence casts a blight over the musical proceedings he interrupts, and no one sings. Dick Swiveller, we are told, is 'a brute only in the gratification of his appetites' (end of Chapter 23, 245). Presumably these included sex as well as food and drink, though we are not told so. No doubt he would follow in the footsteps of Pierce Egan's Tom and Jerry if he could.[47] However, Egan left no such gaps in *Life in London* (1822) which goes into the heroes' meetings with prostitutes in considerable detail. As Wolfgang Iser points out in his discussion of the implied reader, Thackeray believed 'it is the unwritten part of books that would be the most interesting.'[48]

Pendennis (1848-50) and *The Newcomes* (1853-55) share characters, references to song, and also a conscious outlining of the gaps the reader's imagination must be left to fill. This is most prominent in *Pendennis*, where Thackeray complains in the introduction that his audience will not allow him to 'show as they are' 'even the gentlemen of our age', rebuking his lady readers and other subscribers:

> You will not hear ... what moves in the real world, what passes in society, in the clubs, colleges, mess-rooms,—what is the life and talk of your sons.[49]

The heroine of the novel is, ironically, given the name of a famous London courtesan, celebrated in the songs sung in the Cider Cellars, though there is some debate as to whether Laura Bell was known in London at the date of the novel's publication.[50] In *Pendennis*, 'the Back Kitchen' is just part of the normal seamy side of life for the London male, frequently mentioned but not a focal point like the visit to the Cave of Harmony at the beginning of *The Newcomes*. In both, male singing sessions are contrasted with drawing-room singing or playing by women in and for mixed company, and this is part of Thackeray's conscious manipulation and creation of implied readers according to gender.

It is hard work being a reader of Thackeray. One has to be educated and privileged or excluded from part of the narrative viewpoint, and Thackeray exploits the gap between implied and actual readers: 'When you read such words as QVE ROMANVS on a battered Roman stone, your profound antiquarian knowledge enables you to assert that SENATUS POPVLVS was also inscribed there at some time' (*Newcomes,* 297). Does it? Or does the memory of a bit of elementary Latin enable you to believe that you knew that really? If so, you qualify as Thackeray's implied reader, assuming this to be 'the reader whom the text creates for itself' through 'a network of response-inviting structures'[51] which include allusion. R. D. McMaster claims that 'few other novelists in English ... are as allusive as Thackeray.'[52] Thackeray is certainly capable of using allusion to classical texts at various levels to introduce transgressive subtexts, with the assumption that they are only accessible to those with a privileged classical education, and therefore largely male. In *The Newcomes* Thackeray combines classical knowledge with allusion to Fenelon's *Telemaque* in talking of disreputable women, whether gambling at Baden, or when Lord Farintosh takes a too leisurely farewell of his bachelor habits with Eucharis and Calypso at Richmond (356, 782).

The narrator of *The Newcomes* is notoriously Protean.[53] Indeed, at the end he even becomes the reader of his own text (1008). His direct addresses to the reader offer a variety of subject positions linked by class (the class to which actual readers might wish to aspire), religion (emphatically not Jewish), and divided by sex, for example:

> Whereas for you and me, who have the tempers of angels, and never were known to be angry or complain, nobody cares whether we are pleased or not. Our wives go to the milliners and send us the bill, and we pay it; our John finishes reading the newspaper before he answers our bell, and brings it to us; our sons loll in the arm-chair which we should like; fill the house with their young men, and smoke in the dining-room; our tailors fit us badly; our butchers give us the youngest mutton; our tradesman dun us much more quickly than other people's, because they know we are good-natured; and our servants go out whenever they like, and openly have their friends to supper in the kitchen. When Lady Kew said *Sic volo, sic jubeo,* I promise you few persons of her ladyship's belongings stopped, before they did her biddings, to ask her reason (428).

Obviously the implied reader here is male. Equally obviously, elsewhere she is female: 'so charming a lady as yourself' (266). However, the male or masculine reader is the norm, and the narrator has a tendency to invite him to fill out as deliberately constructed void by the exercise of a somewhat salacious imagination, for example, to let his 'naughty fancy' dwell on bathing beauties (114). The female reader could probably construct this picture, but as object rather than as subject, unwilling to share the voyeuristic viewpoint. However, there are some gaps the female reader is ideologically forbidden to fill. One example would be the specificities of the language of Capt. Blackball, who, surveying Ethel, 'examined her points with the skill of an amateur, and

described them with agreeable frankness' (434). Presumably this would be the
Victorian equivalent of 'by 'eck, you don't get many o' them to the pound,' but
Thackeray's implied male readers are here offered a fuller entrée to the irony
than his female ones.

Thackeray opens *The Newcomes* with a set piece about a song and supper
club, the 'Cave of Harmony'. This musical milieu is part of a network of
allusion in the novel, in which certain kinds of music-making are split along
gender lines. Amateur women's singing is a drawing room accomplishment,
often a predictable and limited one. Rosey Mackenzie has stock songs (she
later acquires one more, the sum total of her achievements). These are a
mixture of opera and 'the artless ballads of her native country', Scotland. That
is, not ballads in the sense of the 'muckle sangs' of reiving, murder and incest,
but the brief pieces by known composers more or less in touch with living
tradition which had been popular since the eighteenth century in England, as
part of a supposedly charming artificial Doric pastoral. Thus, the two 'ballads'
mentioned are Scott's 'Jock of Hazeldean' and 'The Bonnets of Bonny
Dundee'.[54]

Incidentally, the taste for Scotch songs transcended gender barriers, and Col.
Newcome's friend James Binnie also sings 'Jock of Hazeldean', as well as
Lady Nairne's 'Laird of Cockpen'.[55] Of course, there are plenty of musical
venues where the masculine and feminine repertoires overlap. However, the
song and supper rooms were exclusively male preserves. The narrator's
depiction of them is infused with a nostalgia for the times of his own (and
Thackeray's) youth, a generation earlier than the publication of the novel. The
fictionalised versions of such places are the Cave of Harmony and the Haunt,
visited by the narrator, Clive and Florac later, and the Back Kitchen of the
Fielding's Head in *Pendennis*. Much of the repertoire was harmless enough.
The songs Thackeray specifies are glees either written early in the nineteenth
century or adapted from various earlier sources, for example, the 'Red-Cross
Knight', cut down to three verses from the complex tale in Evans's *Old
Ballads*, or 'The Derby Ram', a traditional song set as a glee by John Wall
Callcott (and somewhat emasculated in the process).[56] 'The Wolf' for which
Sloman was renowned is masculine only because of its bloodthirsty
impersonation of a robber. The song the colonel himself sings, 'Wapping Old
Stairs' is a sentimental piece of around 1810 with a female persona who swears
fidelity to a sailor whose own fidelity is rather more questionable.[57] The
Colonel, who, after some quarter of a century in the Indian Army, is charmingly
if improbably pure, sees no harm in the girl's memory of spending a fortnight
below decks with her Tom. Though a more knowing modern audience might
wonder whether washing his trousers and making his grog were her only
occupations in the world of Nelson's navy, the song was regarded as safely
sentimental. The point that Pen makes is that for most of these songs 'a lady's

school might have come in, and ... taken no harm by what happened' (9). He asks, 'Why should it not always be so?'

The answer to this lies in the need of those Victorians who were not members of a lady's school for some way of defining themselves against its values. Throughout the novel the singing of songs in convivial male company is part of a homosocial bonding ritual that cements friendships between Clive, Pen and his companions, and other young men, part of a way of life conventionally beyond the ken of respectable woman and the young. The convenient metaphor of sowing wild oats leaves the reader to supply the details in most cases. Even though Barnes Newcome has a working-class mistress and children, the process of oat-sowing is elided; they simply appear fully formed as a political embarrassment. With the hero, the narrator elects to do no more than outline a significant silence; 'over this stage of Clive Newcome's life we may surely drop the curtain' (248).

The ritual singing claims, without constantly exercising, a freedom from the constraints of respectable Victorian discourse. A crucial point of the performance, then, is the *possibility* of transgressing the taboos of mixed or feminine society. Temporary restraint is feasible. Jones sends a note to Hoskins, the master of ceremonies at the Cave of Harmony, to say a boy is in the room, and a gentleman, who was quite a greenhorn, and hence that the songs had better be carefully selected. As R. D. McMaster points out, the context of Jones's quotation from Juvenal is particularly apt, since it continues, 'Away, whores! Away with the songs of night-revelling parasites.'[58] Captain Costigan, however, is not to be restrained, and sings 'one of his prime songs'. What this is we do not know. Thackeray appeals simultaneously here to two sorts of reader, the knowing and complicit male reader who can fill in the hiatus with his own knowledge of what would constitute a 'prime' song for an all-male gathering in the early 1830s, and the female or young reader, for whom Thackeray's text reproduces the lacuna in their knowledge of life demanded by Victorian ideology. The Colonel is on the side of the angels: 'Does any man who has a wife and sisters, or children at home, say "Go on" to such disgusting ribaldry as this?'

The text presents Newcome as making an heroic stand for modern Christian decencies here. However, beneath this impeccable approval is a disturbing undercurrent. The Colonel's complaint that Costigan 'defile[s] the ears of young boys with this wicked balderdash' is countered with 'why do you bring young boys here, old boy?' This neatly implies that the Colonel's fastidiousness is a sign of an imperfect masculinity; he is not a man, but, ironically, an 'old boy'. Thus, the Colonel's expectations of gentlemanliness are answered by a refutation of his own manliness. The position the reader is being invited to assume is undecided. Clive is embarrassed and the narrator says the Colonel's rebuke 'had somehow fallen on the back of every man in the room.' But *every* man includes our worldly-wise narrator. The rest of the text offers the explicitly or implicitly male reader a flawed subject position throughout. Either he opts for a vulnerable innocence or for the taint of worldly experience. Accepting the narrator's stance leaves us as his accomplices in a morally unjustifiable ideology of masculinity. Were we able as *female* readers to fill that gap, we would be quite beyond the pale. (George Speaight's *Bawdy Songs of the Early Music Hall* contains songs known to have been sung at the Cider Cellars, for any female readers undisturbed by the prospect of losing their femininity.)

Thus, Thackeray is using the song popular in his own class, in an urban setting, as part of his outline of an enjoyable, customary, but morally equivocal system of male-sex bonding that implicates the male reader along with the narrator and characters but excludes the female (or, at least, feminine) reader. Where Dickens uses Wegg to articulate class anxieties, Thackeray uses the Cave of Harmony (which might be regarded as a sexual metaphor in its own right) to create a subtext about a sexuality which the novel forbids itself to discuss. Where Scott and Hardy use specific traditional texts to generate this sort of meaning (and Dickens uses specific popular songs to much the same purpose with Dick, but more fuzzily), Thackeray invokes a more generalized kind of discourse. He is thus inviting the reader to construct his own guilty position and thus to discover his own complicity with a sexual double standard—though it has to be said that Thackeray is more concerned to uncover this double standard than to undermine it.

Endnotes

1.   J. F. C. Harrison, *Early Victorian Britain 1832-1851* (1979), 26.
2.   L. Shepard, *The Broadside Ballad* (1962), 79-84; Shepard quotes Dickens's cheerfully ironic description of the ballad trade in Seven Dials from *Sketches by Boz*. For more detail, see Shepard's *John Pitts: Ballad Printer of Seven Dials, London, 1765-1844* (1969) and C. Hindley, *The History of the Catnach Press* (1887).
3.   H. Mayhew, *London Labour and the London Poor*, intro. J. D. Rosenberg (1968 repr. of edition of 1861-62), **3**, 196.
4.   Definition summarized from entry in *The New Grove Dictionary of Music and Musicians*, ed. S. Sadie (1980), **7**, 430-31.
5.   R. Pearsall, *Victorian Popular Music* (1973), 18. Chapter 1 contains the description of the song-and-supper rooms summarized in this paragraph.
6.   G. A. Sala, *Twice Round the Clock*, intro. P. Collins, (1971 repr. of 1859 text), 333-46. Thackeray, 'A Night's Pleasure', *The Oxford Thackeray*, ed. G. Saintsbury (1908), **8**. Gordon Ray discusses the relation between the originals and Thackeray's fictionalized versions in *Thackeray: the Uses of Adversity 1811-46* (1955), 462.
7.   Mayhew, op. cit., **3**, 159, 163, 196.
8.   *The Newcomes*, ed. A. Sanders (1995), 236; 7, 150. 'The Wolf' is by J. O'Keefe, music W. Shield; see Baring-Gould, *English Minstrelsie*, **1**, 61-65. 'The Red-Cross Knight' was cut down from a ballad by J. W. Callcott; for his version, see *A Collection of Glees,*

Canons and Catches composed by the late John Wall Callcott, ed. W. Horsley (1824), **2**, 27.

9. 195-96. For song, see E. Duncan, *The Minstrelsy of England*, **1**, 271; hereafter *MoE*. (Hardy mentioned this as one of his mother's favourite songs; see Chapter 8, below).

10. Mayhew, op. cit., **3**, 58. For the original song, see F. Kidson & M. Shaw, *Songs of Britain* (1913), 90-91.

11. J. Ashton, *Modern Street Ballads* (1888), ix.

12. H. Stone, *Dickens and the Invisible World* (1979).

13. 'The Ivy Green' appeared on broadsides; for a song text, see *MoE*, **1**, 286-88.

14. Both essays in *Sketches by Boz* in *Sketches by Boz and Other Early Papers*, ed. M. Slater (1994), 127, 106.

15. *'The Amusements of the People' and Other Papers*, ed. M. Slater (1996), 201.

16. 'The Amusements of the People I', op. cit. note 15, 180.

17. Op. cit., note 15, 198.

18. R. Pearsall, *Victorian Popular Music*, 189.

19. *The Uncommercial Traveller and Reprinted Pieces*, New Oxford Illustrated Dickens (1964), 150, 153. E. Johnson, *Charles Dickens: His Tragedy and Triumph* (1979), 17-19.

20. He is particularly amusing on painting and John Carey gives a sharp analysis of the basis of his humour on this topic in *The Violent Effigy* (1979), 57-58.

21. R. Collison, *The Story of Street Literature* (1973), 36.

22. M. Cotsell, *The Companion to Our Mutual Friend* (1986), 55-57. Cotsell reprints the text of this and of the words of the songs mentioned in the novel. See also Ashton, 160, and P. Ward, *Cambridge Street Literature* (1978), 25.

23. *Hard Times*, ed. D. Craig (1969), 67 (Book **1**, Chapter 5).

24. For original, see J. Orchard Halliwell, *Nursery Rhymes of England, Collected Principally from Oral Tradition* (1842), 129. Dickens makes approving references to other nursery rhymes in the novel, as well as to fairy tales.

25. For the discussion of 'knowable community', see Raymond Williams, *The Country and the City* (1975), 202-3.

26. *Our Mutual Friend*, ed. S. Gill, Penguin (1971), 758.

27. 96; this song is one of the few not identified by the notes in the Penguin edition, but it is in Cotsell, 59. It is by T. H. Bayly and G. A. Lee; tune and text in M. R. Turner, *The Parlour Song Book* (1974), 74-76; it was published on broadsides. Wegg does the same thing with Charles Dibdin's 'Then farewell my trim-built wherry' (237; see *The Songs of Charles Dibdin*, coll. G. H. Davidson [1848], **1**, 45, 49). This personalisation was something Dickens saw as a kind of moral blackmail, smothering protest, in 'Nurse's Stories'.

28. 230 (Book **1**, Chapter 15). The original words to 'The Light Guitar'/'O, Leave the Gay and Festive Scene' are by H. S. Van Dyke, music John Barrett. It appeared on broadsides, though, like many of these Victorian popular songs, it is elusive in book form, but see *Cyclopaedia of Popular Songs* (c. 1835), **2**, 269-70.

29. 236 (**1**, 15), 'The Poor Peasant Boy', set to music by John Parry. Like the above, found on broadsides rather than in books.

30. 236, 'Eveleen's Bower', by Moore. This too appeared on song sheets; for a tune, see *120 of Thomas Moore's Irish Songs*, 51.

31. The Cotsell notes make actual or putative identifications for all these and give part words. They can be found in, respectively, *The Songs of Charles Dibdin*, **1**, 241-44, 'The Tar for All Weathers' [?]; R. Smith, *The Scotish Minstrel*, **3**, 43—there is a traditional version in Greig-Duncan, **3**, 553, but this isn't the one Wegg knows; *SMM*,

5, no. 413, Baring-Gould, *English Minstrelsie*, **3**, 10; *MoE*, **1**, 10, John Gay, *The Beggar's Opera* (1728), **2**, 3, p. 22, air 3; C. O Lochlainn (ed.), *Irish Street Ballads* (1978), no. 96 (not the same song as 'Eveleen's Bower'); *MoE*, **1**, 308.

32.   From a Stuart catch, according to Cotsell, op. cit., 140, but also a nursery rhyme by this period: Collison, 110.

33.   *OMF*, 607, note on 908. 'Old Towler', words J. O'Keefe, music W. Shield (*MoE*, **1**, 116-17) and 'The Fox Chase', anon. (J. L. Hatton & E. Faning, *Songs of England*, **2**, 190).

34.   *MoE*, **1**, 134.

35.   Cotsell, op. cit., 253. J. W. T. Ley discusses the various versions of this and other songs in Dickens in 'Sentimental Songs in Dickens', *The Dickensian*, **28** (1932), 313-21.

36.   *The Old Curiosity Shop*, ed. A. Easson, Penguin (1972), 159.

37.   Both sing 'Away with Melancholy', anonymous, but included in Mozart's *Magic Flute*; a good example of high-culture music also appearing on broadsides; *OCS*, 533; *OMF*, 348; see *Cyclopaedia of Popular Songs*, **1**, 73-74. Dick's songs also overlap with those known to Augustus Moddle in *Martin Chuzzlewit*, to George Sampson in *OMF*, to Gaskell, and to Kingsley.

38.   See J. W. T. Ley, 'The Songs Dick Swiveller Knew', *The Dickensian*, **27** (Spring 1931), 215; J. T. Lightwood, *Charles Dickens & Music* (1912), 158.

39.   'Timothy Briggs the Barber': S. Richards & T. Stubbs (eds), *The English Folksinger* (1979), 134.

40.   R. D. McMaster, *Thackeray's Cultural Frame of Reference* (1991), 78. This also identifies songs mentioned in Thackeray's novels.

41.   *The Oxford Thackeray*, ed. G. Saintsbury (1908), **7**, 148-234.

42.   D. A. Haury, 'Thackeray's "An Excellent New Ballad about a Lord and a Lawyer"', *Notes and Queries*, n.s. **28** (Oct. 1981), 404-5; *The Oxford Thackeray*, **7**, 98.

43.   W. P. Frith, *My Autobiography and Reminiscences* (1887), **1**, 107. *The Red, White and Blue Monster Song Book*, 736; some evidence of oral circulation.

44.   J. T. Law, 'Thackeray and the Uses of Opera', *Review of English Studies*, n.s. **39**, no. **156** (Nov. 1988), 502-12.

45.   E.g. Law, op. cit., R. Bledsoe, '*Vanity Fair* and Singing', *Studies in the Novel* **13** (1981), 51-63, E. F. Harden, *Annotations for the Selected Works of William Makepeace Thackeray* (1990).

46.   *The Oxford Thackeray*, **8**, 233.

47.   P. Egan, *Life in London, or, the Day and Night Scenes of Jerry Hawthorn, esq. and his Elegant Friend Corinthian Tom ...* (1822).

48.   W. Iser, *The Implied Reader* (1978), 119.

49.   *Pendennis*, ed. J. Sutherland, World's Classics (1994), lvi-vii .

50.   For discussion on dating, see M. C. Clarke, *Thackeray and Women* (1995), 142-42.

51.   R. Selden, partly quoting Iser, *A Reader's Guide to Contemporary Literary Theory* (1985), 112.

52.   McMaster, *Thackeray's Cultural Frame of Reference*, 1.

53.   E.g. discussion by I. Ferris, 'The Reader in the Rhetoric of Realism: Scott, Thackeray and Eliot', in *Scott and His Influence*, ed. J. H. Alexander & D. Hewitt (1983), 382-92.

54.   Smith, *Scotish Minstrel*, **5**, 80; N. Gatherer (ed.), *Songs & Ballads of Dundee* (1986), 24.

55.   *Scotish Minstrel*, **3**, 37.

56.   Both adapted by Callcott: see note 8 above, and Chapter 5, note 22.

57. C. Chilton (ed.), *Victorian Folk Songs* (1965), 8. Thackeray himself pastiched this song in 'The Knightly Guerdon' (*The Oxford Thackeray*, 7, 144) and made it one of Amelia's songs in *Vanity Fair*, suggesting ambivalence about its sentimentality.

58. McMaster, *Thackeray's Cultural Frame of Reference*, 29.

7

Jefferies

By the time Richard Jefferies (1848-87) started writing he could reckon on a predominantly urban audience, since the 1851 census marks the point at which the bulk of the British population turned out to be living in towns rather than the countryside. The son of a farmer near Swindon, Jefferies started work as a journalist and at the age of eighteen was already writing descriptive articles about his local area. His first book publications were fiction, and he continued to write novels for the rest of his life, but he rose to public attention in the late 1870s and 1880s as an essayist on country life.

As a writer about the countryside Jefferies found an audience with a strong taste for nostalgia that he could choose either to exploit or to challenge. J. Arthur Gibbs, a fellow countryside writer, defended the first policy when he wrote in 1898:

> It is often said that in books like these we paint arcadias that never did and never could exist on earth. To this I would answer that there are many such abodes in country places, if only our minds are such as to realise them. And, above all, let us be optimists in literature even though we may be pessimists in life. Let us have all that is joyous and bright in our books, and leave the trials and failures for the realities of life.[1]

Jefferies, however, used both strategies. His inconsistencies are not due to the difference between fiction and essay writing but to political choices

Like his predecessors, Jefferies knew the evocative power of allusion to a traditional ballad (though Jefferies had little concern as to its original provenance). Sometimes he will focus on one ballad text evocative of a world of past romance. Bevis's boyish imagination lights up in response to 'King Estmere' with its theme of two young men slowly forging their fortunes, and Jefferies quotes extensively from the ballad.[2] Sometimes he even feels the need to create a ballad to provide the proper emotional authentication for his story, as in the prentice work *Who Will Win* (1866). The hero's ancestor is supposed to have been immortalised in black-letter ballad form after encountering the heroine bathing in the nude (Ch. 1). These lines are written tongue-in-cheek by Jefferies, as is obvious from the other authenticating evidence he offers from coins representing an event several hundred years after they were struck.[3] The tone of the passage, though sardonic, does not suggest that the eighteen-year-old Jefferies is trying to undermine his hero's status. The epigraph to *The Gamekeeper at Home* (1878) is from 'Guy of Gisborne'. In introducing *Red*

Deer he says that 'there is in every respect an exact parallel between the hunt in the days of Chevy Chase and the hunt of the present time'. The deer are as wild and free as in the days of Otterburn, when

> The dryvars thorowe the woodes went
> For to reas the dear;
> Bomen bickarte uppone the bent
> With ther browd aras cleare.[4]

He is offering a 'literary' reinforcement of the value of the activities he is celebrating (whether the intertext is real or invented). In quoting the *Reliques* he is quoting Percy spelling for spelling and punctuation mark for punctuation mark. Jefferies is both asserting his cultural credentials as a writer and appealing to a sense of cultural community. By the time that Jefferies quotes them, these ballads were no longer part of living oral tradition in southern England[5] but the property of the mildly scholarly private reader. In no way is Jefferies countenancing them as examples of verbal culture produced for ordinary people by ordinary people.[6]

To me, one of the least sympathetic sides of Jefferies is his devaluation of popular culture. There are exceptions to this, of course, and I shall be discussing them later. I also hope to elucidate some of what I take to be Jefferies' justification for this unsympathetic procedure. However, there certainly are numerous examples of this devaluation by either denigration or denial. His substantial collections of essays *Hodge and His Masters* (1880) and *The Toilers of the Field* (1874) provide plenty. In 'The Low "Public"' he notes the singing in the 'low public' bar of 'the stave of a song shouted in one unvarying key'.[7] I don't think Jefferies means this—the song would hardly be improved if the singer kept changing key—but the hostility to the mode of performance is obvious. A further taint is provided by the note that the place is 'a nest of agitation' (183). The agricultural girl in 'Field-Faring Women' (1874) 'chants snatches of rural songs, and sometimes three or four together, joining hands, dance slowly round and round, singing slowly rude rhymes describing marriage—and not over decent some of these rhymes are.'[8] In 'The Labourer's Children. Cottage Girls', 'the children weave their flowers and chant some old doggrel rhymes with little or no meaning' (*HM*, Chapter 22; or **2**, 159). Jefferies stresses what he sees as the ameliorating influences of members of more respectable classes: the clergyman in 'Modern Clergy' 'causes sweeter music and singing' (*HM*, Chapter 25, or **2**, 250). No doubt the clergymen in his audience were also gratified to have the initiative in social music-making ascribed to them:

> Some of the cottagers who show a *little* talent [my italics] for music
> combine under the leadership of the parish clerk and the patronage of the
> clergyman, and form a small brass band. ('The Labourer's Daily Life'
> [1874], *TF*, 89)

Although Jefferies is quite capable of recording sympathetically
customs such as apple wassailing,[9] he more commonly denigrates examples of
a wide range of popular culture, for example, in 'Village Organisation', where
he describes the dinner of the village benefit club as

> a woeful spectacle to eyes that naturally look for a little taste upon an
> occasion of supposed festivity. What can be more melancholy than a
> procession of men clad in ill-fitting black clothes, in which they are
> evidently uncomfortable, with blue scarves over the shoulder, headed
> with a blatant brass band, and going first to church, and then all round
> the place for beer?[10]

He then seems to contradict his account of the trials endured by the participants
in this social event by claiming, 'there is no social band of union,
no connection'. Even what little culture the labourer's life holds is not his
own; it is derived from a degenerate and alien way of living and not original:

> The songs sung by the labourer at the alehouse or the harvest home are
> not of his own composing. The tunes whistled by the ploughboy as he
> goes down the road to his work in the dawn were not written for him.
> Green meads and rolling lands of wheat ... have never yet inspired those
> who dwell upon them with songs uprising from the soil. The solitude of
> the hills over whose tops the summer sun seems to linger so long has not
> filled the shepherd's heart with a wistful yearning that must be expressed
> in verse or music ... These people have no myths; no heroes ... No; nor
> even a ballad of the hearth, handed down from father to son, to be sung at
> home festivals, as a treasured silver tankard is brought out to drink the
> health of an honoured guest. Ballads there are in old books ... but they
> are dead. A cart comes slowly down the road, and the labourer with it
> sings as he jogs along; but, if you listen, it tells you nothing of wheat, or
> hay, or flocks and herds, nothing of the old gods and heroes. It is a street
> ditty such as you may hear the gutter arabs yelling in London, and
> coming from a music hall. ('The Cottage Charter', *HM*, Chapter 24, or **2**,
> 203-4.)

This view is reinforced in 'The Labourer's Daily Life':

These English agricultural labourers have no passion plays, no peasant plays, no rustic stage and drama, few songs, very little music ... They have no appreciation of beauty (*TF*, 99-100).

Why should Jefferies want to be so emphatic in his insistence on the lack of popular culture? To answer this question we first need to gauge his accuracy. There might be three reasons for his denial:
   a) that what he says is true,
   b) that he is wrong; there was a popular song and music culture, but he knew nothing of it,
   c) that he suppressed what knowledge he had.

Let us now look at these three possibilities in order. Was Jefferies telling the truth? It is here that we want to call in the evidence of other writers, either Jefferies' near-contemporaries, or his near neighbours, writing about the same part of the country, or both. As we have seen, Thomas Hughes has left a spirited testimony to the strength of local tradition near Jefferies' home territory in his *Scouring of the White Horse*. This account is datable to an actual scouring in 1857. But one could argue that twenty five years later, when Jefferies is writing, this facet of country life was fast dying away. Indeed, Hughes himself suggests this in his preface to the 1889 edition. On the other hand, if we look at the work of W. H. Hudson, whose *A Shepherd's Life*, dealing with the Wiltshire downs, first appeared in 1910, he seems to suggest the continuity of tradition. Unlike Hughes, Hudson is not particularly interested in folk song and folk customs and his references to men singing to their oxen or horses as 'not unusual' have a casualness about them which tends to confirm their veracity.[11] His shepherd learned traditional songs from his father Isaac and sang them himself as a grown man (71). Tark was another singer of the old songs who 'seemed to know them all' and danced to his own cymbal playing (275).

More substantially, we have the work of Alfred Williams in collecting his *Folk Songs of the Upper Thames* (1923). He maintains in his preface that it was impossible 'to leave a permanent record of the language and activities of the district ... *without* [my italics] treating of the folk songs'.[12] Some caution is necessary here. Neither Hudson nor Williams is specific about what period he is referring to. Williams' use of the past tense is significant, but also vague. However, both he and Hudson wrote a considerable time after Jefferies— Williams some forty years afterwards—and this leaves us with compelling reasons for believing that if Williams could record over 700 versions of songs, some 260 of which he published in his book, songs which were passed on as far as we can tell substantially through oral tradition, then it is most unlikely that these old songs and more were not current in the area of Coate when Jefferies was growing up and after.

However, he might still not have encountered them, and this is my second point. Was Jefferies simply ignorant of the tradition? After all, Alfred Williams, who was making it his business not only to observe but actively to research the life of his home area near Swindon did not come upon this material all at once. He says in his Preface:

> The existence of the songs is not obvious. You may pass through hundreds of villages, with eyes wide open and wits alert, without finding one ... It is only when you have pored over a scene, or a village, and become thoroughly intimate with its people that you can discover them. A countryman never sings to a stranger ... A villager seldom, if ever, offers you a song. You must ask him for it. You will be sure to get a negative reply at the outset. And blunt questions and imperative requests will never succeed (9-10).

Women had songs of their own, which men seldom sang, and naturally these were even more difficult for a male recorder to obtain (19-20). Admittedly Williams is thinking of the whole history of the songs, but he does add that few if any of them 'figure in the literature of their time' and that therefore 'we must conclude that they were unknown to the educated' (14). Though not a stranger to his community Jefferies was an 'educated' man—certainly a man who liked to present himself as educated—and much more aloof from it than Williams was. It is difficult to imagine Jefferies having the sort of rapport with his informants that we see in Williams, for example in his account of bringing Christmas presents to Granny Hunt, aged 96, including a sprig of mistletoe to kiss her under (*In a Wiltshire Village*, 142-43.)[13]

Jefferies makes a similar acknowledgement of the difficulties of entering into popular culture in *Red Deer*:

> Not one word of superstition, or ancient tradition, or curious folk-lore, can a stranger extract ... By mutual consent they steadfastly refrain from speaking in their own tongue and of their own views to strangers (202).

Nor is this simply because Jefferies is not writing of the people of his home area. A similar remark occurs in *Round About a Great Estate*, in the context of herb lore:

> It would be possible for any one ['middle-class' is implied] to dwell a long time in the midst of a village, and yet never hear anything of this kind and obtain no idea whatever of the curious mixture of the grotesque, the ignorance and yet cleverness, which go to make up hamlet life.[14]

Such remarks imply an answer to my third point: Jefferies is aware of the existence of a separate subculture—one towards which he has rather ambivalent feelings, but of which he knows enough to make judgements. Indeed, he goes on to present the reader with some examples of it, but because he wants to maintain his position as an unimpeachable middle-class observer he can't present either himself, or his representative self in this book, Cicely, as direct participants. He goes on to say, 'But so many labourers and labouring women were continually in and out of the kitchen at Lucketts' Place that I had an opportunity of gathering these items from Mrs. Luckett and Cicely' (80-81). Cicely doesn't join in with the cottagers' children's games but 'used to watch their romping dances and picked up the old rhymes they chanted' (29). In *Field and Hedgerow* ('Cottage Ideas') Louisa the maid chants a traditional sheep-stealing song to the child on her knee and Jefferies fortuitously overhears it as he is 'passing by the kitchen door':

Feyther stole th' Paarson's sheep,
A merry Christmas we shall keep;
We shall have both mutton and beef—
But we won't say nothing about it.[15]

The slight nervousness implied here in the characterisation of the narrator's social position is something Jefferies shares with Thomas Hardy in his creation of his autobiography, as discussed below.

Alfred Williams offers us an independent check on what Jefferies probably did know in that he had some knowledge of people and places very close to Jefferies. Williams had a great admiration for Jefferies, though he knew nothing of his work until he was over thirty, i.e. more than twenty years after Jefferies' death (*In a Wiltshire Village*, 92). He specifically mentions Henry Brunsden of Coate, 'who nursed the infant Richard Jefferies', as one who quotes, recites and composes rhymes. He is not specific about their contents but the context makes it obvious that he is not thinking entirely of the culture of the establishment (160-61). Two of the songs in *Folk Songs of the Upper Thames* (101, 168) came from Coate, and Williams collected ten songs from singers named Jefferies, from Longcot and Highworth, though I have not been able to trace any family connection.

Not only is it *prima facie* unlikely that Jefferies could have avoided all contact with the culture of the ordinary people of his area, but his own words often suggest knowledge of it. His reasons, therefore, for declaring that 'in the life of the English agricultural labourers there is absolutely no poetry, no colour' ('The Labourer's Daily Life', *TF*, 97)—by which he means no recognisable culture—is not ignorance. My examples have no doubt already suggested inconsistency in Jefferies' procedures.   Sometimes he made statements as unequivocal as this; sometimes he notes, even sympathetically, such features of rural culture as mumming, carolling and the apple wassailing already mentioned. Both the fact that Jefferies suppresses or downplays his knowledge and the fact that he is inconsistent about this suggest that he is manipulating his material for effect. The following examples may explain why.

First, one ought to acknowledge that Jefferies did not much like what he heard. Keeper Matthew in *Greene Ferne Farm* made himself a fiddle from maple and played it (46). In the novel this suggests both industry and talent but in *The Dewy Morn* he grants that the fiddles made by northern labourers are a kind of art, but says that he doesn't 'care twopence for a fiddle as a fiddle'.[16] I don't think Jefferies was being untrue to himself when he criticised the musical effect of various features of village life, from the children carolling[17] or the 'rude voices' and 'hoarse, harsh notes' of the village choir (*GFF*, 21-22) to Old Tim's 'mumbling' of 'the tag-end of an old song' ('A True Tale of the Wiltshire Labourer', *TF*, 265-66). When the old woman mentioned both in 'Three Centuries at Home' and less sympathetically in *WSC* (84) offers to sing 'The Leathern Bottel' for him or to tell him a tale Jefferies' interest is in the tale—he omits reference to the song in the essay he chose to print.[18] The tale turns out to be something which can be related to high culture because a version of it is to be found in the *Pentamerone*.[19] Jefferies assumes that the traditional version must have come from Basile's 1637 collection of stories rather than the other way round. The evaluations he makes here are very different from those of, say, Hardy and would not be those of my own taste. But I don't think Jefferies is warping his own taste to fit what he assumed to be that of middle-class readers, or what middle-class readers would have felt they ought to appreciate. Jefferies probably really did feel that it would be a good thing for a village to have a harmonium, at least for secular music (*HV*, 205, 'Village Organisation'). (His view about church music in 'Gaudy as a Garden' [1876] seems more in line with—or derived from?—that of Hardy in *Under the Greenwood Tree*).[20] It is rare for Jefferies to stress cultural relativity as he does in the late essay 'One of the New Voters' (1885) when he talks of the conversation of Roger and his friends at the pub: '*their* conversation, not *your* conversation ... talk in which neither you nor any one of your condition could really join.'[21] Note that the choice of pronoun leaves the narrator out of the analysis. He does this for a particular political purpose: to retain sympathy for the workers even when they commit that heinous Victorian crime of making frequent visits to the alehouse. This political purpose usually operates in favour of the suppression of Jefferies' knowledge, and I will deal with it again in my concluding remarks.

Before that, though, it is worth considering some of the occasions on which Jefferies does pay attention to popular culture, and to ask, again, why? The answers to lie with Jefferies' concern to earn his living as a writer. To succeed he naturally had to consider the taste of the rather varied readership of the many periodicals and publishing firms for whom he produced work. Part of this consideration involved assessing the success of other writers. The most important of the models available to him as writer about the countryside, at least in fiction, was his immediate predecessor and contemporary Thomas Hardy. Moreover, Hardy was dealing with a region not so far from Jefferies' own homeland. I am not going to accuse Jefferies of plagiarism: far from it. There is a school of criticism which seems to believe that no one can ever reinvent the wheel, that of two writers describing the same sort of life in similar parts of the country at almost the same time, one must always be the originator and the other the copyist, rather than their drawing on mutually available material. This is not the case, and, even if it were, Jefferies would by no means always be the one at the disadvantage. Relative dating suggests that if Jefferies might have learned from Hardy the value of describing sheep-dipping or a shepherd's superior knowledge, Hardy might have learned from him how to describe a tomb worn away by the feet of village boys or the decay of old families to the level of labourers.[22]

Such coincidences are legion. I have chosen examples from only one book by Jefferies, and that a collection of essays. However, there are parts of his work for which one feels Jefferies was taking a cue from Hardy as to the marketability of intertextual allusion to songs. The marked difference between *Green Ferne Farm* (1880) and Jefferies' earlier fiction certainly suggests that Jefferies had noted the success of novels such as *Far From the Madding Crowd* (1874) as well as the success of his own country essays—he used the same publisher for both, Smith Elder.[23] Hardy and Jefferies met in 1880, and the book that had impressed Hardy as being worthy of note was *The Gamekeeper at Home*.[24] Both authors wrote essays on the labourers of their respective districts, published within a few months of each other by Longman's, and displaying some consciousness of each other's writing.[25]

Greene Ferne Farm is the most Hardyesque of Jefferies' novels, with its rural set pieces, use of dialect for the rural chorus, and its references to song. Gentry and workfolk seem linked through their enjoyment of song, which takes on an emblematic value as a sign of wholeness of community. Felix comments on Geoffrey's favourite ballad 'The Bailiff's Daughter of Islington':

> no sign of study in those old ballads, no premeditation, no word-twisting and jerking; rugged metre so involved that none can understand it without pondering an hour or two (99).

and compares it with Tennyson. As criticism this is absolute nonsense. Tennyson's metrics are far smoother even in his experimental verse than those of the ballad. The ballad can get away with 'rugged metre' because it is accommodated to a tune. And a couple of the lines Jefferies quotes earlier (38) display 'word-twisting and jerking' in rhyming 'also' and 'know', which involves a wrenching of the accent. What is interesting about the comment is its Romantic stress on the value of time-honoured simple and popular forms to express basic emotions. There is no suggestion here that Jefferies the narrator does not agree with Felix. The whole community of the novel is markedly more musical than Jefferies usually represents it as being—a milker sings to his cows (50) and the farm workers, notably Jabez, lift up their voices conspicuously. If this were a Hardy novel we would find an accurate social placing of the characters through the songs they are given to sing. Something similar happens in *Greene Ferne Farm*. Geoffrey, Felix and Margaret live in a world of conspicuously literary song. Jefferies makes their key song the ballad 'The Bailiff's Daughter of Islington', which was very widely reproduced in collections although it is also recorded from popular tradition in Southern England.[26] May and Margaret also sing 'Come Live with Me and Be My Love', which is more exclusively literary (*GFF*, 178).

If we look at Jabez's songs we find two which are supposed to be characteristic of the region, a shearing song and 'George Ridler's Oven'. Alfred Williams records the latter, though he puts it together from several sources (*FSUT*, 291-92). We might assume that Jefferies is straightforwardly recording the traditional song culture of his area. There is, however, a snag to making this assumption. First, Jefferies has chosen songs in dialectal spelling, thus stressing the split between the verbal culture of the middle-class characters and that of the labourers, who are made to appear quaint, as demonstrated by this sample of 'Gaarge Ridler's Oven':

> When I goes dead, as it med hap,
> Why, bury me under the good ale-tap!
> Wi' voulded arms there let me lie,
> Cheek by jowl, my dog and I. (290)

Secondly, it is doubtful whether the examples he uses are selected from personal observation of the available material. Both are apparently taken from the work of Thomas Hughes. The lines above from 'George Ridler's Oven' are not quite word for word, but there were plenty of other sources, such as Scott's *Fair Maid of Perth*.[27] If Jefferies is doing any more than tinkering with lines for which he only had safe literary sources, then it is an astounding coincidence that the only songs he gives Jabez are also found in Hughes. This is especially the case since, as far as I can discover, the shepherd's song is *only* to be found in Hughes, although it sounds genuine.

Moreover, Jefferies was an admirer of Hughes's work and commends *The Scouring* in *A History of Swindon and its Environs* (1867).[28] In the same work he uses two quotations from supposed ballads quoted in the work of Walter Scott (of whom he was also fond) to authenticate and give emotional substance to his historical remarks (117, 166). He does something similar in discussing the honest country squire in 'The Future of Country Society' (1877) and in 'The Old Mill' (1878) he refers us to both Tennyson and to a snatch of the ballad 'The Berkshire Tragedy' which he appears to quote, without acknowledgement, from *The Scouring*.[29] The reason I claim it is the same is that the Hughes version is a very odd one containing some corrupt or archaic words and spellings which Jefferies has reproduced. The quotations in the essays are obvious claims of cultural solidarity between the writer and the reader, who is expected to approve if not to recognize the cultural resources being drawn on. In the novel we might assume that Jefferies is providing an uncomplicated reflection of country life, but I would argue that he is artfully selecting what he quotes for a similar purpose to that found in the essays. He is working in a mode that has already found some acceptance in Hughes's work. Though *The Scouring* was not a particularly popular book, Hughes was an author well-known and respected for *Tom Brown's Schooldays* (which also quotes 'George Ridler's Oven', in Chapter 1). Jefferies is working very much within an established literary tradition rather than being simply a realistic reflector of life.

What Jefferies is doing in *Greene Ferne Farm* is not, however, something he often does. The only other two pieces that cannot pass without comment are both in essays, 'The Midsummer Hum' (1876) from *Chronicles of the Hedges*, and 'A True Tale of the Wiltshire Labourer' in *The Toilers of the Field*. The first has a heroine who is the obviously literary Lucy Lockett. The piece includes a mason singing a verse from 'Jones's Ale' which had previously been used by Hardy with rather more point in *Desperate Remedies* (Chapter 17).[30] Lucy's charm is partly due to her snatches of song and the old posy sent to her by her lover Absalom. Absalom pops up again in the grimmer and more realistic 'A True Tale of the Wiltshire Labourer'. His beloved Madge is given traditional literary approval as a 'lovely nut-brown maid' (*TF*, 262).[31] At the celebrations of 'hay home' Jefferies lists some of the songs performed (265-66). Though he obviously doesn't think much of them he chooses a likely repertoire: 'Dame Durden', 'Lord Bateman and his Daughters' (though the daughters are a good deal less famous than their father—in fact I've never found a version of the ballad with this addition; it may be a later parody but there are supposed to be thirty verses) and 'The Leathern Bottel' again. All three are in *FSUT* (129, 147, 244). 'The Leathern Bottel' is perhaps the most literary but Williams testifies to its widespread popularity. 'Dame Durden' has been little printed and is almost exclusively an oral piece.[32] It is also used by Hardy. Jefferies may well not have known a printed version except the one

Hardy uses in the almost exactly contemporaneous *Far from the Madding Crowd*, Chapter 8. The song stresses hard work and sex:

> Dame Durden kept five servant-maids
>   To carry the milking-pail,
> She also kept five labouring men
>   To use the spade and flail:
>   'Twas Moll and Bet, Doll and Kit,   And Dorothy Draggletail,
> John and Dick, Joe and Jack,
> And Humphrey with his flail.
>
>   John kissed Molly,
>   Dick kissed Betty,
>   Joe kissed Dolly,
>   Jack kissed Kitty,
>   And Humphrey with his flail
>   Kissed Dorothy Draggletail,
> And Kitty she was a charming maid to carry the milking-pail. (*FSUT*, 147.)

So, Jefferies knew, then, that a moderate portion of folk song allusion could make part of a saleable item and it seems likely that he did have at least some knowledge of local tradition. Indeed, as a very young man and a less guarded or more pastoral author he hints so himself, in *Traits of the Olden Time* (1866):

> It has often been remarked that all nations when in an uncultivated, semi-civilised state, hand down their knowledge or their sentiments by songs or ballads to their descendants. This is true even of England. Many of these old songs often of a highly comic, though rather coarse character, yet remain, and for a quart of ale or a pipe of tobacco, may be unearthed from the budgets of the grey-haired agricultural labourer. The milker sings at the pail even when his breath is frozen upon his chin, and the roaring chorus of 'The Leathern Bottel' may still be heard from a village tavern here and there, while the song itself is yet fresh in the memories of men whose singing days have long gone by ... the agricultural labourer ... lives in the past. All his traditions, histories, songs and customs, have been handed down to him from time immemorial, his talk is of his forefathers, and he is himself becoming antiquated and out of date. (*Early Fiction*, 13-14.)

There are even occasions in later years when he admits the possibility of an active local song culture, for example in 'Midsummer Pests' (1877) some milkers 'have a tune or sing a ballad' (*CH*, 169). And the sheep-stealing verse already discussed was recorded by Jefferies in his note-books as coming from

Wiltshire and Sussex, and in fact the only independent version I have found was from Eastbourne.[33]

Why then, the inconsistent denials at other times? Edward Thomas suggests that in his early work 'it is hard in places to tell whether he is expressing his own opinion or those of the farmers whom he has consulted; and he still writes as one of an agricultural community who is to remain in it' (*HV*, xvi). This is a just criticism, but I think another answer lies in a continuation of the long passage from *Traits* just quoted. The tone of the essay is generally rather sceptical about how 'good' the 'good old times' really were. However, Jefferies is aware that the existence of a lively song culture which gave expression to the feelings of every day life was one feature of past times that might make them 'good', as in his remarks on apple-wassailing that it seems natural 'that the events of the year should be met with a song. But somehow a very hard and unobservant spirit has got abroad into our rural life, and people do not note things as the old folk did' (*FH*, 96). Jefferies also wants to contrast past and present, and however suspicious of the past he may be this contrast is to the disadvantage of the present. Hence Roger in 'One of the New Voters' has drunk deep of poor beer, not 'jolly "good ale and old"'. [34] Jefferies refuses to let a song cliché manipulate the view of the agricultural labourer's lot.

It would be impossible to argue that Jefferies was the unvarying champion of the labourer—any one reading *Hodge and his Masters* on this assumption would be sadly disappointed. However, there can equally be no doubt that this was sometimes the position he adopted. Sentimental idealisation of either past or present did not help his purpose here. As he says in the Preface of *Round About a Great Estate*, he makes notes on the former state of things but he does not want it thought that he wishes this state 'to continue or return' (vii). However, the present state of the labouring man is not an improvement, and to represent the tradition of the past continuing into the present is to undermine his case, which is that modern labour relations have brutalised the country workers. Their way of life engenders 'dumb, sullen churlishness' and 'a corresponding dulness as regards all moral and social matters' (*TF*, 95-96). The result of harvest piece-work is 'no song, no laugh, no stay' (*FH*, 132). To claim in this context that some of the traditional culture of the poor lingered on and had a positive social function would be to saw off the branch he was sitting on. If the worker needs a full belly to appreciate art (*Dewy Morn*, Chapter 47 or **2**, 239), and if Jefferies wants to argue that the worker is unable to get a full belly he can hardly argue that the worker already has a living art of his own, especially if he doesn't happen to be all that convinced that it is an art anyway. In conclusion then, Jefferies' work shows a complex mixture of prejudices and of inconsistencies produced by development and uncertainty in himself, and by a bid to please varying audiences that make his references to and use of popular culture contradictory but neither incomprehensible nor necessarily unsympathetic.

Endnotes

1. J. Arthur Gibbs, *A Cotswold Village* (1983), x.
2. R. Jefferies, *Bevis* (1882), **1**, 13-14, 250, 255; **2**, 32, 43. Since there is no standard edition of Jefferies' complete works, the first edition will be used, and where the essays or stories are available in collected form, the first collected edition. For dates of first publication, see G. Miller & H. Matthews, *Richard Jefferies. A Bibliographical Study* (1993). The ballad is C60, *Reliques*, **1**, 62-76. Some editions quote it in an appendix.
3. *The Early Fiction of Richard Jefferies*, ed. G. Toplis (1896), 92-93.
4. *Red Deer* (1883), 4, 21; hereafter *RD*. The lines he actually quotes, however, are from 'Chevy Chase', *Reliques*, **1**, 5.
5. Though they may have been elsewhere. See B. H. Bronson, *The Traditional Tunes of the Child Ballads*, for C161, C162.
6. Jefferies' use of the word 'ballad' is a loose one, though one quite typical of his time. Thus, in *Greene Ferne Farm*, Margaret sings what Jefferies calls 'the beautiful old ballad "Come live with me and be my love"', which is not a ballad, and is by a known writer, Christopher Marlowe, with an answer by Raleigh (1880 edn, 178).
7. *Hodge and his Masters* (1880), **2**, 183; hereafter *HM*.
8. *The Toilers of the Field* (1892), 128; hereafter *TF*.
9. 'Summer in Somerset', *Field and Hedgerow* (1889), 278; hereafter *FH*.
10. *The Hills and the Vale* (1911), 166.
11. W. H. Hudson, *A Shepherd's Life* (1910), 143. (Partly issued as 'A Shepherd of the Downs', *Longman's Magazine*, October and November 1902.)
12. A. Williams, *FSUT*, 9.
13. A. Williams, *In a Wiltshire Village*, condensed by M. J. Davis (1981), 142-43.
14. *Round About a Great Estate* (1880), 80; hereafter *RGE*.
15. *FH*, 192. Compare, 'Mother! father's stole a sheep!/We shall have good mutton & beef./A Happy Xmas we shall have/But you mus'nt say nothing about it O!' sent to the EFDSS in 1914. I am indebted to the English Folk Dance and Song Society and the Vaughan Williams Memorial Library for permission to quote this (Library Collection MPS 60 [31] p. 301).
16. *The Dewy Morn* (1884), **2**, 242; hereafter *DM*.
17. *Wild Life in a Southern County* (1879), 99; hereafter *WSC*.
18. *The Old House at Coate and Other Hitherto Unpublished Essays*, ed. S. J. Looker (1948), 142. However, Jefferies had a fondness for 'The Leathern Bottel' and mentions it on several other occasions (*TF*, 176-78; *Early Fiction*, 13, 52). Widely available in print in various versions from D'Urfey onwards (**3**, 247). Williams says 'few folk-songs, perhaps, enjoyed more popularity' but that it had dropped out of favour (*FSUT*, 244-45).
19. Jefferies says he 'readily recognised' this obscure source. The only translation of G. Basile's *The Pentamerone* before Jefferies was that of J. E. Taylor's bowdlerized version in 1848. The story is 'Vardiello' (48), though Jefferies' memory of it is inaccurate. Taylor's introduction makes it clear that the stories are from tradition, not invented by Basile. There is a full modern edition of R. Burton's 1893 translation by E. R. Vincent (1952).

put up thuck hurdy-gurdy in the Church, an' I arn't never bin thur'. Hereafter *CH*. For Hardy discussion, see Chapter 8 of this book.

21. 'One of the New Voters', *The Open Air* (1885), 107, hereafter *OA*.

22. Compare *WSC* 68-69 and 95-98 with *Far from the Madding Crowd*, Chapters 19, 21, 36; *WSC* 81, with the earlier *Return of the Native*, Book **1**, Chapter 3 but also the poem 'The Children and Sir Nameless' published much later; *WSC* 91 with *Tess*, Chapter 1.

23. W. J. Keith, *Richard Jefferies* (1965) , 40, 124, 126.

24. F. E. Hardy, *The Life of Thomas Hardy* (1972), 134; J. Ebbatson, 'Hardy and Richard Jefferies', *Thomas Hardy Society Annual Review* (1976), **1:2**, 59. The latter provides a useful summary of connections and similarities.

25. Keith, *Richard Jefferies*, 36.

26. E.g. *Reliques*, **3**, 135-57; *FSUT*, 174-75, D228 in the manuscript collection made by H. D. Hammond and held in the Vaughan Williams Memorial Library, the Library and Archive of the EFDSS.

27. It is possible that Jefferies had heard both these songs and was remembering them from oral tradition, but the balance of evidence suggests not. I suspect the first and fourth lines from 'George Ridler's Oven' came basically from Hughes and the second and third from Scott (*Fair Maid of Perth*, Chapter 16).

28. *Jefferies' Land. A History of Swindon and its Environs*, ed. G. Toplis (1896), 126.

29. *Landscape and Labour*, ed. J. Pearson (1979), 79, 40.

30. *CH*, 200. This is the most radical verse in the whole song, and S. Baring-Gould notes that 'the verse best remembered by our peasantry is that of the Mason, which, curiously enough, does not appear in any printed copy' though he has heard it sung in various places (*A Garland of Country Song* [1895], 12).

31. 'The Nut-brown Maid', *Reliques*, **2**, 27-43.

32. However, there is a version in *The London Songster* (1821), 128-34, and various undated broadsides.

33. *The Notebooks of Richard Jefferies*, ed. S. J. Looker (1948), 160.

34. *OA*, 95. The phrase comes from 'The Jolly Ale-Drinker' or 'Back and Side Go Bare', and is at least as old as the play *Gammer Gurton's Needle* (1575) in which it appeared (Chappell, *Popular Songs*, **1**, 72-73).

8

Hardy

Hardy's Background and Musical Milieux

Much criticism of the works of Thomas Hardy has been based on the recognition of his interest in music. He was responsive to a wide variety of musical genres, but it was the traditional music and song of his own region that stirred him most deeply. This interest was maintained throughout his life. As a boy, alone or in the company of his father, he played the fiddle at rural celebrations.[1] At the age of seventy-seven he demonstrated fiddle tunes and dance steps for the local dramatic society, and in his eighties he played traditional dance tunes and discussed folk music with Jessica Vera Stevens.[2] His ear was exceptionally acute and his sensitivity to musical influence abnormally marked.[3] This latter peculiarity provided him with definitive images and situations for use in both verse and prose, and these have been extensively but by no means exhaustively discussed by previous critics.

Such investigations tend to fall into three main categories: first, the amassing of lists of songs referred to in his novels; secondly, the noting of musical metaphors and the discussion of possible analogues between his literary work and music; and thirdly, the study of thematic and structural analogues between his work and 'the ballad as such'.[4] The first operates by quantity rather than by assessing the quality of Hardy's use of musical reference; the other two suffer from a lack of specificity, and may even mislead the reader about the nature of the formative musical influences on Hardy and the use he makes of them. My concern is largely with the third category, though my discussion recognizes that the use of folk songs can only be seen in terms of Hardy's response to a whole traditional musical milieu. We need, therefore, to know what this milieu was.

Although there was far more literacy in both words and music than is sometimes assumed, and although ordinary working people were capable of enjoying and playing the music popular in higher classes than their own,[5] the most widespread and deeply permeating music and song culture of people like Hardy's main characters was passed on by ear, not picked up solely from printed texts. Hardy himself was part of this culture, not just an interested observer like other regional novelists such as Gaskell.

Critics discussing the influence of folk song on Hardy have stressed his debt to the traditional ballad.[6] Insofar as the ballad is, like the novel, a verbal art, this emphasis is appropriate. The point of this discussion is not to suggest that the comparisons made are false, for they can often be extremely illuminating, but to try to show more precisely what the influences of verbal music on Hardy really were and what he did with them in specific terms. Discussions of Hardy such as those by Thom Gunn or Donald Davidson, which reinforce their generalizations about ballads by reference to particular examples, tend to use, as standard, examples from the Scottish border. If references are given they are usually to the edition of such ballads by Professor F. J. Child, *The English and Scottish Popular Ballads* (1882-98).[7] However, as the very title suggests, these ballads have a geographical bias. If we are to do as Davidson suggests and 'make a justifiable inference from the snatches of balladry in the novels and tales' (13), we certainly can *not* conclude that he owed much to ballads like Gunn's examples 'Sir Patrick Spens', 'Edward', or 'The Laily Worm and the Machrel of the Sea' as they are recorded by Child. The first, 'Sir Patrick Spens' (C58), is represented by eighteen versions, all Scottish; 'Edward' (C13) by three, all Scottish; and 'The Laily Worm' (C36) by one, also Scottish. What is more, Child himself had very definite ideas about what constituted a ballad, ideas that demonstrate biases resulting from his position as a middle-class American literary scholar. In spite of his sporadic praise of oral tradition, he frequently distrusted it and showed little sense of its creative potential. Dave Harker comes to the conclusion that

> we may continue to use the texts as highly mediated examples of the kinds of songs described by late nineteenth century English-speaking literary scholars as 'ballads'. About the lives, interests and general culture of the people who made, remade and used these songs, however, a compilation such as Child's can tell us almost nothing.[8]

Indeed, it does not even tell us anything about non-balladic traditional song and music which may have been just as important a part of Hardy's background.

Another objection to the use of references to Child alone must be obvious. Hardy's opportunities of being influenced during his formative years by Border ballads were virtually non-existent. It is therefore necessary for the critic to show that the examples used for comparison were current in some cognate form in mid-nineteenth-century Dorset. In his creative published work and in his *Life*, Hardy quotes or refers to some forty-eight songs, some only in a very fragmentary form, which might loosely be classified as folk songs, that is, songs originally composed by authors now anonymous, or working in or close to tradition, and which apparently have a life of their own, being reproduced by oral tradition and developing different variants over time. He also mentions nine carols and forty-seven tunes likely to be in the repertoire of a traditional performer of the early nineteenth century. Hardy's selection of songs has a wide range of tone and apparent provenance. Seven of them are heavily and obviously associated with Scotland. These are 'O Waly, Waly', 'O Nannie',

'It's Hame and it's Hame', 'The Lass of Gowrie', 'Auld Lang Syne', 'Bonnie Peg', and 'Tibbie Towler' (or 'Fowler').[9] All but the first—an epigraph for Chapter 32 of *A Pair of Blue Eyes*—are sung by Farfrae. The last four are attributed to known authors or adaptators: Lady Nairne and (for the last three) Burns. 'O Waly, Waly' is a lyrical piece associated with 'Jamie Douglas' (C204), which had been widely printed. Another five songs are Irish, but none of these is included in Child's standard collection since he was not concerned there either with lyrical pieces or with Ireland.[10] Of the remaining songs, four can be compared with ballads in Child. 'The Light of the Moon', used by Hardy in *The Dynasts*, is a lyrical version of the song sometimes known as 'The Grey Cock' (C248). 'The Boy and the Mantle' is C29 and 'Queen Eleanor's Confession' is C156. What seems to have been Hardy's favourite ballad, 'The Outlandish Knight', is C4.[11] Considering the claims that are made about Hardy and the ballad, this seems a disappointingly meagre haul.

In later years he certainly displayed an interest in printed ballad texts, including Child's. Hardy owned a copy of *The Ballad Minstrelsy of Scotland*, now in the Dorset County Museum, that he annotated with variants from his own locality.[12] However, it cannot be shown that Hardy used this book in his writing. As his annotations show, such collections merely reinforced what he already knew from his own experience.

To what, then, can Hardy's use of traditional music and song be traced? There are four main categories of source with which such links can be made: some printed texts in edited collections, family manuscript books, a collection made by Hardy himself, and songs from Wessex taken down from oral tradition by later collectors.

First, printed sources known to have been in Hardy's possession and now in the Thomas Hardy Memorial Collection in the Dorset County Museum: these are Percy's *Reliques of Ancient English Poetry* and John Hullah's *The Song Book* (1866).[13] His copy of the *Reliques* is only slightly marked by him. Apart from 'O Waly, Waly', he seems to have used it for the text of Mrs. Durbeyfield's 'ballad of the mystic robe' in Chapter 32 of *Tess*.[14] In the serial version of the novel he quotes two extra verses very close to Percy.[15] 'Queen Eleanor's Confession' in *The Return of the Native* (46-47, 54) probably also came from Percy. Hullah's *Song Book* is a collection of supposedly national songs, heavily reliant on William Chappell's *Popular Music of the Olden Time* (1855-59) and reproducing from it several traditional songs used by Hardy. Hardy's copy of Hullah has pencil notes, mostly in the English section, apparently indicating singers of the various songs known to him. If he had wanted them he could have found in the *Song Book* texts of 'Auld Lang Syne' and 'Tibbie Fowler'. Though we cannot be sure when he acquired the book there is little doubt that he used it in his old age when pressed for a text for songs. The Album Book, H/1956.101.1 in the Thomas Hardy Memorial

Collection in Dorset County Museum, contains tunes, songs, and dance notations provided by Hardy for the Hardy players.[16] ''Twas Down in Cupid's Gardens' (*Return of the Native*, 399; *Tess*, 294, 365) bears the note 'as sung at Casterbridge, Mellstock, Weatherbury + Longpuddle, 1840-50', but the text given is almost word for word from Hullah, and the tune too has obviously been copied straight out, even though there is a version in one of the family manuscript books discussed below.   Even the note just quoted is one made in pencil in Hullah.   The *Song Book* is also the likely source for the Wedding Song sung to Wildeve and Tamsin in *The Return of the Native* (71)[17] though Hardy has refashioned it to give an impression of happiness foreign to the original.

The fact that a song can be found in a printed source owned and even annotated by Hardy does not, of course, prove that he used that version.   He had other, older, more intimate sources.   Some notion of the musical traditions he could have absorbed from his family can be seen in the manuscript books belonging to them and now preserved in the Dorset County Museum.   Among these are a book of carols and songs belonging to his grandfather containing bass parts and a carol book of his father's with fuller part settings.   As Hardy explains in the preface to *Under the Greenwood Tree*, it was the custom to use one end of such books for sacred music and the other for secular,

> to inscribe a few jigs, reels, hornpipes, and ballads in the same book, by beginning it at the other end, the insertions being continued from front to back till sacred and secular met together in the middle, often with bizarre effect, the words of some of the songs exhibiting that ancient and broad humour which our grandfathers, and possibly grandmothers, took delight in, and is in these days unquotable (28).

The first of these manuscript collections is in this format.   This remark shows Hardy's consciousness of the moral unpalatability of older songs for contemporary taste (though they would seem only mildly risqué to us.)   There is also a book of tunes and songs copied from a complation by James Hook, (a local man, not the composer) probably made about 1820.[18]   As well as these, tunes familiar to Hardy may be found in a manuscript collection belonging to the family called *Tunes for the Violin*, which is in the Lock Collection in the Dorset County Library, Dorchester.[19]   Between them these four volumes provide evidence of the Hardy family's knowledge of eight out of his nine carols, thirty-four out of the forty-seven dance and march tunes, and six of the forty-eight folk songs.[20]

These books were not made for each musician to play from directly, but rather served more as memorials.   The reason for the low proportion of folk songs is not far to seek.   The books did not set out to record what was common knowledge around them in the way of song, and in spite of the Hardy family's instrumental prowess none were noted singers. There are a few pieces that achieved oral currency, but the songs are heavily influenced by art songs, that is, songs with a known author and composer, usually designed for instrumental accompaniment, for town rather than country consumption, and for the more prosperous levels of society. Examples include such favourites of Hardy's mother as 'Why are you wandering here, I pray' which Fancy sings to Dick in *Under the Greenwood Tree* (146).[21] Some of these more artificially contrived songs were obviously beginning the process of oral diversification. 'O Nannie' in *The Mayor of Casterbridge* (83) is an English song adopted by the Scots.[22] 'Jockey to the Fair' is a set of rather artificial words set to a preexisting tune, which is played by Gabriel Oak at the hiring fair and in the malthouse in *Far From the Madding Crowd* (75, 97), probably just as a tune.[23]

The third kind of record of music influences on Hardy was made by the novelist himself. He heard what were undoubtedly traditional ballads and songs from his mother and people like the fieldwomen mentioned in the *Life* 'who had been young women about twenty when he was a child' (223). Hardy made his own small collection that he titled 'Country Songs of 1820 onward—killed by the Comic Songs of the Music Hall', which was finally put together in 1926 though it was probably made piecemeal over some years.[24] By 1871 he was already 'writing down such snatches of the old country ballads as he could hear from aged people' (*Life*, 84). His diary for 11 November 1894 notes several fragments such as a couple of lines of a song known as 'Gown of Green': 'Somebody here has been .../Or else some charming shepherdess/That wears the gown of green' (*Life*, 267). Hardy's little collection includes fragments of twenty-three songs, without tunes. Only two of them coincide with entries in Child (C250, 289). Probably Hardy did not record songs that he knew well; he certainly knew many more than these twenty-three, of which he only uses two in his work; nor are the three mentioned in the diary entry found in this collection.

Hardy's own efforts as a recorder were too little, but not entirely too late, though he thought so. He records with a particular insistence in the *Life* his attendance in 1847 at a harvest supper, 'among the last at which the old traditional ballads were sung, the railway having been extended to Dorchester just then, and the orally transmitted ditties of centuries being slain at a stroke by the London comic songs that were introduced' (20). This notion, fruitful as it was for the development of themes of social conflict in his novels, was overdramatic. However, Hardy certainly saw a significant transformation in traditional modes of social music during his lifetime. Indeed, Cecil Sharp, one of the most authoritative of later collectors, shared his view, noting that 'the last generation of folk-singers must have been born not later than sixty or seventy years ago—say 1840.'[25]

1840, of course, was the year of Hardy's birth. But this 'last generation' survived into the twentieth century and provides the fourth and in some ways most important clue to what may have influenced Hardy. From 1905 to 1908 Henry Denison Hammond, assisted by his brother Robert and by George B. Gardiner, collected 918 versions of folk songs from the southwest of England, 764 of them from Dorset. Many of them came from people of Hardy's own age and up to twenty years older. Gardiner himself collected over one thousand further song versions from other counties in or near Hardy's Wessex. Some of their findings have been published but often in collated forms.[26]   In this discussion, however, I refer to the versions in manuscript and typescript in the Vaughan Williams Memorial Library, the Library and Archive at the headquarters of the English Folk Dance and Song Society in London.[27]

One of Hammond's best informants was Robert Barrett (or Barratt: the spelling of the name is variable). Barrett came from Puddletown (Hardy's 'Weatherbury') and was some four years older than Hardy. One of the fieldwomen Hardy says that he heard songs from was Anna Barrett; she and most of those he mentions are traceable in the records for the parish of Puddletown now in the County Records Office in Dorchester. The 1851 census records an Ann Barrett of the right age (the only one in the village) living next door to Robert Barrett; she may have been his sister, or possibly his aunt. Hardy mentions four of the songs that Hammond later collected from Barrett, and the lines he quotes from 'Gown of Green' in the *Life* are identical with those in the version collected by Hammond from Barrett. The three lines sung by the Deserter in *The Dynasts* are very similar to the ending of verse four of Barrett's rendering of 'The Grey Cock' (D248).[28] The sources of Hammond's collection, then, probably include informants from whom Hardy himself could have heard songs.

The work of Hammond in Dorset (and of Hammond and Gardiner elsewhere) shows that traditional songs in Wessex had a wide range of tone and apparent provenance. Hardy's choice of material is an accurate reflection of this. Hammond confirms the currency in Dorset of such great standard tragic ballads as 'Lord Randal' (C12), 'Lord Thomas and Fair Eleanor' (C73), and 'The Unquiet Grave' (C78). Both Hardy and Hammond collected versions of 'Henry Martin' (C250), 'Polly Vaughan', and 'Scilly Rocks'. Another thirteen of Hardy's 'Country Songs' seem to be ballads, not necessarily tragic. None of these is in Child but seven of them were found by Hammond or Gardiner. For one fragment of four and half verses I have found no close analogues at all, and for some others only widely differing versions. This suggests that Hardy knew some ballads local to his area but not common elsewhere. When discussing how he responded to song tradition, therefore, it would be more useful critically to cite versions of songs that he is likely to have been familiar with. This is particularly important since many of these ballads have been pared down to a lyric ('The Grey Cock'/'The Light of the Moon' is a good example), as is typical of southern tradition in the nineteenth century. We also find in

Hammond large numbers of lyrical pieces (with which Child was not concerned). Many of the Hammond songs were Irish in origin, probably picked up from itinerant workers, but there was very little Scottish influence. There is a fair sprinkling of composed pieces being subjected to the diversifying processes of oral transmission, like some of those in the Hardy family manuscript books.

Given that a search in Child for analogues of the forty-eight folk songs Hardy used directly is surprisingly unrewarding, we must see what a comparison with the Hammond material involves. Admitting the fragmentary nature of some, it seems reasonable to connect twenty of those forty-eight with Hammond's Dorset collection, often in more than one version, and a further nine with Hammond and Gardiner's work in nearby counties (mostly Irish songs). Remove the seven specifically Scottish songs used by Hardy and the two ballads he seems to have had only literary sources for, and we can link twenty-nine songs out of thirty-nine with locally collected versions. Of the twenty-three songs in 'Country Songs' two are found in Child but fourteen were collected by Hammond in Dorset.

Clearly, then, we can gain a much better idea of the formative folk song influences on Hardy by studying these four groups of material. If we add a few broadsides in miscellaneous collections we can gain a virtually complete view. Now it is possible to look in more detail at the very significant ways in which Hardy uses references to the individual pieces and to their precise social context in his novels. We can begin by noting what he left out. The five conspicuously Irish songs (four found by Hammond or Gardiner in tradition) he only mentions in his poems 'Donaghadee' and 'Sitting on the Bridge'.[29] In spite of their frequency in the tradition and their occurrence in his *Country Songs*, Hardy never uses traditional sea songs, even in *The Trumpet-Major*. By these omissions he is shaping the outlines of his Wessex: essentially English, looking inward, sufficient unto itself.

Hardy's Wessex is overflowing with characters with the same sensibilities as the author. Musicality is a prominent feature in most of the novels, and in *The Hand of Ethelberta* the hero is a musician. Though it is difficult for us to feel that the characters in the minor novels are motivated by a peculiar passion, in the Novels of Character and Environment this is a major factor in character presentation, motivation, and thematic development. Not only do we meet personalities like William Dewy or Laban Tall, who cannot tear himself from Oak's music, but many of Hardy's characters are actually betrayed by their sensibility. Tess's 'innate love of melody, which she had inherited from her ballad-singing mother, gave the simplest music a power over her which could well-nigh drag her heart out of her bosom' (113). She and Angel are mutually attracted through susceptibility to sound. He is looking over music when he notices her 'fluty voice' (147), and she is fascinated by his harp playing, bad as it is (150). In *The Mayor of Casterbridge* it is Farfrae's readiness with a song that wins him acceptance into the local community, that helps to entrance Lucetta, and that binds Henchard to him. As Henchard later claims, 'it was partly by his songs that he got over me, and heaved me out' (243). Moreover, in each of these novels, as in others, the type of music to which the characters respond is a very precise moral and social touchstone.

To understand fully what Hardy is doing it is necessary to examine the origin and range of his references. In this analysis I shall concentrate on Hardy's use of orally transmitted song and its likely audience and producers.

Church Bands

First I would like to discuss Hardy's use of a form of music very much associated with his writing but not what is usually understood as folk music, that is, the music performed by the local bands in church, often in a separate gallery, or on carol rounds. Hardy's own family had been famous as the key figures in such a band, set up by his grandfather at Stinsford, which was a linch pin in both the sacred and the secular music of the village, though Hardy was too young to have had personal experience of the church side (*Life*, 12-13). In fact, Hardy was one of the later writers to use the fairly popular topic of class tension in church music-making, whether Church of England or non-conformist. By the 1870s even ecclesiastical writers were starting to sound nostalgic about the old church bands.[30] The setting-up of a separate choir in church was a bone of contention even early in the eighteenth century.[31] As we have seen, George Eliot touched on it as part of her pastoral nostalgia, so did Samuel Butler, writing *The Way of All Flesh* at much the same time as Hardy, and so did Jefferies. The topic had been popular in earlier descriptive essays: Washington Irving's *The Sketchbook of Henry Crayon, Gent.* (1819-20), William Howitt, *The Rural Life of England* (1838), 'Church Music and Other Parochials' in *Blackwoods Magazine* (April 1838), William Gardiner, *Music and Friends* (1838), Joseph Gostick's 'The Organ at Great Muggleton' in *The People's Journal*, **2** (1847), 130-31.[32]

In historical terms these bands were not repositories of a 'pure' tradition in the sense of one whose music was generated initially by ordinary people; they were usually influenced in style of composition and performance by the musical interests of the middle-class and gentry in the eighteenth century. Thus 'country church music', as Nicholas Temperley calls it, does not fit easily into either the category of 'art music' or that of 'folk music'.[33] The choir for voices was 'generally accepted in country churches by the middle of the eighteenth century' and Dorset had a strong choir psalmody tradition by the 1730s.[34] Church bands, with treble and bass instruments, were uncommon before 1770 and flourished between 1780 and 1830.[35] Many country musicians were musically literate.

However, this music, especially the carols, was transmitted through several generations by a mixture of oral and written means. It had a traditionary status and a socially cohesive function within predominantly working-class communities. Dave Townsend insists on the overlap between oral and written transmission, pointing out that, while 'English village music of the 18th and 19th centuries was rarely out of touch with the presences of written music', it was still part of 'a true musical tradition'. Transcribers, including Hardy's father, seem to have made deliberate creative adaptations while copying.[36]

The band members were largely the more prosperous members of the working class, artisans and tradesmen, perhaps, as Vic Gammon suggests, because of the cost of instruments.[37] Typically, there would be from three to six of these, often violin or cello and one or more wind instruments such as clarionet, flute or serpent, though the Hardy family band was strings only. The most vital feature was a bass instrument, usually cello or bassoon.[38]

Opposition to these quires (a spelling often used now to differentiate them from the conventional idea of a church choir) reached a head in the 1830s through the influence of the Tractarian movement, as Gillian Warson explains.[39] By 1838, the choir led by William Gardiner's father in a dissenting congregation was already gone.[40] The Stinsford quire was to go in 1841. The reasons for the demise of such quires were political rather than musical, though the musical side was often used as a pretext. Nicholas Temperley argues that standards were variable, though they could be high (and the Hardy family band seems to have been an accomplished one.)[41] More positively, and from a less conventional perspective, Vic Gammon believes that 'the reformers constantly confused style and competence'. Hence, 'it is most likely that the hostile witnesses were generally correct about the style' but 'what they considered vices may have been virtues' and were certainly features of a consistent style of 'full-voiced heterophonic polyphony'.[42] On the one hand, Gardiner was at pains to validate the music socially by stressing the respectability of the performers and their middle-class connections. On the other, he was no admirer of traditional music or singing styles generally and part of him wanted to see it dead and buried: 'I would recommend country gentlemen to disband these rural musicians and set up a barrel organ, which requires no other performer than the sexton to turn it' (*Music & Friends*, **1**, 45, 389, **2**, 593). John Hullah's political (and personal?) interest masqueraded as moral indignation in 1853 when he argue that '*any* inconvenience, any sacrifice of mere musical effect, must be made rather than perpetuate the evils of the singing gallery.'[43] These evils boiled down to the singers not knowing their place. If they sang from the gallery they literally looked down on the rest of the congregation, and the clergyman. This appears as naked class conflict in the remarks of J. A. La Trobe in 1831 as he outlined the reformist vicar's problems:

They murmur their sullen insolence ... if they adopt no more offensive step, [they] desert him altogether, and the singing is in consequence laid aside. It moreover, not infrequently happens, that the low spirit of malignity which boils in the breasts of the common people when thwarted, cannot content itself with inert opposition, but bursts forth in secret or overt acts of annoyance. Not only are his ministrations deserted, but his property injured and his person insulted, by those who once ranked with him in the service of the sanctuary.[44]

In introducing the demise of the church band to his fiction, then, Hardy was picking up on a well-known debate, but from a fresh point of view, that of the performers. His family background determines the placing of his sympathies, even if he disguises them with a little quaint humour. His accounts of the band's music books and carols are straight descriptions of his own father's and grandfather's possessions and practices, even down to the carol numbering. Indeed the loss of the quire and the social impoverishment this implies are the real subject of *Under the Greenwood Tree*, as indicated by its subtitle, *The Mellstock Quire*. The quires he describes in the novel and stories have a typical social mix of members. As was usual, they are all male; the choir in *Two on a Tower*, with its two girls, was uncommon. There was a gender clash as well as a class clash in the replacement of the quire by music in the body of the church with female singers and perhaps a female musician (like Fancy Day). This empowerment of women was the flip-side of a substantial disempowerment of the male leaders of a community whose status was often gained through their band position. The importation of an expensive, dominant, even mechanical, instrument—piano, organ, harmonium, barrel organ—marked an access of control by those prosperous enough to provide it.[45]

The result was the loss of the joyous social harmony which the band represents for Hardy and the other fiction writers. Those mentioned had no orthodox Christian belief; for Hardy especially, the village quire also represents a religious confidence now unrecoverable. Both are depicted most fully in *Under the Greenwood Tree*. The texts and tunes mentioned there can be found in his father's or grandfather's books, except for the favourite number 78, 'Remember, O Thou Man', which is torn out, though there is a loose copy in the Thomas Hardy Memorial Collection. This carol, to be found in Thomas Ravenscroft's *Melismata* (1611), is slightly more admonitory than the rest, which concentrate with a cheerful certainty on the bond between God and Man celebrated at Christmas. A typical text is 'O What Unbounded Goodness, Lord', given here from the manuscript version:

O what unbounded goodness Lord
hast thou this morn Display'd

in Sending here the infant god
Who in a manger Laid.

With pure Delight our bosoms Glow
Our Infant Lord to See
And to the Courtly Stable Speed
With gifts for Christ and thee

O let us loudly now proclaim
Our Adoration here,
And henceforth Worship Well thy Son,
Our Lord and Saviour Dear.[46]

This assurance was a part of community life entered into (however partially) through the music of the villagers, however ordinary or (like Thomas Leaf) humanly inadequate they might be. Hardy has picked on a widespread feature of the disintegration of popular village culture and used it as a focus for fiction rather than just as a minor embellishment of his story.

Traditional Dance and Song

The non-verbal nature of the dance tunes allows for less subtlety of development in the context of fiction, though of course Hardy selects tunes which are highly appropriate to their occasions in both nature and name, such as 'Haste to the Wedding' to mark the marriage of Dick and Fancy and 'The Soldier's Joy' for Troy and Bathsheba.[47] It is the playing of 'Devil Among the Tailors' in church that leads to the downfall of the Longpuddle band.[48] The almost supernaturally seductive fiddler Mop Ollamoor wins Car'line Aspent's affections with 'The Fairy Dance' and 'My Fancy Lad'.[49]

On occasion Hardy uses the actual movements of a dance such as 'The Triumph' in *Under the Greenwood Tree* (66-69). There are instructions for this in the Album Book in the Dorset County Museum.[50] Shiner's not casting off would upset the whole movement of the dance and his assertion of independence of the demands of the dance is a piece of egotistic idiocy. It would leave the dancers numerically ill-assorted and in the wrong relative positions.

As far as the songs go, we need to consider not only what was sung but who was likely to sing it. Hardy's female characters are distinguished with particular niceness through his choice of the songs they sing, which often mark the slight elevation in social position that makes them seem unattainable to their worthier but lower-class suitors. As mentioned earlier, Hardy heard songs from local fieldwomen and from his mother. Pencil jottings in his copy of Hullah and in his own song collection, together with the very humble social circumstances of Mrs Hardy as a child, suggest that his mother's and the fieldwomen's repertoires were similar. But the socially ambitious Hardy did not want to put his own origins on the same level as those of agricultural labourers and the result of this is the calculated and deceptive ambiguity of his account of his mother in the *Life*. Thus, he describes her as 'a woman with an extraordinary store of local memories, reaching back to the days when the ancient ballads were everywhere heard at country feasts, in weaving shops, and at spinning-wheels' (321). He avoids saying that she sang them; instead, he selects as parts of her repertoire composed art songs like 'Isle of Beauty' or 'Why are you wandering here, I pray?' (14).[51] Songs like these also appeared on broadsides and song sheets and might well have been sung by ordinary village singers (though collectors tended to ignore pieces with a known composer). What is important here is that Hardy has chosen to mention *only* those that also formed part of a genteel repertoire, though this is not a feature of his depiction of the rural working-class in his fiction in the way that it is with Mitford. Instead, he uses the traditional pattern of the hero aspiring to a heroine who is his social superior.[52]

The conflict Hardy seems to have felt between cultural tradition and social aspiration is dramatized in the pattern of courtship so often noted in his novels. The 'fieldwoman' type is found in minor characters like Joan Durbeyfield, who picks up songs by ear with amazing rapidity from local residents or passing travellers (*Tess*, 45). (Joan might have found words on broadsides, but there was seldom any musical notation, and, if there was, it tended to be spurious.) But most of Hardy's heroines are at the level of aspirations to a pianoforte at least. As one rises up the social scale, reliance on oral tradition as a mode of learning decreases and reliance on written material increases. In *Under the Greenwood Tree*, for example, Fancy Day sings 'Why are you wandering here, I pray?' to Dick (146) but is too genteel to sing the kind of songs he does. (As Michael Millgate points out, Hardy's revisions to the text increased the social gap between Dick and Fancy.)[53]

Bathsheba's performance of 'The Banks of Allan Water' at the shearing supper in *Far From the Madding Crowd* is greeted with 'that buzz of pleasure which is the attar of applause' (179). This, however, is quite different from the 'silently appreciative gaze' that greets Coggan's performance a little earlier. What she sings is not a folk song, since it was composed by 'Monk' Lewis (1775-1818), but it does rely heavily on ballad situations and it was probably set to a ballad tune.[54] The verse sung by Bathsheba is entirely appropriate to her present situation: gaiety at being flattered by a soldier's winning tongue. What Hardy omits to quote, however, is more ominous. It is an exact description of Fanny Robin's fate; she is deserted by Troy and dies in winter, and at least partly because of the weather. The words of the song, however, specify only that the girl's sorrow is caused by the soldier's falsity—no mention is made of her pregnancy. This softening of the usual folk theme is a common feature of composed pieces with a traditional basis, and Hardy's choice of this song for Bathsheba is appropriate to her social status and also to the later attempt by Gabriel to conceal knowledge of Fanny's child from her.

Eustacia Vye in *The Return of the Native* is supposed to sing ballads on Sundays (93), but we never hear her do so; she is associated by Hardy with military music, and, in a strained and artificial comparison, with the 'march in "Athalie"' and 'the viola' (90). When Anne Garland affects indifference to the news of Bob Loveday's engagement in chapter 35 of *The Trumpet-Major* she sings 'Shall we go dance the round?' (288). Hardy found this song in Hullah, but although it is old—dating back to 1609 at least—it is an elegant little art song, not a folk song. Tess Durbeyfield is obviously the exceptional heroine/singer here. Hardy's breaking of his usual pattern of higher-placed heroine and lower-placed true lover is one indication of the new radicalism of *Tess*. Her songs will be discussed in more detail later.

It might be argued that Hardy's choice of songs for heroines is influenced not only by a desire for accuracy but also by a desire to enlist the reader's sympathetic recognition, for the split between lower-class and genteel culture was a widening one. Traditional folk material was part of the knowledge of a residual rural poor but increasingly separated from the knowledge of likely novel readers. In 1838, just before Hardy's birth, William Gardiner could repeat with some sympathy the claim that 'England has no national music; that it has neither poetry nor songs' but 'Scotland ... [has] ever been famous for ... songs,' yet Gardiner himself had heard traditional songs at harvest homes and singing sessions in public houses, which he had joined in with in his youth.[55] This obtuseness is linked to a patronizing refusal to acknowledge the merits of an alternative culture at one's doorstep, which was accompanied by a sentimental idealization of alternatives as long as they were comfortably distanced. This commonly meant Scotland. As we have already noted, Scottish songs are well represented in music collections of the mid-nineteenth century, while the common songs of servants and the urban or rural poor are not. On the other hand, the collections of Hammond and Gardiner, though they include many songs tinged by the conscious art of the composer, do not include comparable Scottish pieces.

It is not surprising, therefore, that Hardy had little use for Scottish songs in his creation of Wessex except in his treatment of Farfrae. Here his sources seem to have been literary and nonlocal, except for 'O Nannie', and one finds it difficult to imagine that song being widely sung by Wessex labourers, partly because of the range and elaboration of the tune, and partly because of the artificiality of the words. The version given as no. 136 in Hook's compilation has obviously not passed far through the process of oral diversification, though it has been Scotticized. Another of Farfrae's songs, 'It's Hame and it's Hame', is an anonymous Jacobite song. Even though Farfrae may wallow in imaginings of the 'noble martyrs, wha died for loyaltie,' their fate has nothing to do with his own nature or occupations.[56]

As Ian Gregor points out in the New Wessex edition of *The Mayor of Casterbridge*, Hardy is being ironic in making Farfrae sing 'The Lass of Gowrie' just as Lucetta appears in a 'braw new gown' (184). However, to say that it is a traditional Scottish ballad is misleading. Lady Nairne (if she was indeed the author) was working, like Burns, in a vein that was popular in Scotland in the late eighteenth and early nineteenth centuries. But the lighthearted, perfunctory tone of the wooing and the vocabulary of 'rosebud ting'd wi' morning show'r/Blooms fresh within the sunny bow'r' are of an order of conventionalization quite alien to the formulaic phrases of the Scottish narrative ballad.

The three Burns songs, on the other hand, are part of a tradition that Burns may in some measure be said to have created, by adapting (and often trivializing and sentimentalizing) images and situations from the traditional songs of the Scottish countryside. 'Auld Lang Syne' needs no comment, except to note that since the customers of the Three Mariners earnestly request Farfrae to sing it (83), this song at least is presumably already a recognized part of their own cultural knowledge. The adaptations of Burns's 'Bonny Peg' as sung by Farfrae (85, 119) suggest the beginnings of oral diffusion—though not in Wessex. The third Burns song is that requested by Lucetta when Farfrae is depressed by Henchard's antagonism to him (249). It is not, as the note in the New Wessex edition suggests, a variant of 'Bonnie Peg', but of 'Tibbie Towler', which Hardy could have found in Hullah (176-77). Lucetta is thinking of verses three and five:

> There's seven butt, and seven ben,
>   Seven in the pantry wi' her;
> Twenty head about the door,
>   There's one-and-forty wooin' at her ...
>
> She's got pendles in her lugs,
>   Cockle shells wad set her better;
> High-heel'd shoon and siller tags,
>   And a' the lads are wooing at her.

Since it is about a woman with a multiplicity of lovers Lucetta shows some obtuseness in requesting it. The song is comic, but represents Burns in a slightly caustic vein, castigating the value of money in attracting wooers— neither Henchard nor Farfrae is quite indifferent to Lucetta's wealth. The reference to the ballad and its 'owre mony' wooers is made specially pointed by the fact that Henchard arrives a few pages later to retrieve Lucetta's compromising letters and reads extracts from them to Farfrae (252-53).

But in spite of their individual appropriateness, the main point of Hardy's use of Scottish songs is to mark Farfrae out as an alien and perhaps to suggest the slightly superficial or *ersatz* quality of his feelings, which purport to be expressed in verse that depends on or parasitizes older and deeper traditions and that in any case is not an accurate expression of his own nature. The clientele of the Three Mariners notice this. If they receive him with applause and 'a deep silence which was even more eloquent than the applause,' some of them at least are also capable of the recognition, 'be dazed, if I loved my country half as well as the young feller do, I'd live by claning my neighbour's pigsties afore I'd go away!' (81, 82).

Farfrae's kind of music is set against Henchard's. He, though sensitive to all types, is characterized by his feeling for psalms. The grim, dark tones of the Old Testament, particularly those parts associated with Job and Cain, with which Hardy connects Henchard in order to give him the tragic stature of a man of ancient times left stranded by the tides of the present, are reinforced by the psalm Henchard forces the choir to sing in Chapter 33. Hardy emphatically quotes four verses of this to indicate the comprehensiveness of Henchard's bitterness towards Farfrae, and also as a foretaste of his own end, 'And the next age his hated name/Shall utterly deface.' (Given Hardy's predilection for quire music, there may be some nostalgic sense of a dying tradition here too.) The two men are linked by their sensitivity to song—Farfrae's rendering of 'Auld Lang Syne' in Chapter 38 almost deters Henchard from fighting him—but are distinguished by the types of song they choose.

If concentrating on Scotland was one way of distancing popular material, another was to reduce it from live performance to printed texts. These could be consumed by a readership that had no interest in the circumstances of their production. As far as the standard narrative ballads went, this was a process well advanced by the time Hardy wrote his novels, as we have already seen. Some of Hardy's allusions to ballads are essentially literary allusions for a literary audience. For example, the choice of 'The Boy and the Mantle' as a song in Mrs. Durbeyfield's repertoire seems an odd one. This 'ballad of the mystic robe "That never would become that wife/That had once done amiss"' (*Tess*, 234) is an Arthurian story of probable minstrel origin that does not seem to have gained oral currency, and the two extra verses Hardy quoted to make his point clear in the serial version of *Tess* would sound improbable on her lips:

> One while was it gule;
>   Another while was it green;
> Another while was it plaided;
>   Ill it did her beseem.

Another while was it black,
    And bore the worst hue.
'By my troth,' quoth King Arthur,
    'I think thou be not true!'[57]

However, the choice is, thematically, extremely appropriate. Tess is reminded of the words by trying on Angel's gift of wedding clothes and fancying they might betray her by changing colour, as the mysterious gift of the robe found out the ladies of King Arthur's court. In the ballad all ends well for Craddocke's wife (who is compared most favourably with the other ladies) because when the robe begins to crinkle at the hem she confesses to her one sexual misdemeanour—having kissed her husband before they were married. Tess's story ends as it does because she confesses too late; she is not, like Craddocke's lady, instantaneously candid when the need arises. On the other hand, like the lady, Tess is essentially a pure woman in spite of the misdemeanour. The possible changing of the colour of the robe represents the fluctuations of opinion in the eyes of the world as it discovers outward facts about a woman's sexual experience without considering the nature of her inner response and responsibility. Tess's mother could sing this song 'blithely and ... archly,' but Tess's response to the basic situation it deals with, though in a far different world, involves a perception of tragedy not found in this particular ballad.

Hardy's text of 'Queen Eleanor's Confession' (sung by Granfer Cantle in *The Return of the Native*, 46) is so close to that of Percy that it seems most likely that this was his source, especially since Hammond did not record any version and it does not seem to have been extant in English tradition then. However, Hardy has inserted stress marks that reproduce the strong rhythmic emphasis of a country singer. Hardy's use of it has a three-fold purpose: to suggest that Granfer Cantle is a silly old codger whose love of showing off exceeds his capacity to impress; to make the point obliquely through the caustic remarks of the rustics that he is in fact the superannuated representative of a type rapidly becoming extinct, and that insofar as he is typical this loss is in some ways to be regretted; and to reflect proleptically, through a disinterested and ironically inappropriate medium, on the main plot situation, the love triangle between Wildeve, Eustacia, and Clym. Cantle has a real choric function here.

The point of the ballad is that Queen Eleanor has been seduced before her marriage to King Henry by the Earl Marshall. This she confesses to them when they visit her disguised as friars. She also reveals that one of her two sons is the king's and one the Earl Marshall's. Understandably, the king is less than pleased, and only an earlier promise cleverly extorted by the Earl Marshall prevents his execution. Now confession is precisely what Eustacia is bad at, and she not unnaturally fears Clym's wrath, though he, as Hardy insists, is a modern type and hence unlikely to take the drastic courses of action adopted by ballad figures. No mother figure is present in the ballad, the main situation of which allows Hardy one more subtle way of hinting what he could not state openly—that Eustacia had been Wildeve's mistress before her marriage.

Such a technique of oblique reference is common enough in Victorian literature. It was especially useful in dealing with taboo subjects like sexual behaviour. However, allusion to ballads is not common; the alternative culture referred to is often classical or historical, as we have seen with Thackeray. It was often useful to be able to have several layers of reference in a novel so that only those more educated and less vulnerable readers (i.e. upper- and middle-class classically educated men) would understand. Hardy's sense of cultural inferiority led him to overdo general allusions; as Michael Wheeler points out, he collected many ready for *The Return of the Native* and stuffed them in regardless of effect (*Art of Allusion*, 137). His use of classical allusion in a sexual context is limited but it does occur, for example, in the 'Saturday Night in Arcady' sequence included in later versions of Chapter 10 of *Tess*, where he writes of 'Lotis attempting to elude Priapus and always failing' (91) when what he is talking about is the sexual pairings that take place at a Trantridge village dance. But because of his social origins Hardy was both predisposed toward and had access to alternative sources of allusion, some of which were 'below' rather than beyond the cultural aspirations of his readers.

Folk songs were growing less and less familiar to Hardy's likely audiences. The 'ancient ballads' were no longer 'everywhere heard', though versions of their words (often Scottish or Scotticized) might be available to mildly scholarly readers. Many songs were given a wider currency through printed collections, but this was a comparatively new source. It is not until the 1840s that we find many printed collections of songs with music at a reasonable price, in publications like *Davidson's Universal Melodist* (1847). An examination of the *Universal Melodist* confirms Hardy's accuracy in selecting popular songs with a wide social currency when reference to these was appropriate. It includes 'In the Downhills of Life', 'O Nanny', 'O Waly, Waly', 'The Banks of Allan Water', 'Auld Lang Syne', 'Such a Beauty I Did Grow' and 'The Lass of Gowrie'. The high proportion of Scottish or supposedly Scottish songs is interesting. What is even more interesting is what the *Universal Melodist* does not include—the older songs typical of established rural tradition. Except for a few songs like 'The Seeds of Love', which were anthologized in a few collections, the largely middle-class readership that acquired its music in this way would have had no means of knowing many of the songs Hardy mentions without access to oral tradition. This is particularly true of the lyrical pieces rather than the ballads. By 1866 it still seemed a novel venture for John Hullah to popularize such material, and even he thought that Chappell had included in

Popular Music of the Olden Time 'the majority of those English songs and tunes ... which are still current and popular' (Preface). This was not the case. His article in *Macmillan's Magazine* **21** (1869-70) lists as 'popular songs' ones mentioned by Dickens and Hardy (e.g. 'Should he Upbraid', 'O Nanny', 'I'd be a Butterfly', 'O No, We Never Mention Her'), but not folk songs. Outside the tradition most of them remained at best scholars' material until the first decade of this century, the era of Cecil Sharp and (heavily bowdlerized) folk songs for schools. Even then their appearance was much mediated in the interests of a dominant middle class, as Dave Harker has shown.[58] This has, of course, important bearings on the way in which we can read Hardy's references. He seems to be trying to have his cake and eat it, to assert the value and integrity of traditional culture by including references to it in a way less mediated than that used by other novelists, but leaving it sufficiently marginalized to reduce its problematizing capacity to manageable proportions.

Michael Millgate assumes, no doubt correctly, that 'Hardy must have expected some at least of his readers to know' that the ballad Shiner sings in Fancy's presence was a coarse one (*Thomas Hardy*, 47). Yet how many of his readers would that 'some' consist of? Such a question is, finally, unanswerable, yet it is reasonable to suppose also that many of his readers could be expected *not* to know what he was referring to. The way in which Hardy exploits the possibilities of both knowledge and ignorance, the way in which his selection of appropriate songs is far more copious and far more accurate than that of any other regional novelist, and yet also makes concessions to the myth of an unproblematic pastoral—these hint at a radical ambivalence in Hardy towards the fruits of his traditional heritage, an ambivalence that needs to be examined in more detail.

An interesting point that arises from a study of the narrative ballads Hardy uses is that, contrary to expectation, he does not refer unequivocally in his creative prose or verse to any ballad of any antiquity that is in fact fully tragic. We know Hardy knew plenty at first hand; his own collection contains several, including 'Henry Martin' and a version of 'Polly Vaughan', both also collected by Hammond, who found numerous standard tragic ballads current in Dorset even in the early years of this century. The critical commonplace that Hardy's work is much influenced in tone and structure by the traditional ballads heard in his youth can certainly be supported by such evidence. Yet the ballads he referred to specifically were not tragic. The only exception to this is the (ironically) 'cheerful ballad about a murderer' sung in Chapter 17 of *Tess* to make the cows give down their milk (138). This is grim enough, and it has an obvious relevance to the plot insofar as it tells of a lover who murders his partner and is executed. However, this is the only example and it seems to be a comparatively late (eighteenth-century) composition on a common theme.[59]

Much of the world of the earlier ballads is not of much use to Hardy. However grim his world may be, his infanticides are less prominent than in the world of the earlier ballads (except in *Jude the Obscure*, which is not comparable—see below), his 'suicides' often more the result of a continued death wish than of sudden passion, his murders few. Nor does his world consist of fratricide and incest. However, in some areas both ballads and songs did allow him to refer to kinds of experience that would not bear open discussion before a Victorian public.

The frank folk song acceptance of human passion and its consequences was something Hardy did find inspiring. His own collection contains snippets that he might well have put to use but never did, such as 'Miller Brice's song' about going to the green grove on the pretext of listening to the nightingale (D556 and D678 are other versions of this well-known song, 'The Sweet Nightingale'). The 'ballad about the maid who went to the merry green wood and came back a changed state' in *Tess* (120) need not be tragic. Indeed, since the girls who sing it are sympathetic to Tess while they tease her, it probably is not.[60] Hardy only wants to use the widespread metaphor that associates the green of natural growth with human fertility; going to the green wood (like getting a green gown in the song both Barrett and Hardy knew) is a standard traditional way of suggesting the loss of virginity. This is something that these girls accept much more readily and naturally than Tess does. The gap between them and their mothers seems much less wide than the two hundred years that according to Hardy lie between Tess and her own mother in terms of experience; *why* is another question.

If, then, Hardy did not use allusion to traditional material to create an atmosphere of gloom and despondency, what sorts of other uses did he put the material to? It is now worth looking at his uses of local ballads and songs in specific novels.

Desperate Remedies, his first published novel (1871), was written while he was still smarting under the rejection of *The Poor Man and the Lady*, with the 'socialistic, not to say revolutionary' tendency of its writing (*Life*, 61). Although he took to heart Meredith's advice to write a quite different sort of novel, his resentment and iconoclasm managed to sneak through in the use of a couple of songs. In Chapter 17 the postman sings a drinking song of which Hardy quotes the one and only rebellious verse, including the wish 'The Lord make churches and chapels to fall/And there'll be work for tradesmen all.'[61] This seems not only a wry comment on church restoration at the time, as the New Wessex appendix suggests, but also a comment on the state of employment (compare Jude's situation twenty years later) and the expression of a certain anti-clericalism which may have been part of the feeling Hardy had tried to bring out in his rejected novel. This possibility appears in this verse, though not the substance of the song, which is a jolly and rather inconsequential celebration of drink.

Earlier, he had slyly slipped in a reference that his audience would have found quite unacceptable had they known the context. Clerk Crickett has been caustically criticising Miss Aldclyffe and Cytherea Graye with Farmer Springrove and some lesser locals. To illustrate his point that Cytherea displays herself although she has no worldly goods, he quotes

> The chimney-sweeper's daughter Sue,
>   As I have heard declare, O,
> Although she's neither sock nor shoe
>   Will curl and deck her hair, O. (149)

This undercuts the remonstrance of the chivalrous Springrove 'let the maid be a maid while she is a maid' since the full broadside text makes it clear that the hair referred to is not that of the head and that the curling of it is a venereal rather than a cosmetic exercise.[62]

The songs in *Under the Greenwood Tree* are used to characterize Fancy's two rustic lovers. When Dick and Shiner vie with each other over her at the honey-taking, Shiner sings 'King Arthur he had three sons' to demonstrate his command of the situation (151). One hopes that in Fancy's presence Shiner did not sing the words that Hardy himself recorded in September 1889 (*Letters*, **1**, 198):

> King Arthur he had three sons,
> Big rogues as ever did swing,
> He had three sons of [by] wh------s
> And he kicked them all three out-of-doors
> Because they could not sing

but something more like the words of Hammond's D117:

> So in old K. Henery's days,
> And a good old king was he,
> And the old sons of old [sic] they were turnèd out of doors
> Because they could not sing.

However, Hardy's greater familiarity with it makes the first version more likely; he says he thinks the song is only transmitted orally (199). Dick has come to ask for Fancy's hand, but her father wants her to wait for a gentleman. Shiner is proving that, even if better qualified in worldly terms, he is no gentleman, as Michael Millgate points out (*Thomas Hardy*, 47).

It is also worth noting the purely comic treatment of this scene. In a similiar situation in *The Woodlanders* (to be discussed later) the folk song used as a reminder of the honest forthrightness of traditional expression is a source of real social embarrassment. Dick, however, is turned into a sort of Arcadian woodlander on the very first page through the decorative pastoral of the sheep-shearing song he sings. Hammond collected three songs like this; if we examine D358 we can see a sweetly pastoral opening:

> violets}
> Here's the rosebud in June, the sweet meadows} in bloom
> And the birds singing gaily on every green bough
> The pink and the lily and the daffy down dilly
> To adorn and perfume the sweet meadows in June
>   Whilst out o' the plough the fat oxen go slow
>   And the lads and the lasses a-sheep-shearing go.

But this is followed by emphasis on 'the cleanly milk pail ... full of brown ale' and

> Now the shepherds have sheared all their jolly jolly sheep
> What joy can be greater than to talk of the increase?
> Here's the ewes and the lambs, the hogs and the rams
> The fat wethers too, they'll make a fine show.

Hardy has pruned away the more solidly practical emphasis on work, drink, and stock-breeding.

The slight romanticizing of the hero is a process found also in *Far From the Madding Crowd*, another novel with a title taken from the literary pastoral. For all its near-tragic passions, for all its human clashes with a threatening natural world and the fate behind it, this novel also tries to convey the picture of a rural life that is part of a satisfying cycle of seasonal fertility. Consequently it contains quotations from more traditional English folk songs than any other of Hardy's novels. All the rustics seem to sing, from the ploughboy, who is as natural a part of the sound landscape as the sparrows, finches, squirrels and robins, to Gabriel, who plays lighthearted songs of multiple courtship like 'Dame Durden' (97). The song that Jan Coggan sings in his cups when he should be delivering poor Fanny's corpse is a good example of the way in which traditional singers will unselfconsciously adopt any song they happen to care for. This a version of 'The Old Man's Song', an early music-hall piece that was widespread in spite of its rather affected words, and becoming subject to variation through oral transmission. Hardy may have pared away the more literary-sounding parts; the corresponding verse of the version Hammond collected in Blandford ends with words nearly identical to those Hardy quotes, but begins

> From the bleak northern blast may my cot be completely
> Secured by a neighbouring hill,
> And at night may repose steal upon me more sweetly
> By the sound of a murmuring rill.[63]

For both Jan Coggan and Joseph Poorgrass, song is a natural mode of expression even when the singer is completely incompetent. At the shearing supper in Chapter 23 Jan sings the fragment 'I've lost my love and I care not' 'without reference to listeners' (176). Joseph is persuaded to render one of the most beautiful of all lyrics of deserted love, 'I Sowed the Seeds of Love'. Chappell says in *Popular Music of the Olden Time* that this, 'Cupid's Garden' (discussed below), and 'Early One Morning' are 'three of the most popular songs among the servant-maids of the present generation' (735). (This social placing of the song hardly makes it more likely that middle-class young ladies would wish to learn it.) Hammond, who noted it five times, thought it sufficiently popular not to record the words on each occasion, but here is part of D485:

> I sowed the seeds of Love
> And I sowed them in the Spring,
> And I gathered it up in the morning so soon,
> While the small birds sweetly did sing, [bis].
>
> My garden was planted well
> With flowers everywhere,
> But I have not the liberty to choose it for myself,
> Oh! the flower that I love best.
>
> My gardener was standing by
> And I asked him to choose for me,
> He chose me the violet, the lily and the pink,
> But I refused all three.
>
> The violet I did not like
> Because it fades so soon,
> The lily and the pink I really overlooked,
> And I vowed I'd stay till June.
>
> In June there's a red rosebud
> And that's the flower for me,
> And I've oftentimes plucked at the red rose-bush,

Till I gained the willow-tree. ...

Come all you false young men
Don't leave me here to repine,
For the grass that be often trampled underfoot,
Give it time it will rise up again.

Here we can see the metaphors of sowing the seed and of the rose for sexual experience, and that of the willow as a symbol for deserted love.[64] The last line offers us an image of the natural regeneration of human emotion even after the most distressing of experiences (this song is an exact model of what Tess goes through).   Hardy is very daring in allowing Poorgrass to sing it; he is not mocking Poorgrass for trying, and he is certainly not trying to ridicule the song itself, which is thematically appropriate to *Far From the Madding Crowd* in several ways.   Part of the strength of the image of timeless pastoral offered (though not unproblematically) in the novel is that even the Poorgrasses accept this level of poetic expression as normal.   Hardy knows this but perhaps lacks the final courage to make the claim stronger by open quotation, and instead throws a comic cast over the incident.

He represents some features of the workers' culture accurately, such as the conventional (and probably false) introduction to Poorgrass's first song, 'a poor plain ballet of my own composure', and the expectation that everyone is a performer.   On the other hand, he distances himself as a narrator and us as readers by criticism of the music ('the tune consisted of the key-note and another'), the rendering, and the length ('a ballad as inclusive and interminable...').   He appeals to an informed classicism in the reader, comparing Smallbury's piece to 'that with which the worthy toper Old Silenus amused on a similar occasion the swains Chromis and Mnasylus, and other jolly dogs of his day'.   Chromis and Mnasylus are not as obscure as they appear, since they occur in Virgil's Sixth Eclogue, but their names seem deliberately chosen to sound as alien as possible.   Hardy's allusion cuts both ways.   If these latter-day shepherds are to be compared with Virgil's, their tradition is granted the worth and authenticity usually associated with classical authority.   However, Hardy undercuts this with the ironic disparity between reference and vocabulary selection, pastoral 'swains' and masculine dismissive slang, 'old toper' and 'other jolly dogs'.

Hardy was gradually to move away from this rather nervous condescension, but Granfer Cantle in *The Return of the Native* is treated in a similar comic vein, minus the classical allusion; he can sing ''Twas Down in Cupid's Gardens', which uses the same imagery.   (Hammond collected this as D370 and if we compare the Hammond tune with no. 60 in Hook's compilation there are only tiny differences, though the two are separated by at least eighty years.)   The irrepressible Granfer's repertoire includes not only love songs like this and 'The Foggy Dew' and ballads like those already discussed but standard drinking songs like 'The Barley Mow' (399):

> Here's a good health to the barley mow
> The nipperkin and the brown bowl. (D475)

In the ignorant, superstitious, backward but resilient life of the Heath, the life of song is not so moribund as its chief representative would suggest. Even little Johnny Nunsuch sings 'about a sailor-boy and a fair one, and bright gold in store.'[65] The way in which Clym's life is detached from that of the Heath by his experience of the world, even when he seems closest to it, is best illustrated by the fact that when he is furze-cutting he sings a song from an alien genre (comic opera) and even in an alien tongue, 'Le point du jour' (263).

In *The Woodlanders* the same natural world of song, a world that accepts ungrudgingly characters like the Cantles, has become an embarrassment and a threat to the genteel moneyed world that is eventually to destroy it. When Giles's guests sing

> said she,
> "A maid again I never shall be,
> Till apples grow on an orange tree!"

Melbury's hesitations are over. He puts particular stress on the unsuitability of the song for the new type of propriety Grace represents: 'for us old folk it didn't matter; but for Grace—Giles should have known better' (105). What Cawtree and the hollow turner are singing is the standard form of folk lyric lament for lost virginity. It is a floater, that is, a formulaic expression for a particular situation found in a wide range of songs (e.g. D767). It is not, of course, in the least indecent, merely direct; Hardy is showing up the desperate sensitivity of the socially ambitious Melbury. Yet even in a serious collection of folk songs published in 1891 Frank Kidson felt unable to mention the concept of lost maidenhood in this way and bowdlerized the offending lines.[66] The struggle between natural impulse and stringent middle-class morality is a major theme of the novel; Hardy stresses the strains imposed by the latter. He does not, however, advocate complete surrender to the former. Suke Damson's impulsive sexuality (and lack of honesty about it) sours her marriage to Tim Tangs. Hardy gives us evidence as to her nature and to what happens between her and Fitzpiers in her musical invitation to him in Chapter 20 (172). 'The Foggy Dew' was what Granfer Cantle proposed as a serenade for the newly married Venns (*RN*, 399). The exact significance of the 'foggy dew' itself has been much debated, but certainly coming in from it involves the loss of virginity.[67] In the standard version of the song, as found in D406, it is the girl who seduces the young man, and the result is as in *The Woodlanders:*

> In the first part of the night we did both sport and play,
> And in the latter part of the night she slept in my arms till day.

Such sexual spontaneity causes awkward problems in human relationships, it is true, but its naturalness is some guarantee of its worth. This is especially so when it occurs in conjunction with a morally sensitive and responsible character like Tess, the 'pure woman' whom Hardy had originally intended to be seduced instead of possibly raped.[68] Hardy attempts to distil the quintessence of Tess's pastoral charm by quoting extensively one of the songs that attracted Angel:

> Arise, arise, arise!
> And pick your love a posy,
> All o' the sweetest flowers
> That in the garden grow.
> The turtle doves and sma' birds
> In every bough a-building,
> So early in the May-time
> At the break o' the day!   (365-66)

This is a collation of lines from a semi-complete version of a song that Hardy himself collected as an 'Old Song sung at Melbury Osmond about 1820' and annotated with his mother's initials. Hammond also collected a variant that ends with a poignant suggestion of the lovers' parting not found in Hardy's version (D779). What we do find in Hardy's original is the conclusion

> So then he played it over
> All on the pipes of ivory
> So early in the morning
> At the break of the day.

Hardy has excised this delicate euphemism for lovemaking (which is also found in other versions collected elsewhere).[69] Here he wants nothing but the purest pastoral pathos. He was, however, probably safe enough. Angel would presumably not have liked the song if he had understood the reference, and many of Hardy's audience would not have done so either. Hardy seems to have felt it safe to include the flower-gathering symbolism discussed under 'The Seeds of Love', which has the same sort of underlying significance in both 'high' and 'low' culture. It would not be necessary for the audience to respond consciously for such imagery to affect them, as the success of poems like Tennyson's *Maud* indicates. Hardy is engaged in a delicate balancing act between acceptable pastoral and realism. Another example would be the mention of Mrs. Durbeyfield's 'The Spotted Cow', which turns on the pretext of a lover going to the green grove to look for a girl's lost cow (44). Needless to say, the cow is soon forgotten, though the title might lull Hardy's readers into a false sense of security.

Other tunes Angel liked were the ubiquitous ''Twas Down in Cupid's Garden' and 'I Have Parks, I Have Hounds.' The first, as copied by Hardy from Hullah, begins

> 'Twas down in Cupid's Garden
>   For pleasure I did go
> To see the fairest flowers
>   That in that garden grow
> The first, it was the jessamine,
>   The lily, pink and rose ...

The second is a version of 'The Farmer's Toast', which Gardiner found in Portsmouth (H912). It is an idealized celebration of agricultural prosperity:

> I have lawns, I have bowers, I have fruits, I have flowers,
> The lark is my daily alarmer,
> So, my jolly boys, now that follows the plough
> Drink health and success to the farmer.

But Angel is a selective critic; he likes the songs that Tess sings to put forward this sort of image and does not care for the pieces of lighthearted nonsense that are also part of her repertoire, and part of her simplicity. From the critical point of view we can agree with him to some extent, but not humanly. 'The Tailor's Breeches' is just a farcical story about a tailor that was collected by Hammond in two versions, one from Robert Barrett (D238): a tailor proposes to dance in the clothes of a young woman who then runs off with his trousers and valuables. 'Such a Beauty I Did Grow' is an artistically worthless ditty popular on broadsides which Hardy would have known from his father's manuscript book (80-81; see *Tess*, 365). It was certainly found in local tradition, for Hammond recorded a rather different version from Wiltshire (Wr308). The family version begins

> When I was a little boy Some twenty years ago
> I was the pride of Mammy's heart she made me quite a Show
> Such a Beauty I ded grow ded grow ded grow Such a Beauty
>   I ded grow

Straight hair I had and goggle eyes with Such a roguish leer
A broad flat nose turnd up—beside a mouth from Ear to Ear ...

Ruth A. Firor points out that many of the songs Hardy uses are 'degenerate' broadsides, and seems to have a prejudice against both broadsides and oral tradition, as producing crudely unsatisfactory versions of ancient material. Yet she is quite wrong to suggest that we don't hear the later 'ballads' 'on Tess's lips.'[70] We do, insofar as we 'hear' any except for 'The Break of the Day.' The image Firor tries to present of Tess is Angel's image, not Hardy's. Songs like these were alive in the Dorset of Hardy's early years (as Firor points out) and an unsophisticated enjoyment of simple nonsense is part of Tess's rustic character, just as much as her ability to convey artless and natural sexuality through the more lyrical songs. Hardy knows well enough, and in this late novel shows, that Tess's cultural roots are not all amenable to genteel sentimentalization.

Some of Hardy's works have been conspicuous by their absence from this discussion of folk song and there is good reason for this. All the Novels of Character and Environment except *Jude the Obscure* use folk song references; none of the Romances and Fantasies or Novels of Ingenuity does so with any great significance after *Desperate Remedies*. Greatness in Hardy's fiction up to *Jude* largely coincides with the thematic use of the songs that conjured up for him the stable possibilities of a rural environment he half remembered, half created. The great condemnation of the world of *Jude* is that it has no spontaneous song in it. Jude suggests that the creed he has just recited might just as well have been 'The Ratcatcher's Daughter' (143), a music-hall song written by E. Bradley and first published in 1854.[71] Jude's disgust at this sort of harmless production is of a piece with Hardy's. It is not true, as Joan Grundy suggests, that Hardy's rustics are all marked out by their love of music (*Hardy and the Sister Arts*, 137). It is difficult to imagine Widow Edlin giving a catchy rendering of 'The Spotted Cow', yet she would be older than Mrs. Durbeyfield. As Hardy became more and more interested in the social and economic exploitation of the ordinary man he was less and less able either to create what sometimes looks like a separable chorus of quaint, lovable rustics or to allow his main characters to escape into a world that is less and less that of the present. As he develops as a novelist in the Novels of Character and Environment, his settings creep nearer and nearer in both time and feeling to contemporary life. By the time he was writing *Jude* his concern with the injustices of the present made him abandon, however, reluctantly, the world that was two hundred years (as he saw it) behind even Tess. Indeed, he wrote his farewell to that world in Chapter 2 of *Jude*, when he noted that every field had really a rich texture of human associations but that this tradition was simply not available to the young Jude (38-39). Jude's deracination has its cultural aspect as well.

However, it must be said in conclusion that Hardy's feelings about rendering the culture of his boyhood were deeply ambivalent. What he wanted to say about it in his novels could not be separated from the implications his knowledge and sympathy had for his stance as novelist and as aspirant to adoption by the dominant culture of his day. His prentice work *The Poor Man and the Lady* (which Hardy completed in 1868) was supposedly by the Poor Man, 'the tendency of the writing being socialistic, not to say revolutionary.' Its rejection by Meredith and by Macmillan made it clear that this was not the way even to publication, let alone success, though Macmillan praised the description of country life among working men as 'admirable, and ... palpably truthful.'[72] This note was continued by reviewers of the early published novels, who made it clear that picturesqueness was saleable, but anger was not.[73] Hardy was undoubtedly influenced by such views, writing to Macmillan on 17 August 1871 to say that 'upon the whole a pastoral story would be the *safest* venture' (*Letters*, **1**, 12). On the other hand, he retained an impulse to see justice done by his workfolk, expressing a hope for the illustrations to *Far From the Madding Crowd* 'that the rustics, although *quaint*, may be made to appear *intelligent, & not boorish* at all' (*Letters*, **1**, 25). Reviewers, especially in the *Athenaeum*, palpably resisted this enterprise. For example, one fairly favourable review objected that the language of *Far From the Madding Crowd* was not 'possible from the illiterate clods whom he describes' (*Critical Heritage*, 19).

With friends like these Hardy had no need to seek for enemies. His essay 'The Dorsetshire Labourer' (1883) adopts familiar subterfuges to mediate his ploughman's opinions. He cites the radical voice of one dead long enough to be respectably literary: 'in times of special ... stress the "Complaint of Piers the Ploughman" is still echoed in his heart.' Rebellion is privatized, confined 'in his heart'; no hint is given here of any potential for common action.[74] The records of social trivia in the *Life* and his attempts to raise his family's status suggest that Hardy had internalized many of the values of his urban middle-class audience. He was anxious about undermining the system he had fought hard to join. But he never fully capitulated. 'The Dorsetshire Labourer' treats Joseph Arch sympathetically. Dealing with the complaint that country folk are not what they used to be, Hardy says sharply, 'it is too much to expect them to remain stagnant and old-fashioned for the pleasure of romantic spectators' (*Personal Writings*, 181). It is true that he partly betrays the culture he celebrates by the conventions of his mediation, but that betrayal is only partial. Much of his allusion contains subversive messages about class as well as about sex.

Though he is selective about what he chooses to represent that culture, he is too honest and too indebted to it to subdue and trivialize it irredeemably. We cannot know whether the ironies implicit in his choice of texts that could not be fully quoted were intentional, but if they were not their appropriateness is extraordinary. At any rate, they produced two centrally important successes for his art: a thorough and intimate record of at least a section of the ordinary man's rural culture, and the integration of references to that culture into patterns of significance central to the novels. These claims could not be made of any other major nineteenth-century English novelist. However, the reader Hardy implies through his folksong allusions was certainly not among the contemporaries who reviewed his work. Paradoxically, the informed modern reader is probably in a better position to appreciate Hardy's meticulous system of covert allusion than his original audience, although the life he represented still existed in their day. I think this is an irony Hardy would have appreciated.

Endnotes

1.   Florence Emily Hardy, *The Life of Thomas Hardy 1840-1928* (1962), 23; hereafter cited as *Life*.

2.   J. Vera Mardon, *Thomas Hardy as a Musician*, Hardy Monograph series, no. **15**, (1964), 8-12, 20-21.

3.   *Life*, 22, 15.

4.   For an example of the first type, see F. B. Pinion, *A Hardy Companion: A Guide to the Works of Thomas Hardy and their Background* (1968), 187-92, 205-06; for the second, see Joan Grundy, *Hardy and the Sister Arts* (1979), 134-76; for the third, see Thom Gunn, 'Hardy and the Ballads', *Agenda* **10:2-3** (1972), 42.

5.   Possession of family manuscript books by village musicians like the Hardys or John Clare was not uncommon. Obviously, this implies a degree of musical literacy. Roger Elbourne's *Music and Tradition in Early Industrial Lancashire 1780-1840* (1980) provides provocative and well documented discussion of the vexed topic of traditionality: for evidence of the performance of art music (e.g. by the father of the poet Samuel Bamford), see 34-36. See also A. L. Lloyd, *Folk Song in England* (1975) 20-21, for a general discussion.

6.   E.g., Douglas Brown, *Thomas Hardy* (1961), 109-12, 153-59; Samuel Hynes, *The Pattern of Hardy's Poetry* (1961), 80-83; J. R. Brooks, *Thomas Hardy: The Poetic Structure* (1971), 119-21; Donald Davidson, 'The Traditional Basis of Thomas Hardy's Fiction', in *Hardy: A Collection of Critical Essays*, ed. Albert J. Guerard (1963), 10-23; and Gunn, 'Hardy and the Ballads', 19-46.

7.   F. J. Child, ed., *The English and Scottish Popular Ballads*, 5 vols. (1882-98). Short references in the text prefaced by 'C' give the number of the piece in this collection.

8.   'Francis James Child and the "Ballad Consensus"', *Folk Music Journal*, **4:2** (1981), 163. Harker quotes and discusses the examples from Child used in this paragraph and provides a more detailed discussion of Child's limitations. See also his *Fakesong*, Chapters 5 and 6.

9.   For texts and tunes, see J. Hullah, *The Song Book* (1866), 220-21; Percy's *Reliques* (1857 edition; see note 13), xxxi; J. Hogg (ed.), *Jacobite Relics*, **1**, 134-35; W. Mitchison, *Hand-Book of the Songs of Scotland*, 114; Hullah, 174-75; Dick, *Songs*, 23; Hullah, 176-77.

10.   Thomas Hardy, *The Complete Poems*, ed. James Gibson (1981) 456, 797. Some of these titles belong both to a folk song and to one or more art songs.

11. *The Dynasts: An Epic Drama*, ed. Harold Orel (1978), 289. The first two ballads are discussed in context below. See *Tess of the d'Urbervilles* (hereafter *Tess*), 234; *The Return of the Native* (*RN*), 46, 54; and *Life*, 20, 'The Harvest Supper', *Poems*, 778. All page references to Hardy's novels are to the New Wessex edition, General Editor P. N. Furbank (1972-82).

12. *The Ballad Minstrelsy of Scotland*, no editor (Glasgow: Maurice Ogle and Co., 2nd ed., n.d.). Inscribed 'Sgt. Major ... McKay ... Jamaica 1880.' Pencil note states that the book was later published by Alexander Gardner, Paisley and Paternoster Square. There is a London edition of 1893. In a letter to J. J. Foster (?) of 1 September 1889, Hardy mentions the work of Child, first published 1857-59, and extensively revised 1882-98 (*The Collected Letters of Thomas Hardy*, ed. Richard Little Purdy and Michael Millgate, 7 vols. [1978], **1**, 198-99; hereafter cited as *Letters*). Child had republished as far as no. 188 by 1889.

13. *Reliques*, ed. Rev. R. A. Willmott, London: Routledge (1857); *The Song Book*, London (1866). For this chapter only, Percy references will be to this edition.

14. *Tess*, 234; 'The Boy and the Mantle', *Reliques*, 377-82.

15. *The Graphic*, 3 October 1891, 391.

16. I am indebted to the Trustees of the Thomas Hardy Memorial Collection in the Dorset County Museum for permission to consult material in their custody over the past eighteen years. Readers should note, however, that the Album Book is currently unavailable for consultation. For details of Hardy's assistance in local productions, see E. J. Stevens, *Hardy as I Knew Him*, Hardy Monograph series no. **61** (1969).

17   See Hullah, *Song Book*, 84-85, for the song beginning 'As down in the meadows.' According to Chappell, this was used in *Polly* in 1729 (*Popular Music*, **2**, 648). It is to be found in several collections and on many broadsides.

18. These will be referred to as TH 1, TH 2 and Hook. Apart from these, Hardy also owned an early printed music book of tunes (1793-94) and a fragmentary carol book. All these are now available on microfilm, together with other material from the collection (Wakefield: EP Microform Ltd., 1975), film no. 96939, reel 10.

19. I am indebted to Mr. H. E. F. Lock for permission to make use of this collection.

20. Some of the 'songs' are in tune form only. For a technical examination of the music I must thank Mr. A. D. Townsend, co-producer with me of a long-playing record entitled *The Mellstock Quire* (1980) which presents music and song of various kinds associated with Hardy.

21. *Life*, 14.

22. See Percy, *Reliques*, ed. H. B. Wheatley (1876), lxxii; the 1857 edition is less clear— 'Scotch' songs were an English fashion. Tune only, Hook no. 82; words, Hook no. 136.

23. Information about the tune from A. D. Townsend, *pers. comm.* The song text is in TH 1, secular songs end, 16.

24. In the Thomas Hardy Memorial Collection in the Dorset County Museum, and reproduced by permission as an Appendix to this volume. One piece is a verse on tobacco that is obviously not a song, but another item is arguably a mixture of three different songs.

25. *English Folk Song: Some Conclusions*, 3rd edn (1954), 119.

26. Most extensively in four volumes edited by Frank Purslow: *Marrowbones* (1965), *The Wanton Seed* (1969), *The Constant Lovers* (1972), and *The Foggy Dew* (1974). See also James Reeves, *The Everlasting Circle* (1960). Although my own work has been conducted independently of it, R. J. Elliott's unpublished B. Litt. thesis 'Thomas Hardy

and the Ballad' (Oxford, 1974) also discusses Hardy's collection and some parallels with H. D. Hammond. M. Grosvenor Myer's 'Folksong in Thomas Hardy' (*Folk Review* **2:2** [1972], 6) is suggestive but, at only a page, very brief.

27   I am indebted to the librarians there for their help and to Mrs Ursula Vaughan Williams and the EFDSS for permission to make use of the material. My references consist of the number given to each item by Frank Purslow in his catalogue, prefixed by the initial of the county in which it was noted. In the main I shall deal with material collected by Hammond within twenty miles of Dorchester. This distance would represent a good day's walk, and coincides fairly closely with the county boundary. In quoting from the Hammond and Gardiner mss, lineation and the use of '+' for 'and' have been normalized and obvious spelling errors corrected.

28.   *Life*, 223, 267, fragments 1 and 3; *The Dynasts*, 289; 'The Tailor's Breeches', in *Tess*, 294, 365, and in 'A Few Crusted Characters' in *'Life's Little Ironies' and 'A Changed Man'*, ed. F. B. Pinion (1977), 143; compared with Hammond's D224, D229, D248, and D238.

29.   See *Complete Poems*, 796. The songs are 'Irish Molly-O': H (Hampshire) 256, H287, H1182; 'Kathleen Mavourneen': H525; 'Kitty of Coleraine': D146 (the tune alone is no. 112 in Hook); 'Susan, Pride of Kildare': H58, H250, H354, H575, S6. For 'Take Me, Paddy, Will You Now' see note to 'My Husband's Got No Courage in Him' in *Wanton Seed*, 137.

30.   V. Gammon, 'The Performance Style of West Gallery Music', in *The Gallery Tradition*, ed. C. Turner (1997), 50.

31.   N. Temperley, *The Music of the English Parish Church* (1983), 156.

32.   Gillian Warson discusses some of the literary accounts of this music in 'The English Choir-band in Literature', in *The Gallery Tradition*, 9-15.

33.   N. Temperley, 'Present at the Birth', in *The Gallery Tradition*, 2-3.

34.   N. Temperley, *Music of the English Parish Church*, 158.

35.   *Music of the English Parish Church*, 196-97.

36.   D. Townsend, 'Processes of Transmission in the Country Psalmody Tradition', in *The Gallery Tradition*, 27-30.

37.   V. Gammon, '"Babylonian Performances": The Rise and Suppression of Popular Church Music, 1660-1870', in *Popular Culture and Class Conflict 1590-1914*, ed. E. & S. Yeo (1981), 65-66. Sometimes, though, church authorities bought and maintained band instruments; this would have given them more control (C. Turner, 'The Decline of the Gallery Tradition', *The Gallery Tradition*, 74.

38.   *Music of the English Parish Church*, 197.

39.   *The Gallery Tradition*, 13.

40.   W. Gardiner, *Music and Friends* (1838), 44.

41.   *Music of the English Parish Church*, 160-62.

42.   *The Gallery Tradition*, 51.

43.   J. Hullah, *Music in the Parish Church* (1856), 23.

44.   Quoted by Gammon in *Popular Culture and Class Conflict*, 76.

45.   Temperley discusses the rise of the barrel organ in church, *Music of the English Parish Church*, 235.

46.   TH 2, no. 59. This and other carols, tunes and songs from the Hardy family manuscripts can be heard played on authentic instruments on *The Mellstock Quire*, and on The Mellstock Band's *Under the Greenwood Tree* (Saydisc Records, 1986).

47.   *Under the Greenwood Tree* (hereafter *UGT*), 189; *Far From the Madding Crowd* (hereafter *FMC*), 255. 'Haste to the Wedding' is Hook, no. 19, with a note 'as danced

at Mellstock about 1840' on the page preceding no. 1, and in *Tunes for the Violin* no. 1, in a different version. It is in the Album Book in Hardy's hand, with instructions, and he also mentions it in the poem 'In the Small Hours'. 'The Soldier's Joy' is no. 24 in Hook, and nos 44 and 47 in *Tunes for the Violin*. It is played by the King's Own Cavalry in the poem 'The Dance at the Phoenix'.

48.   This is danced at Mrs Yeobright's (*Return of the Native*, 150); 'Absent-Mindedness in a Parish Choir', *Life's Little Ironies*, 173-75. Also called 'The Devil's Dream', it is to be found in *Tunes for the Violin*, no. 21, and in Hook, no. 211, and in the Album Book, in Hardy's hand with dance instructions for a five-handed reel.

49.   *Life's Little Ironies*, 135, Both tunes were favourites of the young Hardy (*Life*, 15, and 'The Dance at the Phoenix'). For 'The Fairy Dance', composed by Neil Gow, see Hook, no. 12 or *Tunes for the Violin*, no. 24. For 'My Fancy Lad', see *Tunes for the Violin*, p. 87.

50.   Hardy wrote a letter to the English Folk Dance Society about this in September 1926, which is cited in the New Wessex edition, 201, but unfortunately this just confuses the issue.

51.   For texts, see E. Duncan (ed.), *The Minstrelsy of England*, **1**, 271; S. Baring-Gould, *English Minstrelsie*, **2**, 27.

52.   This widespread plot motif was one given some personal application by the events of Hardy's own life, such as his early patronage from the lady of the manor, Julia Martin (*Life*, 19) and his eventual marriage to the safely genteel Emma Gifford.

53.   *Thomas Hardy: His Career as a Novelist* (1971), 53.

54.   For a text of the song, see Percy Buck, ed., *The Oxford Song Book* (1916), no. 10.

55.   *Music and Friends*, (1838), **1**, 226; **3**, 46-47, 52-53.

56.   *MC*, 81. Also used by Scott (*Fortunes of Nigel*, Chapter 31 [377]) and Gaskell (*North and South*, Chapter 8 [65]). Authorship uncertain. For text and tune, see W. Mitchison (ed.), *Hand-Book of the Songs of Scotland* (n.d.), 100-01.

57.   See the edition of Child by G. L. Kittredge and H. C. Sargent (1932), xxvii. Bertrand Harris Bronson's monumental companion to Child, *The Traditional Tunes of the Child Ballads* (1959-72), records no tunes for this. In 1892 Hardy told a correspondent to look for it in Percy (*Letters*, **1**, 282). For another discussion, see M. G. Myer, '"Traditional" lullabies in Victorian fiction', *Notes & Queries*, **35:3** (1988), 319-20.

58.   *Fakesong*, chapters 8 and 9.

59.   *Wanton Seed*, 94. Hammond collected three versions of this and Hardy two lines. It goes under various titles, such as 'The Prentice Boy' and 'The Wexford Girl'.

60.   Possible analogues of varying tones can be found in D97, D246, D564, or D719.

61.   The rest of the text of D345 is conveniently quoted in an appendix to the New Wessex edition of the novel.

62.   V. de Sola Pinto and A. E. Rodway (eds), *The Common Muse*, 212.

63.   D105. See *The Foggy Dew*, 22.

64.   Lloyd, *Folk Song in England*, 187-88; Reeves, *Everlasting Circle*, 21-23.

65.   *RN*, 95. Such a common theme could be found (in decreasing order of probability as a source) in D808, D867, D585, D479, D378, or D343.

66.   F. Kidson (ed.), *Traditional Tunes*, 45; cf. D767.

67.   Lloyd, *Folk Song in England*, 200-1.

68.   T. Laird, *The Shaping of 'Tess of the d'Urbervilles'* (1975), 34.

69.   E.g., in spite of his tendency to rewrite texts, S. Baring-Gould, *Songs of the West* (1905), 183.

70.   *Folkways in Thomas Hardy* (1962), 185.

71.   *Victorian Tear Jerkers*, Sounds Like Folk, no. 4 (1974), 19-21. No editor given.
72.   *Life and Letters of Alexander Macmillan*, ed. C. L. Graves (1910), 289.
73.   R. G. Fox, ed., *Thomas Hardy: The Critical Heritage* (1970), 2, 4, 10, 13.
74.   *Thomas Hardy's Personal Writings: Prefaces, Literary Opinions, Reminiscences*, ed. Harold Orel (1967), 171.

9

Conclusion

So, was there a plot?

No, probably not—at least in the sense of a conscious, concerted and malign attempt by the authors discussed here to suppress traditional working-class song culture because it was working-class. Such a theory would offer a neat conclusion to this book, but the truth is more complicated.

Certainly there was no shortage of class antagonism throughout this period, and this provided the matrix within which our writers worked. This had operated through class colonialism from the earliest days of folk song collection. Thus, as Dave Harker points out, Pinkerton (best known for *Select Scottish Ballads*, 1783) was aiming to keep his material out of the hands of the 'vulgar' as part of a literary heritage—although much of it was still in circulation in chapbooks.[1] General class prejudice and bad faith were widespread amongst critics. For example, T. H. Lister pronounced in the *Edinburgh Review* in 1831 that 'experience does not authorize us to regard it as probable, that the world will be favoured with any poetry of very exalted merit from persons in humble life and of defective education.'[2] In 1863, a reviewer in the *Daily News* complained about *Sylvia's Lovers*:

> We do not mean to say that the grandest heroism and noblest virtues may not be exemplified in low life, but it is trying the patience of readers too far to compel them to wade through three volumes of unpronounceable *patois* and miserable incidents in order to follow the trail of persons who display a very ordinary amount of either heroism or virtue.[3]

Hardy's experience with critics has already been noted, and similar examples are legion. All this necessarily had its effect on authors trying to gauge the commercial viability of representing working-class culture in their fiction.

Although collectors were habitually suspicious of oral tradition they were equally suspicious of new popular culture because it wasn't traditional, and seemed dangerous in claiming an independent political viewpoint. John Ashton, the compiler of *Modern Street Ballads* (1888), describes 'The Song of the Lower Classes' by Ernest Jones, a middle-class Chartist whose work was popularized on broadsides, as 'inflammatory rubbish'.[4] Certainly a reminder that an ordinary man can thrust a sword 'thro' the heart of the proudest king' could be regarded as inflammatory, perhaps unusually so,[5] but Jones's point that the workers do not have a fair share of what they produce is unanswerably put:

We're not too low—the bread to grow,
But too low the bread to eat.

Ashton offers a cautious endorsement of the right to strike and quotes what he
sees as the 'fairly typical' political song 'Striking Times' of 1853, but he sees
the antagonism between employer and employed as representative of 'every
civilised society' (17).

Singing in the abstract was regarded as socially ameliorative and reassured
the ruling classes that all was well. One sardonic Chartist song of 1840 was
written in reponse to the 'Accidental perusal of a Whig recommendation to the
sons of toil to "sing" at their labour, and thereby render it "almost a pastime"'
(Kovalev, 80). Where ruling class interests and popular song and music came
into contact, competition and conflict (and the three could become
synonymous), then attempts certainly were made to suppress the music. This
was the case with the struggles over church bands, where a strong if relatively
recent musical tradition became socially evident because it was formally
institutionalized through its relations with the Established Church and various
non-conformist church organisations. In areas where control could be
exercised, it was regarded as desirable that it should be. In 1839 Sir John
Herschel claimed a need for reformation:

> Music and dancing ... have become so closely associated with ideas of riot
> and debauchery among the less cultivated classes, that a taste for them, for
> their own sakes, can hardly be said to exist, and before they can be
> recommended as innocent or safe amusements, a very great change of
> ideas must take place.[6]

By 1856 Hullah was still lamenting, 'We have not yet ... much reason to
congratulate ourselves on the success of our attempts to teach the working
classes how to use their leisure.'[7] E. D. Mackerness discusses the comments of
the new school inspectors and cites T. M. Marshall, who suggested in 1853 that
teachers should censor what might be profane and corrupting while admitting
that many good songs were 'handed on among the poor chiefly by oral tradition,
and ... exist wholly independently of the *musical profession*.'[8]

The writers examined in this volume, however, are mostly not so much those
conspicuous for their class antagonism as those whose sympathies for ordinary
people led them to try to ameliorate class relations. This was true even of those
with conservative views, since the nineteenth century saw some rather
unexpected political alliances. As Roger Elbourne points out, 'it was often the
rural aristocracy which championed traditional ways as a defence against the
rising middle classes.'[9] It is Mitford, according to W. J. Keith, who gives the

best contemporary account of the 1830s Machine Riots.[10]   Kingsley even
refused to become a magistrate lest he be forced to sentence a poacher.[11]   The
problem with good intentions, though, is that they may pave a way to hell for
others as well as for oneself. Thus, Scott distrusted the quality of traditional
oral material. Although he tampered with less than is sometimes supposed, he
felt he could not always trust it to speak for itself.[12] Howitt regretted that there
was 'a vulgarity in most popular customs that offends invariably our present
tastes' and saw the labourer as 'as simple, as ignorant, and as laborious a
creature as one of the wagon-horses that he drives'.[13] Such hostility to various
features of the popular culture these writers not only claimed to champion but
did champion to some degree is common. It is not so surprising once we realize
that it was ideologically necessary for them to reduce some elements of what
was 'other' in working-class culture.[14] Only thus could they make those whose
cause they wished to support appear assimilable to the ruling-class interests they
themselves were part of. Engels seems an unlikely example of political bad faith
towards the working classes, and a still less likely ideological bedfellow of
Richard Jefferies, yet he too represented the workers' life as atomised, deprived
entirely of the culture of 'Merry Old England'.[15]

Did it actually matter? After all, song quotation and allusion is only a tiny
fraction of our texts. Yes, it did matter; Engels might also be our guarantee that
even passing remarks about popular culture contributed significantly to a
dominant misrepresentation of the life of the majority. The idea that whoever
controlled the people's songs was the true popular preacher was one taken
seriously in the nineteenth century.[16] Hence, commentators were anxious to
know what such song was like. The reviewer of Kingsley's *Yeast* for *The
Spectator* said that 'the form of the work is subordinate to the object of the
author' which was 'to exhibit social problems' including 'the brutish abject spirit
but angry discontent pervading the mass, at least of the agricultural labourers.'
To prove this, the reviewer focuses on the Feast, with a column and a half of
illustration, largely the verses and chorus sung by 'Blackbird' the gipsy boy—
the rick-burning song and and the 'poetry' of 'A Rough Rhyme on a Rough
Matter'. The two last are quoted entire. They are taken seriously as the voices
of the 'peasantry', with no suspicion of their authenticity.[17]

As a parallel example in avowedly non-fictional writing it is worth examining
Our Coal and Our Coal-pits (1853) by J. R. Leifchild, who, as Martha Vicinus
points out, 'was considered one of the most reliable and informed reporters
about coal mining for the middle class, and yet he felt it necessary to write fake
songs to gain sympathy for his major points.'[18] The book consists of 243 pages
of statistics and geological reports, but studded with verses. Some are
recognisable adaptations of literary texts, for example, a rewrite of lines from
Gray's 'Elegy' (192). 'The Keel Row' (74-75) is genuine. However, Leifchild
also says, 'Some other keelman's songs which I discovered, are not exactly

poetical or polite.' He quotes one innocuous verse and says, 'I regret that the popular literature is not better than the above shows it to be. It is strange that it should be prized.' (75) He introduces songs with faint and equivocal hints of adaptation: 'Hark! he is singing a song, which I may *thus* [my italics] present to you' or 'let us try and catch the song for publication. Well, it is nearly as follows.' The songs that follow (151, 164-5, 171) have a sprinkling of dialect words and some traditional analogues, but they appear to be heavily manipulated to convey a simplistic quietist message to reassure the reader that the Durham pit-lads, however exploited (and Leifchild does not shirk this point) can still be content with their lot:

> What a merry gay life is that of the Driver,
>   And what if I scarce see the sun,
> I can sing in the dark, and spend my last stiver
>   In sweeties, and frolic, and fun.

Leifchild attempts a similar impersonation of a little trapper's feelings in 'The Trapper's Petition', which is introduced with 'what do you think of the following boy's verses, written after a pit perambulation?' The ambiguous phrasing here implies they were written *by* the boy, but it was Leifchild who was making the perambulation, so he is speaking *for* him:

> Just let me get those pretty flowers
>   Down in the field beside the stream;
> Then I shall wile away the hours
>   As though I lay in pleasant dream (155).

This comes from a man who has pointed out in the previous two pages that boys of ten (and until recently children of about six) are employed as 'trappers' for tenpence a day for twelve hours in darkness operating a ventilation system. The banksman's song supposedly expresses an adult's confidence in the active support of gentlemanly visitors (171).

The preface to Leifchild's subsequent work quotes a tribute from a Government Inspector of Mines, Herbert Mackworth, expressing his pleasure at the previous book 'as giving the most complete and accurate account of a part of our colliery population;.[19] So impressed is Mackworth that he is determined to distribute copies to engineers abroad. One presumes neither man would have dreamed of manipulating the statistics in the same way as the songs.

Oral song culture was thus triply badly served: it was denied, it was censored, manipulated and misrepresented, and it was always reduced by being reproduced shorn of its musical context. Song, like theatre, is a mixed mode of art and is dependent on the affective power of music as well as on its words.

Supposed solecisms of rhythm, rhyme and even grammar vanish when presented in conjunction with an appropriate tune. Of course, the same is true of allusions to other forms of song, but the cultural foundations of, say, opera references are not usually undermined by suspicions of its class origins. Moreover, the audience is more in a position (both ideologically and practically) to resurrect the tunes of songs within their own cultural experience. Thus, Mrs Hogg had grounds for her suspicions that printed forms of songs with words only relegated a still-living culture to the past. By claiming them for literature, collectors preserved them in both senses of the word. Ballad quotations in realist texts almost always represent a displacement of the culture that created them into the 'past' of the fiction, even if the 'past' the ballads come from is actually the chronological future in terms of the novel's setting, as with *Quentin Durward*, *The Fair Maid of Perth*, or *Hereward the Wake*.[20] Ironically, some of those who wanted to defend the songs of the people helped to create the cultural impoverishment they sought only to record.

From this, the literary critic might learn for the future to be alert to the voices of orature—from whatever source—in modern texts. The past we cannot change, but we may at least be able to retrieve some extra voices in the polyphony of discourses offered by nineteenth-century realist writers.

Endnotes

1. *Fakesong*, 23.
2. Quoted by Vicinus, *The Industrial Muse*, 1.
3. Quoted by Uglow, *Elizabeth Gaskell*, 530.
4. J. Ashton (ed.), *Modern Street Ballads* (1888), 338; includes text.
5. For selections of Chartist verse, see Maidment, *The Poorhouse Fugitives*, 23-59, and Y. V. Kovalev (ed.), *An Anthology of Chartist Literature* (1956). In spite of the influence of oral forms on this kind of verse it was, of course, first and foremost consciously modelled on high-culture poetry (Maidment, 37-38). Its rhetoric tends to be compromised by vagueness; 'blood' is mentioned fairly frequently, but it is not always obvious whose blood is in question, and whether, or how, any of it gets spilt.
6. Pearsall, *Victorian Popular Music*, 199.
7. Hullah, *Music in the Parish Church*, 27.
8. E. D. Mackerness, *A Social History of English Music* (1964), 159.
9. Elbourne, *Music and Tradition in Early Industrial Lancashire*, (1980), 34.
10. Keith, *The Rural Tradition*, 97. The essay is in *Our Village*, 5.
11. H. Hopkins, *The Long Affray*, 26.
12. M. R. Dobie, 'The Development of Scott's "Minstrelsy"', 83-85, E. Johnson, 1, 197, *Letters*, 120.
13. *The Rural Life of England* (1838), 2, 151; 1,157.
14. I use the term 'ideologically' here in an enabling rather than a deprecatory sense. For a discussion of various implications, see T. Eagleton, *Ideology: an Introduction* (1991), Ch. 1, and sections on Gramsci and Althusser, 115-18, 148-52.
15. J. Lucas, *The Literature of Change* (1977), 48.

16.   Kingsley's formulation (see Ch. 4, n. 50) but echoing Andrew Fletcher of Saltoun's famous declaration that 'if a man were permitted to make all the ballads, he need not care who should make the laws of a nation.'

17.   *The Spectator*, **24**, March 22, 1851, 281-82.

18.   J. R. Leifchild, *Our Coal and Our Coal-pits; the People in them, and the Scenes around them* (1853); Vicinus, *The Industrial Muse*, 87.

19.   J. R. Leifchild, *Cornwall: Its Mines and Miners* (1855), ix.

20.   *Hereward the Wake* is set shortly after the Norman Conquest, *Quentin Durward* in 1468, and *The Fair Maid of Perth* in the late fourteenth century, but all quote ballads not recorded in writing before the Elizabethan period, or, usually, much later. The nineteenth-century belief that ballads as we know them are a product of the Middle Ages is erroneous, but in any case the writers are being deliberately anachronistic.

Appendix 1

Tunes for the song sequence in *Redgauntlet*

The following tunes cover all but one of the songs quoted in this sequence. I have not given the psalm tune. The tunes are given in their original keys. In order to place them together in sequence for singing or playing it is necessary to transpose them into compatible keys. A few errors of musical grammar relating to time values have been silently corrected, and modern conventions of notation have been employed.

ARMSTRONG'S GOODNIGHT   *SMM* 6, NO. 600

COCK UP YOUR BEAVER   JAMES HOGG, *JACOBITE RELICS* 2, 127

MY HEART'S IN THE HIGHLANDS   *SMM* 3, NO. 259

FOR A' THAT

RELICS 2, 55

JOHNNIE O' BREADISLEE

NLS MS 843, fol. 22

KIND ROBIN

SMM 5, NO. 478

I'LL NEVER LEAVE THEE

THOMSON, NO. 21

Appendix 2

[This collection was compiled by Thomas Hardy about 1926. Some songs are pasted in in two or three columns, which makes ordering uncertain. To avoid confusion, they are reproduced here in one column only; otherwise, the typography imitates Hardy's writing as far as possible.]

COUNTRY SONGS OF 1820 ONWARDS
Killed by the Comic Song of the Music Hall.

John Dart's song:

> "She hears me not
> She fears me not
> Nor does she care what comes to me
> While here I lie
> Alone to die
> Beneath the willow tree"

Miller Brice's song:

> Come, come my brave boys,
> Let us sing + rejoice
> To the yonder green grove let us go,
> To hear the fond tale
> Of the sweet nightingale
> Singing down in the valleys below.

———————

Farmer Coggan's song:

> I saw a maid stripped to her smock
> As she was a-raking (all round) the hay-cock
>   (around)
> I said 'Fair maid, lay down your rake
> And go with me to yonder wake.

————

> "If I should leave my master's hay
> He'll stop my wage[s] + turn me away"
> "I'll give thee rings jewels + a costly robe."
> By this he gained the fair maid's love.

————

> With kisses close + words so kind
> To go with him she had a mind:
> She put on her gown and laid by her rake
> And went with the soldier to yonder wake.

- - - - - - - - - - - - - -

G. M.'s + G.'s

> I wish I was a fisherman by yon river side
> And Polly a salmon swimming in the tide,
> I'd throw out my fish-net, catch her in a snare,
> And bring home my Polly I vow + declare.

———

<u>Will the Weaver</u> — (old Dorset song)

> "Loving son what is the matter
> Does she frown or does she flatter
> Or does she a-gadding run?
> Tell me, tell me loving son?"

———

(Old Jacob's <u>Sargent's and Becky Swetman</u>'s song:)—

> I'll go to fair Floro + to her I'll say
> "Come, let us be happy; it wants but one day."
> One day, said the fair one The day comes too soon,
> To marry so early my age is too young.

——

> I'll first go to service, + when I return,
> Then we will be married all in the next town
> What, will you go to service + leave me to sigh?
> O yes, loving shepherd, I'll tell you for why.

——

> So a short time after to service she went,
> To wait on two ladies it was her intent.
> To wait on two ladies — two young ladies gay,
> Who clothéd fair Floro in costly array.

——

> In one twelvemonth after a letter he sent,
> It was two or three lines for to know her intent,
> She answered she lived so contented a life
> That never would she be a poor shepherd's wife.

——

> My flocks + my herds I will bid, then, adieu,
> My sheep-crook + black dog I'll leave here with you,
> My sheep-crook + black dog I'll leave here behind.
> Since Floro, fair Floro, has prov'd so unkind.

——

The Bold Friar

Somebody knocks, ma'am (bis)
See who it is, Betty (bis)
It's the bold Friar, ma'am (bis)
What does he want, Betty? (bis)
What do you want, Sir? (bis)
Want to come in, Betty. (bis)
Wants to come in, ma'am. (bis)
He may walk in, Betty. (bis)
You may walk in, Sir (bis)
        So the bold Friar walked in.

———

Old Dorset Song.

"To sell things the cheaper
Your tailors steal the stuff
That game a-played with readymade
Suits pedlars well enough
With my nick-nack, tic-tac, raddy-oody-i-do."

Old song: — Nell.

It happened on a certain time
        A lawyer in London town did dwell
He kept a handsome housekeeper
        Her name was Nell.

    asks
[She ~~tells~~ the sweep to lend her his clothes to personate the
Devil; + to lend him his boy—]

"In stepping o'er to shun the dirt
        As I to you may tell,
She quickly catchd him by the coat!
        Sing, O brave Nell!
         . . . . .

And don't you see that little devil
        Sitting on yonder tree
If ever you sh^d break your vows
        As sure as h— is h—
That little d— shall fetch you
        If you slight poor Nell

"He went to wed a gay lady
        And left poor Nell."

"Good master devil spare me now
        And mind but what I tell
+ I to morrow by break of day
        Will wed poor Nell.

"The lawyer he went trembling home
        In a most dreadful fright
And early the next morning
        As soon as it was light
With trem § joints + staring eyes
        And cheeks both wan + pale
He came to her with humble voice
        Good morrow dear Nell.

"She never told a friend or foe
        The trick that she had played
        Till 8 or 10 weeks after
When she was put to bed
She told it at her gossiping
Which pleased the wenches well
Her husband laughed + thus he said
        Twas well done Nell!

Old Dorset ballad:

Greenland is a barren place,
[And] a place that bears no green:
Nothing but ice and snow,
Where the whale-fish do blow,
And the daylight's seldom seen
                              Brave boys,
And the daylight's seldom seen

———
. . . . . .

When the sad news to Plymouth came
        Our gallant ship was lost,
Caused many a valiant seaman bold
        To mourn for their sad loss

———

As for the light that shone so bright
        We thought all dangers past,
But we, poor souls, that very night
        On Scilly rocks were cast.
                . . . .

———

On Friday morn as we set sail—
        Not far was it from land—
When there we spied a fair mermaid
        With the comb + glass in her hand.

———
. . . .

'Twas to the Indies we were bound,
        Our gallant ship to steer,
And all along as we sailed on
        I thought of Polly dear.

———
. . . .
. . . .

Nov. 1872. <u>Jacob Childs's song, + also that of Dorset weavers</u>:

> I'm a cobbler bold
> Just come from roamen,
> And there I fell in love
> With a clever woman
> Wi' my ring-ting tiddle-iddle-ing
> Wi' my ring-ting-tear-O,
> Wi' my ring-ting tiddle-iddle-ing,
> Ah, she's my dear O.

———

> I went to her father's house
> To ask his favour
> And he gie'd me consent
> That I should have her
> Wi' my ring-ting, &c.

———

> Ten pound I got by her
> Besides some leather,
> Also a pair of shoes
> In a lump together
> Wi' my ring-ting, +c.

———

> 'Od zooks, 'ch'ave a-lost my wex
> What is become on't?
> 'Tis enough to make one vex.
> Look, here's a crumb on't.
> Wi' my ring-ting, +c.

———

Another:—

> Goodmorrow, Moll, and from the skies
> I'm glad th'st a-come this way.
>   . . . .
>
> My head-clothes must cost pounds a year,
> Or ever I am thine.

———

Fragments of another ballad:

. . . . .

A coffin then they did contrive
And threw her in the sea alive.

. . . . .

The captain + his men did stare
To see a coffin floating there;
They took it up, I do declare
And in it found a damsel fair.

. . . . .

The captain proved to her most kind,
And unto him she told her mind,
How she was banisht from her love
Whose parents they did cruel prove.

. . . . .

Unto the raging seas he went
With sorrow, grief, and discontent,
This merchant ship he did espy,
And on his true love fixed his eye.

. . . . .

With joy + love they married were,
And banisht all their grief + care:
He then was lord + duly heir,
And she was then his lady fair.

———
———

Jan. 19. 1896

Melbury Ballads.

"There were four drunken maidens
Came from the Isle of Wight
They drank from Monday morning
Till Saturday at night.

"Till Saturday at night
Before they would give out.
The four drunken maidens
Would have their randy out.
Shall

"In came Peggy Saunders
So blithe as any broom
Said turn about fair maidens
So . . .
And make for me some room
For I'll be worthy of my room
Before I will give out
Or
And the four drunken maidens
   Have had
   Shall have their randy out."

——

Up on Tipple Tor
There were three trading women
Jen and Madam Carey
Dressed in silver trimmen
So for the Royal Briton
{Jen
{Gin and gin for ever
How I love {the gin
   {thee Jen

——

I cal-led for a can-dle, to light myself to bed,
For the burning flames of torment before my eyes did shine.

from F. B. (1907)

                              {decrie
"All daintie meats I doe {decry
              feed
Which ~~make~~ men fat as swine;
Who lives more frugally than I
That on a leaf can dine?
              I need no dripping panns or crocks,
Have no greased hands to wipe,
              My larder is a littel box,
              My kitchen is a pipe!

                    (Quaint lines on Tobacco.
                         Old paper 1826)

                         ————

Old Song sung at Melbury Osmond about 1820

                    One Midsummer morning
                    As I was a-walking
                    The fields + the meadows
                    A-covered all with green
                    The turtledoves + small birds
                    On every bough a-building
                    So early in the morning
                    By
                    At the break of the day

                         ————

                    Arise, arise, arise!
                    And pick your love a posy
                    All of the sweetest flowers
                    That in the garden grow
                    And I did pick the posies
                    Sweet lily, pinks, and roses
                    So early in the morning
                    By
                    At the break of the day

                         ————

                    ....
                    ....
                    ....
                    ....
                    So then he played it over
                    All on the pipes of ivory
                    So early in the morning
                    By
                    At the break of the day

                         ————

<u>Sung by Mary Gapper</u>

> Young Jimmy went a-fowling
> > With his dog + his gun
> And he fowled all the day
> > Till the evening came on

———

> Then home to his father
> > Young Jimmy did run
> Saying O my dear father
> > Do you know what I've done!

———

> Her apron was round her
> > And I took her for a swan
> I've shot my dear darling
> > My love Polly Wann!

———

<u>Sung by Nance Bishop.</u>   M. a v<u>ery</u> little girl.

> In Scotland lay brothers all three . . . .
> And each of the three . . . .
> They all did cast lots cast lots to see
> Which should go robbing all on the salt sea.

———

> . . . . the lot it did fall
> On Henry Martin the youngest of all
> That he should go robbing all on the salt sea
> . . . . to maintain his two brothers and he

Let's go a shooting said Richard to Robin
Let's go . . . . Robin to Dobbin
Let's . . . . { John all}
                              {Dan'l}   alone
Let's . . . . every one.

What shall we shoot . . .
We'll shoot the devil . . .
How bring him home . . .
Borrow a cart . . .
A cart will not do . . .
Borrow a waggon . . .
How get him indoors . . .
Pull down the door
How shall we boil him
Put him in the crock . . .
A crock will not do . . .
Borrow a furnace . . .
A furnace will do . . .

———————

Fragment of a quaint Ballad
Sung by Wessex weavers about 1820.

....

         her
"'Od zooks!" said ~~the~~ father; "what ails my dear daughter,
    And what hath she under her apron so clean?"
" — 'Tis my lily white gown that is too long for wearing,
    And I was afeard that the tail 'uld get green;
                keep from that
          So to ~~hinder the~~ blunder
          I rolled it up under,
    And tied wi' the string o' my apron so clean."

....

But when she was standing upstairs on the landing,
    The cry of a suck-child was heard in the hall:
"'Od zooks!" said he, staring; "this thing is past bearing!
    O bain't ye ashamed, wench?" —She said, "Not at all.
          I found it out walking,
          So sadly a-squawking,
    And brought it home with me, the swaddlings + all."

....

Caetera desunt

———————

Bibliography

[This is a select bibliography of works cited in or consulted for this book and most likely to be of specific—rather than general—use to readers.]

Published Sources

Ainsworth, W. H., *Rookwood*, ed. F. Swinnerton, London: Dent, 1954.

Alexander, J. H. & Hewitt, D. (eds), *Scott and his Influence: Papers of the Aberdeen Scott Conference 1982*, Aberdeen: Association for Scottish Literary Studies, Occasional Papers 6, 1983.

Alexander, J. H. & Hewitt, D. (eds), *Scott in Carnival: Selected Papers from the Fourth International Scott Conference*, Edinburgh, 1991, Aberdeen: Association for Scottish Literary Studies, 1993.

Altick, R., *The English Common Reader*, Chicago & London: University of Chicago Press, 1963.

Anderson, W. E. K. (ed.), *The Journal of Sir Walter Scott*, Oxford: OUP, 1972.

Anon., *A Short History of Cheap Music, as Exemplified in the Records of the House of Novello, Ewer & Co.*, London and New York: Novello, Ewer, 1887.

Anon. (ed.), *Cyclopaedia of Popular Songs*, London, 2 vols, n.d. but c. 1835.

Anon. (ed.), *Temperance Rhymes*, London: Simpkin, Marshall, 1839.

Anon. (ed.), *The Ballad Minstrelsy of Scotland*, Glasgow: Maurice Ogle, n.d. but before 1880.

Anon. (ed.), *The Edinburgh Musical Miscellany: a Collection of the Most Approved Scotch, English, and Irish Songs, Set to Music*, Edinburgh, 1804.

Anon, 'The History of the Young Coalman's Courtship to the Creelwife's Daughter', Niddry's Wynd: n. pub., n.d.

Anon. (ed.), *The Red, White and Blue Monster Song Book*, London: J. A. Berger, n.d. but post 1865.

Ashton, J., *Modern Street Ballads*, London: Chatto & Windus, 1888.

Auster, H., *Local Habitations: Regionalism in the Early Novels of George Eliot*, Cambridge: Harvard UP, 1970.

Baker, W., *The Libraries of George Eliot and George Henry Lewes*, Victoria: English Literary Studies Monograph Series **24**, 1981.

Bakhtin, M., *Problems of Dostoevsky's Poetics*, ed. and trans. C. Emerson, Manchester: MUP, 1984.

Bakhtin, M., *The Dialogic Imagination*, ed. M. Holquist, Austin: University of Texas Slavic Series, no. 1, 1981.

Bamford, S., *Homely Rhymes, Poems and Reminiscences*, London, and Manchester: Simpkin, Marshall & Co., and A. Ireland, 1864.

Bamford, S., *Hours in the Bowers*, Manchester, 1834.

Bamford, S., *Miscellaneous Poetry*, London: T. Dolby, 1821.

Baring-Gould, S. and Fleetwood Sheppard, H. (eds), *A Garland of Country Song: English Folk Songs with their Traditional Melodies*, London, 1895.

Baring-Gould, S. (ed.), *English Minstrelsie*, Edinburgh, 8 vols, 1895.

Baring-Gould, S., Fleetwood Sheppard, H., & Bussell, F. W. (eds), *Songs of the West*, London: Methuen, [1905].

Barry, P., 'The Part of the Folk Singer in the Making of Folk Balladry', in *The Critics and the Ballad*, ed. M. Leach & T. P. Coffin, Carbondale: S. Illinois UP, 1961, 59-76.

Basile, G., *The Pentameron*, trans. R. Burton, intro. E. R. Vincent, London: William Kimber, 1952.

Basile, G., *The Pentamerone*, trans. and ed. J. E. Taylor, London, 1848.

Bell, J. (ed.), *Rhymes of the Northern Bards*, Newcastle, 1812.

Bell, S. P. (ed.), *Victorian Lancashire*, Newton Abbot: David & Charles, 1974.

Bentley, N., Slater, M. and Burgis, N. (eds), *The Dickens Index*, Oxford: OUP, 1988.

Berger, D., '"Damn the Mottoe": Scott and the Epigraph', *Anglia*, **100:3-4** (1982), 373-96.

Bledsoe, R., 'Vanity Fair and Singing', *Studies in the Novel*, **13** (1981), 51-63.

Borrow, G. (ed.), *Romantic Ballads*, Norwich, 1826.

Borrow, G., *Lavengro*, ed. F. Hinde Groome, London: Methuen, 1901.

Borrow, G., *Lavengro*, ed. W. I. Knapp, London: John Murray, 1900.

Borrow, G., *Romano Lavo-Lil*, London, 1874.

Borrow, G., *The Romany Rye*, ed. W. I. Knapp, London: John Murray, 1900.

Borrow, G., *The Zincali, or An Account of the Gypsies of Spain*, London: John Murray, 2 vols, 1841.

Bratton, J. S., *The Victorian Popular Ballad*, London: Macmillan, 1975.

Brewer, W., *Shakespeare's Influence on Sir Walter Scott*, Boston: Cornhill, 1925.

Broadwood, L. (ed.), *English County Songs*, London, 1893.

Bronson, B. H. (ed.), *The Traditional Tunes of the Child Ballads*, Princeton: Princeton UP, 4 vols, 1959-72.

Brontë, E., *Wuthering Heights*, ed. I. Jack, Oxford: OUP, 1981.

Brooks, J., *Thomas Hardy: The Poetic Structure*, New York: Cornell UP, 1971.

Brown, D., *Thomas Hardy*, London: Longman, 1961.

Buchan, D., 'History and Harlaw', in *Ballad Studies*, ed. E. B. Lyle, The Folklore Society, 1976, 29-40

Buchan, J., *Sir Walter Scott*, London: Cassell, 1932.

Buck, P. (ed.), *The Oxford Song Book*, London: Oxford UP, 1916.

Burns, R., *The Merry Muses of Caledonia*, ed. James Barke & Sydney Goodsir Smith, Edinburgh: Macdonald, 1982.

Callcott, J. Wall, *A Collection of Glees, Canons and Catches Composed by the Late John Wall Callcott*, ed. W. Horsley, London, 2 vols, 1824.

Carey, J., *The Violent Effigy*, London: Faber, 1979.

Carlisle, J., *The Sense of an Audience: Dickens, Thackeray and George Eliot at Mid-century*, Athens, Georgia: Georgia UP, 1981.

Carlyle, T., 'Corn-Law Rhymes', Edinburgh Review, no. **110**, vol. **55** (1832), 338-61.

Chappell, W. (ed.), *A Collection of English National Airs*, London, 2 vols, 1840.

Chappell, W. (ed.), *Old English Popular Music*, London, 2 vols, 1893.

Chappell, W. (ed.), *Popular Music of the Olden Time*, London, 2 vols, 1855-59.

Child, F. J. (ed.), *English and Scottish Ballads*, Boston, 1857-59.

Child, F. J. (ed.), *The English and Scottish Popular Ballads*, ed. G. L. Kittredge & H. C. Sargent, Boston: Houghton Mifflin, 1 vol., 1932.

Child, F. J. (ed.), *The English and Scottish Popular Ballads*, Boston & New York: Houghton, Mifflin, 1882-98.

Chilton, C. (ed.), *Victorian Folk Songs*, London: Essex Music, 1965.

Chitty, S., *The Beast and the Monk*, London: Hodder & Stoughton, 1974.

Clancy Brothers & Tommy Makem Songbook, The, New York: Oak, 1964.

Cobbett, W., *Rural Rides*, ed. G. Woodcock, Harmondsworth: Penguin, 1967.

Cochrane, J. G., *Catalogue of the Library at Abbotsford*, Edinburgh, 1838.

Collison, R., *The Story of Street Literature*, London: Dent, 1973.

Colloms, B., *Charles Kingsley:The Lion of Eversley*, London: Constable, 1975.

Cooper, T., *The Purgatory of Suicides. A Prison-rhyme*, London, 1845.

Corson, J. C., 'Scott's Boyhood Collection of Chapbooks in Abbotsford Library', *Bibliotheck*, **3:6** (1962), 202-17.

Cotsell, M., *The Companion to Our Mutual Friend*, London: Allen & Unwin, 1986.

Craig, D., *Scottish Literature and the Scottish People 1680-1830*, London: Chatto & Windus, 1961.

Craik, D. M., *The Woman's Kingdom: A Love Story*, London: Hurst & Blackett, 3 vols, 1869.

Crawford, T., *Scott*, Edinburgh: Oliver & Boyd, 1965.

Croker, T. Crofton, *My Village versus 'Our Village'*, London, 1833.

Cruse, A., *The Victorians and their Books*, London: Allen & Unwin, 1935.

Culler, J., *Structuralist Poetics*, London: Routledge, 1975.

Cunningham, A. (ed.), *The Songs of Scotland, Ancient and Modern*, London: John Taylor, 3 vols, 1825.

Dallas, K. (ed.), *The Cruel Wars*, London: Wolfe, 1972.

Davidson, D., 'The Traditional Basis of Thomas Hardy's Fiction', in *Hardy: A Collection of Critical Essays*, ed. A. J. Guerard, Englewood Cliffs: Prentice-Hall, 1963.

Davidson's Universal Melodist, Consisting of the Music and Words of Popular Standard and Original Songs, London: G. H. Davidson, 2 vols, 1847.

de Sola Pinto, V. (ed.), *The Common Muse*, Harmondsworth: Penguin, 1965.

Deacon, G., *John Clare and the Folk Tradition*, London: Sinclair Brown, 1983.

Devlin, D. (ed.), *Modern Judgements: Scott*, Nashville: Aurora, 1968.

Dibdin, C., *The Songs of Charles Dibdin*, coll. G. H. Davidson, London, 2 vols, 1848.

Dick, J. C. (ed.), *Notes on Scottish Song by Robert Burns, Written in an Interleaved Copy of The Scots Musical Museum with Additions by Robert Riddell and Others*, London: Henry Frowde, 1908.

Dick, J. C. (ed.), *The Songs of Robert Burns*, London: Henry Frowde, 1903.

Dickens, C., *'The Amusements of the People' and Other Papers*, ed. M. Slater, London: Dent, 1996.

Dickens, C., *Hard Times*, ed. D. Craig, Harmondsworth: Penguin, 1969.

Dickens, C., *Our Mutual Friend*, ed. S. Gill, Harmondsworth: Penguin, 1971.

Dickens, C., *Sketches by Boz and Other Early Papers*, ed. M. Slater, London: Dent, 1994.

Dickens, C., *The Old Curiosity Shop*, ed. A. Easson, Harmondsworth: Penguin, 1972.

Dickens, C., *The Uncommercial Traveller and Reprinted Pieces*, intro. L. C. Staples, New Oxford Illustrated Dickens, London: OUP, 1964.

Dibdin, C., *The Songs of Charles Dibdin*, coll. G. H. Davidson, London, 2 vols, 1848.

Dixon, J. (ed.), *Ancient Ballads and Songs of the Peasantry of England*, London: Percy Society Transactions, **17**, 1846.

Dixon, J. (ed.), *Ancient Ballads and Songs of the Peasantry of England*, ed. R. Bell, London, 1857.

Dobie, M. R., 'The Development of Scott's "Minstrelsy", an Attempt at a Reconstruction', *Transactions of the Edinburgh Bibliographical Society*, n.s. **2** (1940), 67-87.

Donaldson, W., *The Jacobite Song: Political Myth and National Identity*, Aberdeen: Aberdeen U.P., 1988.

Dugaw, D., *Warrior Women and Popular Balladry*, Cambridge: CUP, 1989.

Duncan, E. (ed.), *The Minstrelsy of England*, London: Augener, [c. 1905].

Dunstan, R. (ed.), *The Cornish Song Book*, London: Reid Bros, 1929.

D'Urfey, T., *Wit and Mirth, or, Pills to Purge Melancholy*, London, 4th ed., 6 vols, 1719-20.

Eagleton, T., *Ideology: an Introduction*, London: Verso, 1971.

Ebbatson, J., 'Hardy and Richard Jefferies', *Thomas Hardy Society Annual Review*, **1:2**, 1976, 59-61.

Edgeworth, M., *Castle Rackrent*, London: Dent, 1910, repr. 1972.

Egan, P., *Life in London, or, the Day and Night Scenes of Jerry Hawthorn, esq. and his Elegant Friend Corinthian Tom, Accompanied by Bob Logic, the Oxonian, in their Rambles and Sprees through the Metropolis*, London, 1822.

Elbourne, R., *Music and Tradition in Early Industrial Lancashire*, Woodbridge, Suffolk: D. S. Brewer, 1980.

Eliot, G., *Adam Bede*, ed. S. Gill, London: Penguin, 1980.

Eliot, G., *George Eliot: Essays*, ed. T. Pinney, New York: Columbia UP, 1963.

Eliot, G., *Scenes of Clerical Life*, ed. D. Lodge, Harmondsworth: Penguin, 1973.

Eliot, G., *Silas Marner*, ed. Q. D. Leavis, Harmondsworth: Penguin, 1967.

Elliott, E., *Poetical Works*, Edinburgh: William Tait, 1840.

Ellis, S. M., *William Harrison Ainsworth and his Friends*, London: John Lane, 2 vols, 1911.

English Folk Dance and Song Society, *Victorian Tear Jerkers*, London: EFDSS, Sounds Like Folk, no. **4**, no author or editor given, but music arranged K. Harris, 1974.

Evans, E. L., *My Father Produced Hardy's Plays*, Beaminster, Dorset: Toucan Press, Hardy Monograph Series, no. **17**, 1964.

Evans, T., *Old Ballads, Historical and Narrative, with Some of Modern Date*, London, 2 vols, 1784

Farmer, J. S. (ed.), *Musa Pedestris. Three Centuries of Canting Songs and Slang Rhymes (1536-1896)*, privately printed, 1896.

Firor, R. A., *Folkways in Thomas Hardy*, New York: A. S. Barnes, 1962.

Foner, P. S. (comp.) *American Labor Songs of the Nineteenth Century*, Urbana: Illinois UP, 1975.

Forbes, J. (ed.), *Cantus, Songs & Fancies* [also known as *The Aberdeen Cantus*], Aberdeen, 1666.

Fox, R. G. (ed.), *Thomas Hardy: The Critical Heritage*, London: Routledge Kegan Paul, 1970.

Fox, W. J., 'Reports of Lectures, Addressed Chiefly to the Working Classes. On Living Poets—their Influence on the Course of Political Freedom and Human Progress', in *The People's Journal*, ed. John Saunders, **1** (1846), 201.

Frith, W. P., *My Autobiography and Reminiscences*, London, 1887.

Frykman, E., *John Galt's Scottish Stories 1820-1823*, Uppsala: A.-B. Lundequistska Bokhandeln, 1959.

Galt, J., *Ringan Gilhaize: or the Covenanters*, ed. D. S. Meldrum & W. Roughead, Edinburgh: John Grant, 2 vols, 1936.

Galt, J., *The Entail or the Lairds of Grippy*, ed. I. A. Gordon, London: Oxford U.P., 1970.

Gardiner, W., *Music and Friends*, London: Longman, 2 vols, 1838, 3rd vol., 1853.

Gaskell, E., *Mary Barton*, ed. E. Wright, Oxford: OUP, 1987.

Gaskell, E., *North and South*, ed. A. Easson, Oxford: OUP, 1982.

Gaskell, E., *Ruth*, ed. A. Shelston, Oxford: OUP, 1985.

Gaskell, E., *Sylvia's Lovers*, ed. A. Sanders, Oxford: OUP, 1982.

Gaskell, E., *The Letters of Mrs Gaskell*, ed. J. A. V. Chapple & A. Pollard, Manchester: MUP, 1966.

Gaskell, E., *The Works of Mrs Gaskell*, ed. A. W. Wright, Knutsford edition, London: Smith, Elder, 8 vols, 1906.

Gatherer, N. (ed.), *Songs and Ballads of Dundee*, Edinburgh: John Donald, 1986.

Gay, J., *The Beggar's Opera*, London, 1728.

Gibbs, J. A., *A Cotswold Village*, Hemel Hempstead: Dog Ear Books, 1983.

Gifford, D., *James Hogg*, Edinburgh: Ramsay Press, 1976.

Gillington, A. E., *Songs of the Open Road: Didakei Ditties & Gypsy Dances*, London: J. Williams, 1911.

Goldstein, K. (coll.), *Lucy Stewart*, Folkways Records, FG 3519, vol. 1 'Child Ballads', 1961.

Gordon, R. K. (1942), 'Shakespeare's Henry IV and the Waverley Novels', *Modern Language Review*, **37** (1942), 304-16

Gordon, R. K., *John Galt*, Toronto: Toronto UP, 1920.

Graham, G. F. (ed.), *The Songs of Scotland*, Edinburgh: Wood & Co., n.d. but before 1869.

Gray, B., *George Eliot and Music*, Basingstoke: Macmillan, 1989.

Green, H., *Knutsford, its Traditions and History*, London, 1859.

Groome, F. Hinde, *In Gipsy Tents*, Edinburgh, 1881.

Grundy, J., *Hardy and the Sister Arts*, London: Macmillan, 1979.

Gunn, T., 'Hardy and the Ballads', *Agenda*, **10**: **2-3** (1972), 19-46.

Haber, T., 'The Chapter-Tags in the Waverley Novels', *Publications of the Modern Language Association of America*, **45** (1930), 1140-9.

Halliwell, J. O. (ed.), *Nursery Rhymes of England Collected Principally from Oral Tradition*, London: Percy Society, Percy Society Publications, **4**, 1842.

Handley, G., 'Mrs Gaskell's Reading', *Durham University Journal*, **59** (June 1967), 131-8.

Harden, E. F., *Annotations for the Selected Works of William Makepeace Thackeray*, New York: Garland, 2 vols, 1990.

Hardy, F. E., *The Life of Thomas Hardy*, London: Macmillan, 1962.

Hardy, T., [Family ms books] Wakefield: E. P. Microform, Film no. 96939, Reel **10**, 1975.

Hardy, T., *Desperate Remedies*, New Wessex edn, London: Macmillan, 1975.

Hardy, T., *Far From the Madding Crowd*, New Wessex edn, London: Macmillan, 1975.

Hardy, T., *Jude the Obscure*, New Wessex edn, London: Macmillan, 1975.

Hardy, T., *Life's Little Ironies and A Changed Man*, New Wessex edn, London: Macmillan, 1977.

Hardy, T., *Tess of the d'Urbervilles*, New Wessex edn, London: Macmillan, 1975.

Hardy, T., *The Complete Poems*, ed. J. Gibson, London: Macmillan, 1981.

Hardy, T., *The Dynasts: An Epic Drama*, ed. H. Orel, London: Macmillan, 1978.

Hardy, T., *The Mayor of Casterbridge*, New Wessex edn, London: Macmillan, 1975.

Hardy, T., *The Return of the Native*, New Wessex edn, London: Macmillan, 1975.

Hardy, T., *The Woodlanders*, New Wessex edn, London: Macmillan, 1975.

Hardy, T., *Under the Greenwood Tree*, New Wessex edn, London: Macmillan, 1975.

Harker, D., 'Francis James Child and the "Ballad Consensus"', *Folk Music Journal*, **4:2** (1981), 146-64.

Harker, D., *Fakesong: The Manufacture of British 'Folksong' 1700 to the Present*, Milton Keynes: Open University Press, 1985.

Harrison, J. F. C., *Early Victorian Britain 1832-1851*, Bungay: Fontana, 1979.

Hart, F. R., *The Scottish Novel*, London: John Murray, 1978.

Hatton, J. L. & Faning, E. (eds), *Songs of England*, London: Boosey & Co., n.d.

Haury, D. A., 'Thackeray's "An Excellent New Ballad about a Lord and a Lawyer"', *Notes & Queries*, n.s. **28** (Oct. 1981), 404-5.

Hawker, J., *A Victorian Poacher*, ed. G. Christian, Oxford: OUP, 1978.

Hawker, R. S., *Cornish Ballads and Other Poems*, Oxford, 1869.

Hayden, J. (ed.), *Scott: The Critical Heritage*, London: Routledge Kegan Paul, 1970.

Hazlitt, W., *Lectures on the English Poets and The Spirit of the Age*, intro. C. M. Maclean, London: Dent, 1967 repr.

Hecht, H. (ed.), *Songs from David Herd's Manuscripts*, Edinburgh & London, William Hay, Sampson Low, Marston & Co., 1904.

Henderson, G., *Lady Nairne and her Songs*, Paisley: Alexander Gardner, 5th edn, 1908.

Herd, D. (ed.), *Antient and Modern Scotish Songs*, Edinburgh, 2 vols, 1791.

Hillhouse, J. T., *The Waverley Novels and their Critics*, Minneapolis: University of Minnesota Press, 1936.

Hindley, C., *The History of the Catnach Press*, Detroit: Singing Tree Press, 1969 repr. of 1889 ed.

Hogg, J. (ed.), *Jacobite Relics of Scotland*, Edinburgh: Blackwood, 1819-21.

Hogg, J., *Memoirs of the Author's Life and Familiar Anecdotes of Sir Walter Scott*, ed. D. S. Mack, Edinburgh: Scottish Academic Press, 1972.

Hogg, J., *The Brownie of Bodsbeck*, ed. D. Mack, Edinburgh: Scottish Academic Press, 1976.

Hogg, J., *The Three Perils of Man: War, Women and Witchcraft*, ed. D. Gifford, Edinburgh: Scottish Academic Press, 1972.

Hogg, J., *The Three Perils of Woman: Love, Leasing and Jealousy*, ed. D. Groves, A. Hasler & D. Mack, Edinburgh: Edinburgh U.P., 1995.

Hollingworth, B. (ed.), *Songs of the People*, Manchester: MUP, 1982.

Holloway, J., & Black, J. (eds), *Later English Broadside Ballads*, London: Routledge & Kegan Paul, 2 vols, 1979.

Hone, W., *The Every-day Book*, London, 2 vols, 1825-26.

Hopkins, H., *The Long Affray: The Poaching Wars 1760-1914*, London: Macmillan, 1986.

Howitt, W., *The Rural Life of England*, London, 1838.

Howitt, W., *The Rural Life of England*, London, 2nd ed., 1840.

Howitt, W. & M., *Visits to Remarkable Places*, London, 1840.

Howitt's Journal of Literature and Popular Progress, 1847-48.

Hudson, W. H., *A Shepherd's Life*, London: Methuen, 1910.

Hughes, T., *The Scouring of the White Horse* and *The Ashen Faggot: A Tale for Christmas*, London, 1889.

Hughes, T., *The Scouring of the White Horse*, Cambridge, 1859.

Hughes, T., *Tom Brown's Schooldays*, London: Macmillan, 6th edn, 1889.

Hullah, J., 'Music in the Parish Church, a Lecture Delivered at Newcastle-on-Tyne at a meeting of the Durham and Northumberland Association for the Promotion of Church Music', London, 1856.

Hullah, J., 'Popular Songs of the Last Half Century', *Macmillan's Magazine*, **21** (1869-70), 127-34.

Hullah, J., *The Song Book*, London: Macmillan, 1866.

Hustvedt, S. B., 'George Borrow and his Danish Ballads', *Journal of English and Germanic Philology*, **22** (1923), 262-70.

Hynes, S., *The Pattern of Hardy's Poetry*, Chapel Hill: University of N. Carolina Press, 1961.

Ibbetson, W., 'Songs of the English Gipsies', *Notes & Queries*, Series 7: **4** (1887), 397.

Irving, W., *The Sketch Book of Geoffrey Crayon, Gent.*, London: Oxford UP, 1912.

Iser, W., *The Implied Reader*, Baltimore and London: John Hopkins UP, 1974.

Jackson-Houlston, C. M. & Townsend, D., *The Mellstock Quire*, Poole: Forest Tracks, (Long-playing record FT 3016), 1980.

Jacobson, R., 'Closing Statement: Linguistics and Poetics', in *Style in Language*, ed. T. Sebeok, New York: Massachusetts Institute of Technology, 1960.

James, L., *Fiction for the Working Man*, Harmondsworth: Penguin, 1974.

Jamieson, R. (ed.), *Popular Ballads and Songs from Tradition, and Scarce Editions; with Translations of Similar Pieces from the Ancient Danish Language, and a Few Originals by the Editor*, Edinburgh, 2 vols, 1806.

Jauss, H. R., 'Literary History as a Challenge to Literary Theory', in *New Directions in Literary History*, ed. R. Cohen, London: Routledge Kegan Paul, 1974, 11-41.

Jefferies, R., *Bevis*, London, 3 vols, 1882.

Jefferies, R., *Chronicles of the Hedges and Other Essays*, ed. S. J. Looker, London: Phoenix House, 1948.

Jefferies, R., *Field and Hedgerow*, London, 1889.

Jefferies, R., *Greene Ferne Farm*, London, 1880.

Jefferies, R., *Hodge and his Masters*, London, 1880.

Jefferies, R., *Jefferies' Land: A History of Swindon and its Environs*, ed. G. Toplis, London, 1896.

Jefferies, R., *Landscape and Labour: Essays and Letters*, coll. and intro. J. Pearson, Bradford-on-Avon: Moonraker, 1979.

Jefferies, R., *Red Deer*, London, 1883.

Jefferies, R., *Round About a Great Estate*, London, 1880.

Jefferies, R., *The Dewy Morn*, London, 2 vols, 1884.

Jefferies, R., *The Early Fiction of Richard Jefferies*, ed. G. Toplis, London, 1896.

Jefferies, R., *The Hills and the Vale*, ed. E. Thomas, London: Duckworth, 1911.

Jefferies, R., *The Notebooks of Richard Jefferies*, ed. S. J. Looker, London: Gray Walls, 1948.

Jefferies, R., *The Old House at Coate and Other Hitherto Unpublished Essays*, ed. S. J. Locker, London: Lutterworth Press, 1948.

Jefferies, R., *The Open Air*, London, 1885.

Jefferies, R., *The Toilers of the Field*, London, 1892.

Jefferies, R., *Wild Life in a Southern County*, London, 1879.

Jefferies, R., *World's End*, London, 1877.

Jeffrey, F., review of T. Bowdler's edition of Shakespeare, *Edinburgh Review*, **36** (October 1821) 52-54.

Johnson, D., *Music and Society in Lowland Scotland in the Eighteenth Century*, London: Oxford UP, 1972.

Johnson, D., *Scottish Fiddle Music in the Eighteenth Century*, Edinburgh: John Donald, 1984.

Johnson, E., *Charles Dickens: His Tragedy and Triumph*, Harmondsworth: Penguin, 1979.

Johnson, E., *Sir Walter Scott: The Great Unknown*, London: Hamish Hamilton, 2 vols, 1970.

Johnson, J. (ed.), *The Scots Musical Museum*, Edinburgh, 6 vols, 1787-1803.

Karpeles, M., 'The Distinction between Folk and Popular Music', *Journal of the International Folk Music Council*, **20** (1968), 9-12.

Keith, W. J., *Richard Jefferies*, University of Toronto Press, 1965.

Keith, W. J., *The Rural Tradition*, Brighton: Harvester, 1975.

Kelly, G., *English Fiction of the Romantic Period*, London: Longman, 1989.

Kidson, F. & Shaw, M. (eds), *Songs of Britain*, London: Boosey & Co., 1913.

Kidson, F. (ed.), *Traditional Tunes*, Wakefield: E. P. Publishing, 1891, repr. with foreword by A. E. Green, 1970.

Kingsley, C., *Alton Locke*, ed. E. A. Cripps, Oxford: OUP, 1983.

Kingsley, C., *Hereward the Wake*, London, 1866.

Kingsley, C., *Literary and General Lectures and Essays*, London, 1890.

Kingsley, C., *Poems of Charles Kingsley*, London: Oxford UP, 1913.

Kingsley, C., *Two Years Ago*, Cambridge, 1857.

Kingsley, C., *Westward Ho!*, Cambridge, 1855.

Kingsley, C., *Yeast: a Problem*, London, 1851.

Kingsley, F. (ed.), *Charles Kingsley: his Letters and Memories of his Life*, London: Henry King, 1877.

Kinloch, G. R. (ed.), *Ancient Scottish Ballads*, London, 1827.

Kinloch, G. R. (ed.), *The Ballad Book*, London, 1827.

Kovalev, Y. V. (ed.), *An Anthology of Chartist Literature*, Moscow: Foreign Languages Publishing House, 1956.

Laird, J. T., *The Shaping of "Tess of the d'Urbervilles"*, Oxford: Clarendon Press, 1975.

Lamont, C., 'Jacobite Songs as Intertexts in Waverley and The Highland Widow', in *Scott in Carnival*, ed. J. H. Alexander & D. Hewitt, Aberdeen: Association for Scottish Literary Studies, 1993, 110-21.

Lamont, C., 'The Poetry of the Early Waverley Novels', *Proceedings of the British Academy*, **61** (1975), 315-36.

Lansbury, C., *Elizabeth Gaskell: The Novel of Social Crisis*, London: Elek, 1975.

Law, J. K., 'Thackeray and the Uses of Opera', *Review of English Studies*, n.s. **39**: no. **156**, (Nov. 1988), 502-12.

Leifchild, J. R., *Cornwall: Its Mines and Miners. With Sketches of Scenery, Designed as a Popular Introduction to Metallic Mines*, London, 1855.

Leifchild, J. R., *Our Coal and Our Coal-pits; the People in them and the Scenes around them*, London, 1853.

Leland, C., Palmer, E. H., & Tuckey, J., *English-Gipsy Songs in Rommany with Metrical English Translations*, London: Trübner & Co., 1875.

Leland, C., *The English Gipsies and their Language*, London: Trübner & Co., 1873.

Lewis, M. E. B., '"The Joy of my Heart": Robert Burns as Folklorist', *Scottish Studies*, **20** (1976), 45-67.

Ley, J. W. T., 'Sentimental Songs in Dickens', *The Dickensian*, **28** (1932), 313-21.

Ley, J. W. T., 'The Songs Dick Swiveller Knew', *The Dickensian*, **27** (Spring 1931), 205-18.

Ley, J. W. T., 'The Songs of Silas Wegg', *The Dickensian*, **26** (1930), 111-17.

Lightwood, J. T., *Charles Dickens and Music*, London: Charles H. Kelly, 1912.

Lloyd, A. L., *Folk Song in England*, St. Albans: Paladin, 1975.

Lockhart, J. G., *The Life of Sir Walter Scott*, London: Dent, 1906.

Lodge, D., *After Bakhtin*, London and New York: Routledge, 1990.

Lodge, D., *The Modes of Modern Writing*, London: Edward Arnold, 1979.

Lucas, J., *The Literature of Change*, Sussex: Harvester, 1977.

MacCue, K., 'Burns, Women and Song', in *Robert Burns and Cultural Authority*, ed. R. Crawford, Edinburgh: EUP, 1997.

Mack, D., 'The Rage of Fanaticism in Former Days', in *Nineteenth-century Scottish Fiction*, ed. I. Campbell, Manchester: Carcanet, 1979, 37-50.

Mack, E. C., & Armitage, W. H. G., *Thomas Hughes*, London: Ernest Benn, 1952.

Mackerness, E. D., *A Social History of English Music*, London: Routledge Kegan Paul, 1964.

Macmillan, A., *The Life and Letters of Alexander Macmillan*, ed. C. L. Graves, London: Macmillan, 1910.

Maidment, B. (ed.), *The Poorhouse Fugitives*, Manchester: Carcanet, 1987.

Maidment, B., 'Essayists and Artisans—the Making of Nineteenth-century Self-taught Poets', *Literature & History*, **9:1** (Spring 1983), 74-91.

Maidment, B., 'Magazines of Popular Progress and the Artisans', *Victorian Periodicals Review*, **17:3** (Fall 1984), 83-94.

Maidment, J. (ed.), *A North Countrie Garland*, Edinburgh, 1824.

Mardon, J. V., *Thomas Hardy as a Musician*, Beaminster, Dorset: Toucan Press, Hardy Monograph Series no. **15**, General Editor J. Stevens Cox, 1964.

Martin, R. B., *The Dust of Combat*, London: Faber & Faber, 1959.

Martineau, H., *Deerbrook*, London: Edward Moxon, 1839.

Mayhead, R., *Walter Scott*, London: Routledge Kegan Paul, 1968.

Mayhew, H., *London Labour and the London Poor*, intro. J. Rosenberg, New York: Dover, 4 vols, 1968 reprint of edition of 1861-62.

McMaster, R. D., *Thackeray's Cultural Frame of Reference*, Basingstoke: Macmillan, 1991.

Mellstock Band, the, *Songs of Thomas Hardy's Wessex*, Wotton-under-Edge: Saydisc Records, CSDL410, 1995.

Mellstock Band, the, *Under the Greenwood Tree; the Carols and Dances of Hardy's Wessex Played on Authentic Instruments*, Wotton-under-Edge: Saydisc Records, SDL 360, 1986.

Miller, G. & Matthews, H., *Richard Jefferies, a Bibliographical Study*, Aldershot: Scolar, 1993.

Millgate, J., *Walter Scott: The Making of the Novelist*, Edinburgh, 1984.

Millgate, M., *Thomas Hardy: His Career as a Novelist*, London: Bodley Head, 1971.

Milner, D., & Kaplan, P. (eds), *The Bonnie Bunch of Roses*, New York: Oak, 1983.

Mitchison, W. (ed.), *Hand-Book of the Songs of Scotland*, Glasgow: Morison Kyle, n.d. but post 1850.

Moffat, A. (ed.), *The Minstrelsy of Scotland*, London, 1896.

Montgomerie, W., 'Sir Walter Scott as Ballad Editor', *Review of English Studies*, n.s. 7 (1956), 158-63.

Moore, T., *120 of Thomas Moore's Irish Songs* (alternative title *The Songs of Thomas Moore*), London: Davidson, n.d.

Moore, T., *The Poetical Works of Thomas Moore*, ed. A. D. Godley, London: Oxford UP, 1910.

Motherwell, W. (ed.), *Minstrelsy Ancient and Modern*, Glasgow, 1827.

Munro, A., '"Abbotsford Collection of Border Ballads": Sophia Scott's Manuscript Book with Airs', *Scottish Studies*, **20** (1976), 91-108.

Myer, M. G., 'Folksong in Thomas Hardy', *Folk Review*, **2:2** (1972), 6.

Myers, A., *Myers' Literary Guide: The North East*, Ashington: Mid Northumberland Arts Group and Carcanet, 1995.

Nelson, H., 'Our Mutual Friend and Mayhew', *Nineteenth-Century Fiction*, **20** (1965), 207-22.

Nettel, R., *A Social History of Traditional Song*, London: Adams & Dart, 1969.

Neuburg, V. E., 'The Literature of the Streets', in *The Victorian City*, ed. H. J. Dyos & M. Wolff, London: Routledge Kegan Paul, 2 vols, 1973, **1**, 191-209.

O Lochlainn, C. (ed.), *Irish Street Ballads*, London: Pan, 1978.

Oliphant, M., *Chronicles of Carlingford: Miss Marjoribanks*, Edinburgh: Blackwood, 1866.

Opie, I. & P. (eds), *The Oxford Dictionary of Nursery Rhymes*, Oxford: OUP, 1952.

Orel, H. (ed.), *Thomas Hardy's Personal Writings: Prefaces, Literary Opinions, Reminiscences*, London: Macmillan, 1967.

Palmer, R. (ed.), *A Ballad History of England from 1588 to the Present Day*, London: Batsford, 1979.

Palmer, R. (ed.), *A Touch on the Times: Songs of Social Change 1770-1914*, Harmondsworth: Penguin Education, 1974.

Palmer, R. (ed.), *Everyman's Book of English Country Songs*, London: Dent, 1979.

Palmer, R., *The Sound of History. Songs and Social Comment*, Oxford: OUP, 1988.

Parkinson, K., & Priestman, M. (eds), *Peasants and Countrymen in Literature: A Symposium Organised by the English Department of the Roehampton Institute, Roehampton, 1981*, [London: Roehampton Institute,1982].

Pearsall, R., *Victorian Popular Music*, Newton Abbot: David & Charles, 1973.

People's & Howitt's Journal, The, 1849-51.

People's Journal, The, 1846-49.

Percy, T. (ed.), *Reliques of Ancient English Poetry*, London, 1765.

Percy, T. (ed.), *Reliques of Ancient English Poetry*, London, 4th ed., 1794.

Percy, T. (ed.), *Reliques of Ancient English Poetry*, ed. R. A. Willmott, London: Routledge, 1857.

Percy, T. (ed.), *Reliques of Ancient English Poetry*, ed. H. B. Wheatley, London: Bickers & Son, 1876.

Peters, C., *Thackeray's Universe: Shifting Worlds of Imagination and Reality*, London: Faber & Faber, 1987.

Pickering, M., *Village Song and Culture*, London: Croom Helm, 1982.

Pinion, F. B., *A Hardy Companion: A Guide to the Works of Thomas Hardy and their Background*, London: Macmillan, 1968.

Praz, M., *The Hero in Eclipse in Victorian Fiction*, London: Oxford UP, 1956.

Pritchett, V. S., *The Living Novel*, London: Chatto & Windus, 1966.

Purdy, R. L. & Millgate, M. (eds), *The Collected Letters of Thomas Hardy*, Oxford: OUP, 7 vols, 1978.

Purslow, F. (ed.), *Marrowbones*, London: English Folk Dance and Song Society, 1965.

Purslow, F. (ed.), *The Constant Lovers*, London: EFDSS, 1972.

Purslow, F. (ed.), *The Foggy Dew*, London: EFDSS, 1974.

Purslow, F. (ed.), *The Wanton Seed*, London: EFDSS, 1969.

Raleigh, J. H., 'What Scott Meant to the Victorians', *Victorian Studies*, 7 (1963-64), 7-34.

Ramsay, A. (ed.), *The Evergreen*, Edinburgh, 1724.

Ramsay, A., *The Tea-table Miscellany*, London, 5th edn, 1730.

Ramsay, A., *The Tea-table Miscellany*, Edinburgh, 13th edn, 1762.

Rawlins, J. P., *Thackeray's Novels: a Fiction that is True*, Berkeley: California UP, 1974.

Ray, G., *Thackeray: The Uses of Adversity 1811-1846*, London: Oxford UP, 1955.

Reed, J. R., *Victorian Conventions*, Ohio: Ohio UP, 1975.

Reeves, J. (ed.), *The Everlasting Circle*, London: Heinemann, 1960.

Richards, S. & Stubbs, T. (eds), *The English Folksinger*, Glasgow: Collins, 1979.

Ritson, J. (ed.), *Ancient Songs & Ballads from the Reign of King Henry the Second to the Revolution*, London: Payne & Foss, 2nd ed. of below, 2 vols, 1829.

Ritson, J. (ed.), *Antient Songs, from the Time of King Henry the Third to the Revolution*, London, 1792.

Roberts, M. *Tess in the Theatre*, Toronto: Toronto UP, 1950.

Rollins, H. (ed.), *A Pepysian Garland: Blackletter Broadsides of the Years 1595-1659*, Cambridge: Harvard UP, 1971.

Rollins, H. (ed.), *Cavalier and Puritan*, New York: NYUP, 1923.

Roud, S., *The Roud Folksong Index*. Privately published electronic database, regularly updated; available for use in the Vaughan Williams Memorial Library, the Library and Archive of the English Folk Dance and Song Society.

Roud, S., *The Roud Songster Index*. Privately published electronic database, as above.

Russ, J., *How to Suppress Women's Writing*. London: The Women's Press, 1984.

Sadie, S. (ed.), *The New Grove Dictionary of Music and Musicians*, London: Macmillan, 7, 1980.

Sala, G. A., *Twice Round the Clock Or the Hours of the Day and Night in London*, intro P. Collins, Leicester UP, 1971 repr. of 1859 edn.

Scott, D., *The Singing Bourgeois: Songs of the Victorian Drawing Room and Parlour*, Milton Keynes: Oxford UP, 1989.

Scott, W. (ed.), *Minstrelsy of the Scottish Border*, Edinburgh, 3 vols, 1802-3.

Scott, W. (ed.), *Minstrelsy of the Scottish Border*, ed. T. F. Henderson, Edinburgh: Blackwood, 4 vols, 1902.

Scott, W., *A Legend of the Wars of Montrose*, ed. J. H. Alexander, Edinburgh: EUP, 1995.

Scott, W., *Chronicles of the Canongate, First Series*, Dryburgh edn **19**, London & Edinburgh, 1894.

Scott, W., *Count Robert of Paris*, Dryburgh edn **24**, London & Edinburgh, 1894.

Scott, W., *Guy Mannering*, Dryburgh edn **2**, London & Edinburgh, 1892.

Scott, W., *Ivanhoe*, Dryburgh edn **9**, London & Edinburgh, 1893.

Scott, W., *Miscellaneous Works*, Edinburgh, Black, vols **3**, **4** and **6**, 1870.

Scott, W., *Peveril of the Peak*, Dryburgh edn **15**, London & Edinburgh, 1894.

Scott, W., *Quentin Durward*, Dryburgh edn **16**, London & Edinburgh, 1894.

Scott, W., *Redgauntlet*, ed. G. A. M. Wood & D. Hewitt, Edinburgh: EUP, 1997.

Scott, W., *Rob Roy*, Dryburgh edn **4**, London & Edinburgh, 1893.

Scott, W., *The Abbot*, Dryburgh edn **11**, London & Edinburgh, 1893.

Scott, W., *The Antiquary*, ed. D. Hewitt, Edinburgh: EUP, 1995.

Scott, W., *The Black Dwarf*, ed. P. Garside, Edinburgh, EUP, 1993.

Scott, W., *The Fair Maid of Perth*, Dryburgh edn **22**, London & Edinburgh, 1894.

Scott, W., *The Heart of Midlothian*, Dryburgh edn **7**, London & Edinburgh, 1893.

Scott, W., *The Lady of the Lake*, Edinburgh: Ballantyne, 1810.

Scott, W., *The Monastery*, Dryburgh edn **10**, London & Edinburgh, 1893.

Scott, W., *The Pirate*, Dryburgh edn **13**, London & Edinburgh, 1893.

Scott, W., *The Surgeon's Daughter*, Dryburgh edn **25**, London & Edinburgh, 1894.

Scott, W., *The Tale of Old Mortality*, ed. D. S. Mack, Edinburgh: EUP, 1993.

Scott, W., *Waverley*, Dryburgh edn **1**, London & Edinburgh, 1893.

Scott, W., *Woodstock*, Dryburgh edn **24**, London & Edinburgh, 1894.

Seeger, P. & MacColl, E. (eds), *The Singing Island*, London: Mills Music, 1960.

Selden, R., *A Reader's Guide to Contemporary Literary Theory*, Brighton: Harvester, 1985.

'Seleucus', 'Ballad of "The Three Sisters"', *Notes & Queries*, Series **1**, **6**, 102.

Shakespeare, W., *King John*, Arden edn, London: Methuen, 1954.

Shakespeare, W., *The Merchant of Venice*, Arden edn, London: Methuen, 1964.

Sharp, C., *English Folk Song: Some Conclusions*, London: Methuen, 1954.

Sharpe, C. K. (ed.), *A Ballad Book*, Edinburgh, 1823.

Sharpe, C. K. (ed.), *A Ballad Book*, ed. D. Laing, Edinburgh: Blackwood, 1880.

Sharps, J. G., *Mrs Gaskell's Observation and Invention*, Sussex: Linden Press, 1970.

Shaw, J., 'Scott's Influence on the Childhood of the Victorians', *Scottish Literary Journal*, **7:1** (1980), 51-64.

Shepard, L., *John Pitts: Ballad Printer of Seven Dials, London, 1765-1844*, London: Private Libraries Association, 1969.

Shepard, L., *The Broadside Ballad*, London: Herbert Jenkins, 1962.

Shuldham-Shaw, P. & Lyle, E. B. et al. (eds), *The Greig-Duncan Folk Song Collection*, Aberdeen: AUP, 7 vols to date, 1981 onwards.

Simpson, L., *James Hogg: A Critical Study*, Edinburgh: Oliver & Boyd, 1962.

Smith, L. A., *Through Romany Songland*, London: David Stott, 1889.

Smith, M. B., 'Victorian Entertainment in the Lancashire Cotton Towns', in *Victorian Lancashire*, ed. S. P. Bell, Newton Abbot: David & Charles, 1974, 169-85.

Smith, R. A. (ed.), *The Scotish Minstrel*, Edinburgh: J. Purdie, 4th edn, n.d.

[Somerville, A.], *The Autobiography of a Working Man by 'One Who Has Whistled at the Plough'*, London, 1848.

Speaight, G. (ed.), *Bawdy Songs of the Early Music Hall*, Newton Abbot: David & Charles, 1975.

Spectator, The, Review of *Yeast*, 22 March, 1851.

Springer, M., *Hardy's Use of Allusion*, London: Macmillan, 1983.

Stein, R. L., 'Historical Fiction and the Implied Reader: Scott and Iser', *Novel*, **14:3** (Spring 1981), 213-31.

Stevens, E. J., *Hardy As I Knew Him*, Guernsey: Toucan Press, Hardy Monograph Series, no. **61**, 1969.

Stevenson, R. L., *The Master of Ballantrae*, ed. E. Letley, Oxford: OUP, 1983.

Stevenson, T. (ed.), *Choice Old Scottish Ballads*, Wakefield: E.P. Publishing, 1976 repr. of 1868 edn [Contains C. K. Sharpe, *A Ballad Book*; J. Maidment, *A North Countrie Garland*; G. R. Kinloch, *The Ballad Book*; J. Maidment, *A New Book of Old Ballads*.]

Stokoe, J. & Reay, S. (eds), *Songs & Ballads of Northern England*, Newcastle: Walter Scott Ltd, n.d. but post 1882.

Stone, H., *Dickens and the Invisible World*, London: Macmillan, 1980.

Storch, R. D. (ed.), *Popular Culture and Custom in Nineteenth-century England*, London: Croom Helm, 1982.

Swann, C., 'Past into Present: Scott, Galt and the Historical Novel,' *Literature & History*, **3** (1976), 65-82.

Temperley, N., *The Music of the English Parish Church*, Cambridge: CUP, vol. **1**, 1983.

Tennyson, C., *Alfred Tennyson*, London: Macmillan, 1968.

Thackeray, W. M., *Pendennis*, ed. J. Sutherland, Oxford: OUP, 1994.

Thackeray, W. M., *The Newcomes*, ed. A. Sanders, Oxford: OUP, 1995.

Thackeray, W. M., *The Oxford Thackeray*, ed. G. Saintsbury, London: Oxford UP, vols 7, **8**, 1908.

Thomson, W., *Orpheus Caledonius*, London, 1733.

Tomlinson, W., 'A Bunch of Street Ballads,' *Papers of the Manchester Literary Club*, **5** (1886), 305-16.

Townsend, D., & Jackson-Houlston, C. M., 'Village Bands of Hardy's Wessex', *Southern Evening Echo*, 15 January, 1983.

Trumpener, K., *Bardic Nationalism: the Romantic Novel and the British Empire*, Princeton: PUP, 1997.

Turner, C. (ed.), *The Gallery Tradition: Aspects of Georgian Psalmody: Papers from the International Conference Organised by the Colchester Institute, August 1995*, Ketton: SG Publishing, 1997.

Turner, M. R. (ed.), *The Parlour Song Book: A Casquet of Vocal Gems*, London: Pan, 1974.

Uglow, J., *Elizabeth Gaskell: A Habit of Stories*, London: Faber, 1993.

Vicinus, M., *The Industrial Muse*, London: Croom Helm, 1974.

Vizetelly, H., *Glances Back through Seventy Years*, London, 2 vols, 1893.

Warburton, R. E. Egerton, *Hunting Songs, Ballads, etc.*, Chester, 1834.

Ward, P., *Cambridge Street Literature*, Cambridge: Oleander Press, 1978.

Wheatley, H. B., *London Past and Present*, London, 3 vols, 1891.

Wheeler, J. (ed), *Manchester Poetry*, London and Manchester, Charles Tilt, 1838.

Wheeler, M., 'Mrs Gaskell's Reading and the Gaskell Sale Catalogue in Manchester Central Library', *Notes & Queries*, n.s. **24** (1977), 25-30.

Wheeler, M., *The Art of Allusion in Victorian Fiction*, London: Macmillan, 1979.

Williams, A. (ed.), *Folk Songs of the Upper Thames*, London: Duckworth, 1923.

Williams, A., *In a Wiltshire Village*, ed. M. J. Davis, Gloucester: Alan Sutton, 1981.

Williams, D., *A World of His Own: The Double Life of George Borrow*, Oxford: OUP, 1982.

Williams, R., *The Country and the City*, St. Albans: Paladin, 1975.

Williams, R., *The Long Revolution*, Harmondsworth: Pelican, 1965.

Wilson, P., 'Ringan Gilhaize: a Neglected Masterpiece?' in *John Galt 1779-1979*, ed. C. A. Whatley, Edinburgh: Ramsay Head, 1979, 120-50.

Wilson, T., *Companion to the Ballroom*, London: 1816.

Wilt, J., 'Steamboat Surfacing: Scott and the English Novelists', *Nineteenth-Century Fiction*, **35** (1981), 459-86.

Winstock, L. (ed.), *Songs and Music of the Redcoats: A History of the War Music of the British Army 1642-1902*, London: Leo Cooper, 1970.

Witemeyer, H., *George Eliot and the Visual Arts*, New Haven: Yale UP, 1979.

Worth, C., 'Scott, Story-Telling and Subversion: Dialogism in Woodstock', in *Scott in Carnival*, ed. J. H. Alexander and D. Hewitt, Aberdeen: Association for Scottish Literary Studies, 1993, 380-92.

Yates, D., *My Gipsy Days*, London: Phoenix House, 1953.

Yeo, E. & S. (eds), *Popular Culture and Class Conflict 1590-1914 Explorations in the History of Labour and Leisure*, Sussex: Harvester, 1981.

Young, M., 'History as Myth: Charles Kingsley's Hereward the Wake', *Studies in the Novel*, **17:2** (Summer 1985), 174-88.

Zug, C., 'Sir Walter Scott and the Ballad Forgery', *Studies in Scottish Literature*, **8** (July 1970), 52-64.

Zug, C. D., 'Scott's "Jock of Hazeldean": The Re-creation of a Traditional Ballad', *Journal of American Folklore*, **86** (1973), 152-60.

Unpublished sources, theses, and unique collections

Abbotsford Collection, National Library of Scotland. This collection contains a wealth of material likely to be useful to those interested in Scott's knowledge of songs and music. Apart from sources actually cited directly in this book and/or noted separately below, the following are most likely to be of interest: Letters of Scott 1806-32, including a song (MS 855); Seven Ballads and a Song (MS 865); MSS 901, 907, 912; Extracts from Marginal Notes (MS 1571); Commonplace Book including Ballads (MS 1568); a Volume of Airs, mostly Ballads, by Andrew Blaikie, dedicated to Scott in 1824 (MS 1578). There is other similar material also in the care of the NLS, including a Songbook (MS 6299).

Barclay, D. A., 'Enormous Tradition: Literary Allusions in Thackeray and Dickens' (Harvard Ph. D. thesis, 1986).

Borrow, G., Manuscript notes on gipsies (MS 11312), miscellaneous papers including reproductions of various Ballads by George Borrow (MS 11342), 'Songs of Norfolk' [actually almost entirely on names] (MS 11330), Norfolk Record Office, Norwich.

Borrow, G., Miscellaneous notes (1065), manuscript of parts of Romano Lavo-lil (1067) and fragments of the manuscript of the Appendix to The Romany Rye (1068), in the Brotherton Collection, Leeds University Library.

Broadwood, L., The Lucy Broadwood Ballad Sheet Collection, Vaughan Williams Memorial Library, the Library and Archive of the English Folk Dance and Song Society in London.

Cartwright, J. S., 'Elizabeth Gaskell and Charles Kingsley: the Creative Artist's Interpretation of a Working Class World' (Bedford College, University of London, Ph. D. thesis, 1980).

Constable Collection, National Library of Scotland: material associated with Walter Scott, including a Draft of a Prospectus for *Albyn's Anthology*, MS 677.

Coolidge, J. R., 'Life and Letters of Mrs Gaskell', n.d. Typescript, Gaskell Section, Brotherton Collection, Leeds University Library.

Dawson, H. D., 'The Role of the Common Man in Thomas Hardy's Fiction' (University of Texas at Austin Ph. D. thesis, 1976).

Elliot, R., 'Thomas Hardy and the Ballad' (University of Oxford B. Litt. thesis, 1974).

Gammon, V., 'The Broadside Ballad as a Form of Political Propaganda during the English Revolution 1640-1660', 1976. Typescript in Vaughan Williams Memorial Library, P 8184.

Gardiner, G., folk songs collected by him, in the George Gardiner Collection of Manuscripts, Vaughan Williams Memorial Library.

Gaskell, E., the music books of Elizabeth Stevenson, 1825-27 (MS F 823.894 C1), in the Gaskell Collection, Manchester Central Reference Library.

Gray, B., 'The Listening Faculty: Studies in George Eliot's Use of Music, Voice and Natural Sound' (Birkbeck College, University of London Ph. D. thesis, 1986).

Hammond, H. E. D. and R. F., folk songs collected by them in the Hammond Collection, Vaughan Williams Memorial Library.

Hardy, T., Material associated with Thomas Hardy the novelist, especially his family music books, his Library, his own collection of 'Country Songs', and the Album Book H/1956.101.1, in the Thomas Hardy Memorial Collection, Dorset County Museum.

Hardy, T., Programmes for the Hardy Players productions, ephemera, and other material associated with Hardy, in the Hardy Collection, Dorchester Reference Library, Dorset.

Herbert, L. O., 'History and Tradition in the Novels of Thomas Hardy' (Cornell University Ph. D. thesis, 1958).

Inboden, R. L., '"The Music in my Heart I Bore"': the Ballad Revival, Scott, and Wordsworth' (Cornell University Ph. D. thesis, 1985).

James, G. J., 'Walter Scott and George Eliot: a Common Tradition' (Emery University Ph. D. thesis, 1973).

Law, J. K., '"Awfully Fond of Music": Music in Thackeray's Life and Works' (University of Missouri-Columbia, Ph. D. thesis, 1983).

Materials for Border Minstrelsy. Scotch Ballads, MS 877, and Ballads and Songs, Ancient and Modern, MS 893, Abbotsford Collection, National Library of Scotland.

Owens, G., 'Town and Country in the Life and Works of Mrs Gaskell and Mary Russell Mitford' (University of Wales, Bangor, MA thesis, 1953).

Parish registers and census returns for Stinsford and Piddletown and surrounding villages, held by the Dorset Archives Service at Dorset Records Office, Dorchester.

Parish registers and census returns for Coate and surrounding villages, held by Wiltshire and Swindon County Records Office, Trowbridge, and by the Berkshire County Record Office, Reading.

Pietch, F., 'The Relationship between Music and Literature in the Victorian Period: Browning, Hardy and Shaw' (Northwestern University Ph. D. thesis).

Pitcairn, R., Ballads Collected by Robert Pitcairn 1817-23, MS 2914, National Library of Scotland.

Romany Collection, the, Brotherton Library, University of Leeds.

Scott, Lady John, The Lady John Scott Collection of Music, MSS 834-843, National Library of Scotland.

Scott, W., Annotated Copy of *The Pirate*, MSS 5023, 5024, National Library of Scotland.

Sharp, C., Broadside Collections 1991, 2061 and 2062, Vaughan Williams Memorial Library.

Sharpe, C. K., MS Sharpe Ia iv, Edinburgh University Library.

Sharpe, C. K., Songs and Ballads: a Collection in Sharpe's handwriting, chiefly from mss of Scott and others, 1824, MS 210, Lauriston Castle Collection, National Library of Scotland.

'Sheepstealer's Song', written out by Octavia Fossett, manuscript in Vaughan Williams Memorial Library, MPS 60 (31) 301.

Wilkie, T., The Notebooks of Thomas Wilkie: Old Scots Songs, &c, MSS 122 (1814) and 123 (1815), National Library of Scotland.

Williams, A., manuscript songs in the Alfred Williams Collection of Folk Songs, Catalogue no. 2598, Wiltshire and Swindon County Record Office.

Index

Primary sources and secondary sources before 1900 are indexed; secondary sources available in the Bibliography and notes are not. Titles are indexed separately from their authors. Songs, tunes and other short compositions with a musical element are given separate entries under 'songs'. Spelling and punctuation have been standardized, although several variants may occur in the body of the book according to the source quoted. Widely varying titles for the same basic piece have been cross-referenced.

Songs prefixed by * are included in some form in Appendix 2, Hardy's collection of 'Country Songs of 1820 Onwards'. They are cross-referenced to the nearest standard title. Where possible, they have also been cross-referenced to versions collected by Hammond or to standard numbers on the Roud *Folksong Index*.